"You say that you will employ every effort of your mind to remove from the Statute Book, the stigma of piracy on the Slave Trade. . . . The Act of Congress might be repealed but can you repeal history?"

William H. Trescot to
William Porcher Miles,
Barnwell Island, South Carolina
February 8, 1859

A PRO-SLAVERY CRUSADE

THE FREE PRESS New York
Collier-Macmillan Limited, London

RONALD T. TAKAKI

A PRO-SLAVERY CRUSADE

The Agitation to Reopen the African Slave Trade

The Free Press
A Division of The Macmillan Company

866 Third Avenue, New York, New York 10022

Collier-Macmillan Canada Ltd., Toronto, Ontario

Library of Congress Catalog Card Number: 71–136270

printing number
1   2   3   4   5   6   7   8   9   10

ACKNOWLEDGMENTS

Writing can be a lonely experience. Fortunately many friends helped me tighten and enrich my analysis. Charles G. Sellers, Henry F. May, Fawn Brodie, Rudolph Lapp, Raymond Wolters, Alexander Saxton, Nancy Woloch, James M. McPherson, Lawrence Friedman, and my wife Carol read and criticized parts or all of the manuscript. Professor Sellers shared with me his deep and passionate insights into the tragedy of race relations in the South. Professor Friedman and Carol endured many rereadings of the drafts, and offered sharp and creative suggestions for revisions. My thanks to all of them.

PREFACE

The Old South, according to Southern legend, was the best of all possible worlds. There were lovely ladies and gallant gentlemen. There were saucy Scarlett O'Haras flirting with young and handsome Southern Cavaliers at elegant barbecues. There were huge plantations and stately white mansions with Grecian columns and rose gardens and magnolia trees. The planter aristocracy was full of splendor. And the slaves were a happy people. There were the old plantation mammy, who was lovable and loving, and the butler, dedicated and polished. Then there were the field-hands who sang as they picked the cotton. In this Old South, there were also poor whites, content with their whiskey and simple mountain life. Here, then, was the great society!

Actually, the legend of the Old South is just that—a legend. It is more fiction than fact. What particularly concerns us here is the legend's description of the planter class as an established aristocracy. No doubt a number of the Virginia and Charleston planter aristocrats belonged to a long line of wealthy planters. But the planter of the Old South was usually a one-generation planter aristocrat—a rough and highly competitive entrepreneur who overcame the frontier and made a huge fortune. He was Wilbur J. Cash's young Irishman. He began as a lowly yeoman farmer in the Carolina upcountry around 1800. One winter he drifted down the river and found the people at the halfway station of Columbia greatly excited about a new invention— the cotton gin. When he returned home, he bought 40 acres of land, and worked hard to clear the land and cultivate the cotton. Eventually he bought a slave, then more slaves and more land, and built a large and impressive house with white columns. When he died years later, he was the owner of 114 slaves, and was remembered as "a gentleman of the old school." [1] Cash's story about the Irishman graphically illustrates the reality of slaveholding social mobility in the Old South. Yet, as even Cash himself recognized but did not fully appreciate, this slaveholding social mobility had begun to freeze before the Civil War. More importantly, many Southerners *thought* it had. The traditional Southern optimism rooted in the yeoman-to-planter mobility was splintering in the 1850's. This raises highly important and fascinating questions: what happened in the white society of the Old South when the chief basis of economic mobility and the symbol of social status—slaves—were being closed to the white majority? To what extent did the fear of the monopolization of slaves contribute to class conflicts between nonslave-holders and slaveholders below the Mason-Dixon line? How was the agitation to reopen the African slave trade a response to these internal social tensions?

[1] Wilbur J. Cash, *The Mind of the South* (New York: Knopf, 1941), pp. 14–17.

While many Southerners worried about a threatening class upheaval within Southern society, they also felt an anxious concern for a Southern disquietude about the morality of their peculiar institution. As Kenneth M. Stampp, David Brion Davis, and Winthrop D. Jordan have pointed out, the institution of slavery involved a fundamental ambivalence.[2] Slaveholders regarded the slave as property, as a thing. Yet they also regarded the slave as a person, and in certain circumstances the master-slave relationship took place at a human level. While we are not primarily interested here in the ambivalence itself, we are immensely concerned about how this contradiction bothered and gnawed at the Southern conscience, how Southern pro-slavery radicalism was a response to this Southern moral turmoil, and how the new aggressive pro-slavery ideology of the 1850's—the pro-African slave trade argument—had a psychological function for troubled and uneasy white Southerners. Thus, as we shall see, Eugene Genovese crucially misinterprets the Southern defense of slavery when he states: "Slavery may have been immoral to the world at large, but to these men [slaveholders], *notwithstanding their doubts and inner conflicts, it increasingly came to be seen as the very foundation of a proper social order and therefore as the essence of morality in human relationships."*[3] The controversy over slavery was undoubtedly a conflict of world views between the South and the outside world. But Genovese fails to appreciate the importance of the struggle of these very world views within Southern white society and in the minds of many white Southerners, and the relationship between this Southern turmoil and Southern militancy against the anti-slavery values of western civilization.

[2] Kenneth M. Stampp, *The Peculiar Institution: Slavery in the Ante-Bellum South* (New York: Random House, 1956), pp. 192–236; David Brion Davis, *The Problem of Slavery in Western Culture* (Ithaca: Cornell University Press, 1966), pp. 58–61; Winthrop D. Jordan, *White Over Black: American Attitudes Toward the Negro, 1550–1812* (Chapel Hill: University of North Carolina Press, 1968), pp. 104, 322–23.

[3] Eugene Genovese, *The Political Economy of Slavery: Studies in the Economy and Society of the Slave South* (New York: Random House, 1966), p. 8. Italics added.

Actually, to an important extent, slaveholders became increasingly committed to slavery as a moral institution *because of* "their doubts and inner conflicts." They were desperately trying to free themselves from the chains of moral anxiousness based on their ambivalence towards the slave.

Historians have traditionally tended to analyze the Southern pro-slavery movement within the context of the conflict between the North and the South. Obviously we cannot ignore the reality of the sectional crisis. Yet, as Charles G. Sellers and William Freehling have shown in their studies of the Southern defense of slavery, we must also give more serious attention to the inner tensions and problems of Southern society. We must not label this view "guiltomania" and dismiss it as "irrelevant."[4] We must try to deepen our understanding of the Southern predicament and the irony so pervasive in Southern history. This is especially true if we wish to appreciate fully the significance of pro-slavery aggressiveness during the decade before the Civil War.

Thus, in this study of the pro-slavery mind of the South, we shall focus on the agitation to reopen the African slave trade in order to probe a crucial question about the Southern defense of the peculiar institution: how was Southern pro-slavery radicalism of the 1850's not only a reaction to Northern abolitionism, but also a response to the *internal crisis* of the Old South—a crisis based chiefly on the distressing awareness that slaveholding social mobility was tightening, and on the disturbing recognition that white Southerners themselves doubted the rightness of slavery?

---

[4] Charles G. Sellers, "The Travail of Slavery," in Sellers (ed.), *The Southerner as American* (Chapel Hill: University of North Carolina Press, 1960); William Freehling, *Prelude to Civil War: The Nullification Controversy in South Carolina* (New York: Harper and Row, 1966); Eugene Genovese, *The World the Slaveholders Made* (New York: Random House, 1969), pp. 143, 150.

CONTENTS

ONE

PROLOGUE:

THE DESTINY
OF THE
SLAVE STATES

hree years after the fragile and uneasy Compromise of 1850, the young editor of the Charleston *Southern Standard*—Leonidas W. Spratt—published a highly flamboyant and dramatic essay, "The Destiny of the Slave States." [1] This essay was Spratt's clarion call for the reopening of the African slave trade. A few years later Horace Greeley of the New York *Tribune* called the South Carolina fire-eater "the philosopher of the new African slave trade," and Spratt deserved the appellation. [2] Profoundly concerned about the internal crisis of Southern society

[1] Charleston *Southern Standard*, June 25, 1853.
[2] New York *Tribune*, in the Boston *Liberator*, August 19, 1859.

in the tumultuous decade before the Civil War, he had analyzed the African slave trade's essential meaning for the South. He demanded that Southerners confront the moral contradictions of their slaveholding society as well as the social dilemma of Southern white class turmoil threatening to plunge the South into anarchy. His ideological defense of slavery was far more radical than the pro-slavery argument of earlier polemicists like Thomas R. Dew and John C. Calhoun. He zealously agitated for the reopening of the African slave trade until it became a major issue in the press, politics, Methodist Church, and Commercial Conventions of the South. Committed to the African slave trade as the test of his slaveholding society's integrity, Spratt uncompromisingly proclaimed the rightness of the African slave trade and gathered behind him a new and aggressive pro-slavery crusade.

In his opening essay on the African slave trade, Spratt was not merely revolting against the anti-slavery sentiments of the North and Europe.[3] More importantly, he was breaking sharply from a history of Southern opposition to the African slave trade.[4] During the era of the American Revolution, many Southerners had sensed a fundamental contradiction between the principles of natural rights and the institution of slavery. They confessed

[3] William O. Blake, *The History of Slavery and the Slave Trade, Ancient and Modern* (Columbus, Ohio: J. & H. Miller, 1860), p. 250; *De Bow's Review*, XVIII (January, 1855), p. 17; W. E. B. Du Bois, *The Suppression of the African Slave-Trade to the United States of America, 1638–1870* (New York: Russell & Russell, 1965), p. 247; Boston *Liberator*, June 25, 1858; New York *National Anti-Slavery Standard*, June 26, 1857. Before the nineteenth century England and France were deeply involved in the African slave trade. See U. B. Phillips, *American Negro Slavery* (Gloucester, Massachusetts: Peter Smith, 1959), pp. 20–21; Clement Eaton, *A History of the Old South* (New York: Macmillan, 1966), pp. 30–31; Du Bois, *Suppression*, p. 207.

[4] No doubt, there had also been limited Southern support for the African slave trade before 1853. In 1803, for example, South Carolina allowed the importation of African slaves. However, this support was chiefly economic, and did not have the moral and ideological emphases present in Spratt's advocacy. See *The Debates and Proceedings in the Congress of the United States*, 1 Congress, 1 & 2 Sessions (Washington: Gales and Seaton, 1834), p. 336; Phillips, *American Negro Slavery*, p. 136.

3

Prologue: The Destiny of the Slave States

a deep disquietude toward slavery and criticized the African slave trade. In the Virginia House of Burgesses and the Virginia County Conventions, they denounced the importation of African slaves as a "Trade of Great Inhumanity," and demanded the abolition of "such a wicked, cruel, and unnatural trade."[5] After the Revolution, white Southerners continued to lead the efforts to suppress the African slave trade. At the Philadelphia Constitutional Convention of 1787, Southerners like James Madison, George Mason, and Luther Martin spearheaded the drive to write a Constitutional provision for the prohibition of the African slave trade.[6] Twenty years later President Thomas Jefferson, a slaveholder from Virginia, urged Congress to legislate the abolition of the trade which violated the "human rights" of the "unoffending inhabitants of Africa." Congress quickly enacted the President's request. In the House of Representatives, the bill to outlaw the African slave trade was passed by an overwhelming vote of 113 to 5; only three Southerners voted against it.[7] In 1820, again guided by Southern leadership and support, Congress enacted the law declaring the African slave trade piracy and imposing the death penalty upon Americans engaged in the importation of African slaves. This law was advocated by

[5] This opposition to the African slave trade was also based on economic and political concerns. James Curtis Ballagh, A History of Slavery in Virginia (Baltimore: Johns Hopkins University Press, 1902), p. 22; J. Franklin Jameson, The American Revolution Considered as a Social Movement (Boston: Beacon Press, 1963), p. 23; Du Bois, Suppression, pp. 14, 223; David Christy, Cotton Is King, in E. N. Elliott (ed.), Cotton Is King, and Pro-Slavery Arguments (Augusta: 1860), p. 235.

[6] Du Bois, Suppression, pp. 54, 60, 61; Frederic Bancroft, Slave-Trading in the Old South (Baltimore: J. H. Furst, 1931), pp. 607; Blake, Slavery, pp. 396–397. Southerners in the state legislatures, meanwhile, were also trying to suppress the African slave trade. See Du Bois, op. cit., pp. 71–72, 233, 236, 238; Ralph B. Flanders, Plantation Slavery in Georgia, p. 39; Savannah Republican, December 31, 1858, in Richmond Enquirer, January 7, 1859.

[7] The law defined the violation of the prohibition as "high misdemeanour" and provided a fine of $20,000 for fitting out a slave ship and $5,000 for participation in the trade, and a penalty of imprisonment for not more than ten years, nor less than five years. Debates and Proceedings, 9 Congress, 2 Session, Appendix, pp. 1266–1270. See also Debates and Proceedings, 9 Congress, 2 Session, pp. 241, 486–487.

President James Monroe of Virginia, endorsed by cabinet members William Crawford of Georgia and John C. Calhoun of South Carolina, introduced by Charles Fenton Mercer of Virginia, and supported by Southern Congressmen.[8] Clearly white Southerners themselves had stigmatized the African slave trade. Thus, in "The Destiny of the Slave States," Spratt was announcing his radical departure from this part of Southern history. Anxious about the future of his slaveholding society, he was demanding the reopening of the trade which earlier Southerners had condemned, and the reconstruction of Southern values on a definite pro-slavery basis. In almost Emersonianlike rhetoric, Spratt was expressing a romantic Southern nationalism and a hope for a Southern scholar. "The time is coming when we will boldly defend this system of [African] emigration before the world. The hypocritical cant, and whining morality of the latter-day saints die away before the majesty" of our commerce. "We have been too long governed by Psalm-singing School masters from the North. *It is time to think for ourselves.*" The eloquent fire-eater was also asserting a Southern manifest destiny, a Southern city upon a hill. "We, too, are in the hands of a super-intending Providence, to work out the real regeneration of mankind. . . . If the slaveholding race in these States are but true to themselves, they have a great destiny before them. . . . All we want is wisdom and thorough statesmanship to guide and direct us, and we may yet be *a chosen people* for great and wise purposes." [9] In his call for a distinctly Southern and consistently pro-slavery point of view, the daring philosopher

[8] *Debates and Proceedings,* 16 Congress, 1 Session, pp. 2207–2210, 2623–2625; William H. Trescot to W. P. Miles, February 8, 1859, Miles Papers, University of North Carolina Library; Peter Gray, *An Address of Judge Peter W. Gray to the Citizens of Houston, on the African Slave Trade* (n.p. 1859), p. 24; Judge James M. Wayne, "Charge to the Grand Jury of the Sixth Court of the U.S., for the Southern District of Georgia," in *African Repository,* XXXVI, No. 4 (April, 1860), pp. 103, 104, 109.

[9] Charleston *Southern Standard,* June 25, 1853; italics added. For newspaper reactions, North and South, see New York *Tribune,* May 14, 1854, in J. S. Pike, *First Blows of the Civil War* (New York: American News Company, 1879), p. 229; Buffalo *Democracy,* in Jackson *Semi-Weekly Mississippian,* July 14, 1854; *Charleston Standard,* in New York

Prologue: The Destiny of the Slave States

of the African slave trade was asking Southerners to free themselves from distressing feelings of guilt over slavery and to accept their destiny as a slaveholding society.

Spratt's defiant proposal for the reopening of the African slave trade impressed the editor of the secessionist Charleston *Mercury*. "Is it not time," declared the editor in 1854, "to look at this matter [the African slave trade] as involving questions which, stretching beyond the narrow vision of dreamers, demand for their solution calm inquiry and sober discussion?" Like Spratt, the *Mercury* editor saw an important economic as well as moral relationship between the African slave trade and the institution of slavery. "Does not the Slave Trade," he asked, "in supplying to many flourishing States the labor needful for their development, in abundantly furnishing to the world the most useful products of human labor, in bringing the savage within the pale of civilization and Christianity . . . rightfully claim for itself an origin higher than mere avarice, and a recognition at the hands of Government other than is accorded to the buccaneer and pirate? We . . . confidently expect to see the Slave Trade classed among those mysteries which, however repulsive to fastidious eyes, are yet, in the hands of God, the instruments of man's progress." [10] In the editor's judgment, Southerners should acknowledge the vital role of the African slave trade in the development of western civilization, and should shamelessly re-evaluate their moral attitude towards the African slave trade.

The radical demand for the importation of African slaves was soon extended beyond editorial debate and into the political structure of South Carolina. A year after Spratt offered his vision of the Southern destiny, the Grand Juries of Richland and Williamsburg announced their support for the reopening of the African slave trade. The editor of the Abbeville *Banner* applauded the members of the Richland Grand Jury for their

Weekly Tribune, September 8, 1856; Edgefield *Advertiser*, August 10, 1853; Richmond *Enquirer*, September 2, 1853; Abbeville *Banner*, in Boston *Liberator*, November 3, 1854.

[10] Charleston *Mercury*, reprinted in *De Bow's Review*, XVII (December, 1854), p. 612; Charleston *Mercury*, in Edgefield *Advertiser*, November 16, 1854.

singular good sense and independence. He found it "refreshing" to see men in high responsible positions daring to think for themselves. Such brave men, he exclaimed, were truly "the pioneers of approaching moral revolutions." [11] Two years later, in his 1856 message to the South Carolina legislature, Governor James H. Adams gave the prestige of his office to the demand for the reopening of the African slave trade. Newspapers from Washington to Georgia to Tennessee to Texas reprinted the Governor's radical message. The Governor's endorsement represented a significant development in the agitation for the reopening of the African slave trade. Previously the extreme proposal had been championed primarily by adventurous fire-eaters like Spratt and had been confined largely to discussions in the press. In his message, Governor Adams officially recognized the proposal and recommended the reopening of the African slave trade as a legitimate policy of government. [12] Thus the Governor had transformed Spratt's demand for slaves into a political issue.

The politicization of the African slave-trade proposal provoked hostile responses from many Southerners. Expressing the view of many shocked Southerners, Congressman James L. Orr of South Carolina condemned the Governor's recommendation as "monstrous" and "nefarious." The editor of the Savannah *Republican*, remembering South Carolina's extreme behavior during the Nullification Crisis, diagnosed Adams's message as a symptom of the disunionist political distemper afflicting the Palmetto State for the past thirty years. [13] The editor of the New

[11] See "Report of Consul R. Bunch of Charleston," *British and Foreign States Papers, 1854–1855* (London, 1865), XLV, p. 1156; Abbeville *Banner*, in Boston *Liberator*, November 3, 1854.
[12] James H. Adams, "Message to the Legislature, 1856," reprinted in the appendix of Edward B. Bryan, *Report of the Special Committee of the House of Representatives of South Carolina, on so much of the Message of His Excellency Gov. Jas. H. Adams, As Relates to Slavery and the Slave Trade* (Columbia, 1857); Washington *National Intelligencer*, December 1, 1856; *Republican Banner and Nashville Whig*, November 30, 1856; Savannah *Morning News*, November 27, 1856; Jackson *Semi-Weekly Mississippian*, December 5, 1856; Galveston *Weekly News*, December 16, 1856; Richmond *Enquirer*, November 28, 1856.
[13] James Conner to J. J. Pettigrew, December 5, 1856, J. J. Pettigrew Papers, North Carolina Archives; Richard Yeadon, in Charleston

Prologue: The Destiny of the Slave States

Orleans *Picayune* called Adams's supposition that Congress would repeal the federal laws against the trade "the wildest of hallucinations." [14] The Southern protest against the Governor's message almost immediately led to a Congressional resolution condemning the agitation to reopen the African slave trade. Concerned about the agitation of Spratt and Adams, Congressman Emerson Etheridge of Tennessee asked the House of Representatives to declare that the proposal for the revival of the African slave trade was "shocking to the moral sentiment of the enlightened portion of mankind," and that Congressional action "conniving at or legalizing the horrid and inhuman traffic" would warrant "the reproach and execration of all civilized and Christian people throughout the world." After a long emotional debate, the House of Representatives adopted the Etheridge resolution by a vote of 152 to 57. [15] In unmistakably moral terms, Congress denounced the new radical demand for the reopening of the African slave trade.

But Spratt and Adams were not discouraged. Of the 71

Courier, December 1, 1856; James L. Orr to J. J. Pettigrew, April 20, 1857, and January 18, 1858, J. J. Pettigrew Papers, North Carolina Archives; Savannah *Republican,* December 6, 1856, quoted in Henry H. Simms, *A Decade of Sectional Controversy, 1851–1861* (Chapel Hill: University of North Carolina Press, 1942), p. 195; and Robert R. Russel, *Economic Aspects of Southern Sectionalism,* 1840–1861 (New York: Russell & Russell, 1960), p. 214.

[14] New Orleans *Picayune,* December 4, 1856; see also *Republican Banner and Nashville Whig,* November 30, 1856; Charleston *Courier,* November 26, 1856; John B. Adger, *A Review of Reports to the Legislature of South Carolina on the Revival of the Slave Trade* (Columbia: A. W. Gibbes, 1858); Carolina *Times,* in Boston *Liberator,* December 5, 1856; F. Lieber to S. A. Allibone, November 1856; in Perry (ed.), *op. cit.,* p. 292; John Preston to J. L. Orr, December 4, 1857, Orr Papers, University of North Carolina Library.

[15] Emerson Etheridge, in John F. G. Claiborne, *Life and Correspondence of John A. Quitman,* 2 Vols. (New York: Harper and Brothers, 1860), Vol. II, p. 336; a table of the votes may be found in Michael W. Cluskey, *The Political Textbook, or Encyclopedia . . . for the Reference of Politicians and Statesmen* (Philadelphia: J. B. Smith, 1860), p. 589. For some reactions to the resolution, see Jackson *Daily Mississippian,* December 30, 1856; Richmond *Enquirer,* December 30, 1856; Nashville *Union and American,* December 24, 1856; *Republican Banner and Nashville Whig,* January 15, 1857.

Southern Congressmen who voted on the Etheridge resolution, 54 voted nay. The Etheridge resolution was in the tradition of earlier Southern leaders like Jefferson, Monroe, and Calhoun. But most Southern Congressmen were unwilling to support this moral disapproval of the African slave trade. Mississippi Congressman John A. Quitman, for example, declared he was opposed to "lectures" on the immorality of the African slave trade.[16] Meanwhile, advocates of the African slave trade were successfully beginning to politicize their radical proposal in many Southern states, and to draw increasing Southern support for the agitation to reopen the African slave trade.

Clearly white Southerners were engaged in a debate among themselves over the proposal to reopen the African slave trade. And their debate was charged with significance. The issue raised by the youthful philosopher of the African slave trade was forcing Southerners to worry about the internal crisis of their society and to scrutinize their assumptions about the African slave trade and the peculiar institutions. As the pro-slavery radicalism of fire-eaters like Spratt became increasingly aggressive during the decade before the Civil War, Southerners were being compelled to confront the question of the meaning and destiny of their slaveholding society.

[16] Quitman, in Cluskey, *Political Textbook*, pp. 589–591. For reactions of Southern newspapers, see Jackson *Daily Mississippian*, December 30, 1856; Nashville *Union*, December 24, 1856; Richmond *Enquirer*, December 23, 1856.

TWO

THE
YOUNG
FIRE-EATERS

 the agitation for the reopening of the African slave trade was part of a general escalating Southern aggressiveness. Spratt's clamor for African slaves was symptomatic of the pro-slavery militancy demanding the federal protection of slavery in the territories and driving the nation down the road to Fort Sumter. But *why* did the defense of slavery become increasingly aggressive and more intense in the 1850's? No doubt explanations are readily available: the traditional interpretations have focused on the Compromise of 1850 and the loss of Southern power in the United States Senate, the emotional storm over *Uncle Tom's Cabin* ("the book that made this great war"), the sectional bitter-

10

ness and violence over the expansion of slavery and free soilism into Kansas, the emergence of the threatening Republican Party, the bold and dramatic John Brown raid on Harper's Ferry, and Lincoln's election to the Presidency in 1860. Clearly these events contributed to Southern anxiety and aggressiveness and to the breakdown of the democratic process and the destruction of the Union. But surely much more was involved in the development of pro-slavery radicalism during the decade before the Civil War.

A profile analysis of African slave-trade advocates can uncover *new* clues to help us understand the pro-slavery extremism of the 1850's. This study has analyzed biographical data for 97 advocates in order to provide information about the sociology of the African slave-trade agitation and insight into the nature of the pro-slavery defense and the Southern secession movement.[1]

[1] For biographical information, an extensive number of sources was used, including James G. Wilson and John Fiske (eds.), *Appleton's Cyclopædia of American Biography* (New York: D. Appleton & Co., 1888); Allen Johnson and Dumas Malone (eds.), *Dictionary of American Biography* (New York: Charles Scribner's Sons, 1928–1936); Clifford P. Reynolds, *Biographical Dictionary of the American Congress, 1774–1961* (Washington: United States Government Printing Office, 1961); Emily B. Reynolds and Joan R. Faunt, *Biographical Directory of the Senate of the State of South Carolina, 1776–1964* (Columbia: South Carolina Archives Department, 1964); John A. May and Joan R. Reynolds, *South Carolina Secedes* (Columbia: University of South Carolina Press, 1960); Thomas M. Owen, *History of Alabama and Dictionary of Alabama Biography*, 4 Vols. (Chicago: I. J. Clark, 1921); Dunbar Rowland, *History of Mississippi: The Heart of the South*, 2 Vols. (Chicago: J. S. J. Clark, 1925); Dunbar Rowland, *Mississippi*, 3 Vols. (Atlanta: Southern Historical Publishing Association, 1907); Earl W. Fornell, *The Galveston Era, the Texas Crescent on the Eve of Secession* (Austin: University of Texas Press, 1961); Daniel Hollis, *University of South Carolina*, 2 Vols. (Columbia: University of South Carolina Press, 1951); Percy L. Rainwater, *Mississippi, Storm Center of Secession, 1856–1861* (Baton Rouge: Otto Claitor, 1938); Harold S. Schultz, *Nationalism and Sectionalism in South Carolina, 1852–1860* (Durham: Duke University Press, 1950); Avery Craven, *Edmund Ruffin: A Study in Secession* (New York: D. Appleton, 1932); William Dillon, *Life of John Mitchel*, 2 Vols. (London: Kegan Paul, French & Co., 1888); Ottis C. Skipper, *J. D. B. De Bow, Magazinist of the South* (Athens: University of Georgia Press, 1958); Laura A. White, *Robert Barnwell Rhett: Father of Secession* (New York: The Century Co., 1931); Harvey Wish, *George Fitzhugh* (Baton Rouge: Louisiana State University Press,

Spratt's proposal to reopen the African slave trade, to be sure, did not win the support of all Southern fire-eaters. Nevertheless, since the African slave-trade advocates represented an important advance guard of pro-slavery radicalism, a study of these men can offer us a beginning for a more profound understanding of the aggressive slavocracy. The 97 advocates represented all sections of the South— Border, South Atlantic, Gulf, and Southwest.[2] Several leading advocates like John Mitchel, Edmund Ruffin, and George Fitzhugh resided in the border states. Most of the advocates, however, lived in the cotton states, primarily South Carolina, Georgia, and Mississippi. Mitchel, editor of the Knoxville

1943); Reuben Davis, *Recollections of Mississippi and Mississippians* (New York: Houghton, Mifflin and Company, 1891); James D. Lynch, *Bench and Bar of Mississippi* (n.p. n.d.).

[2] List of the selected 97 advocates according to states:

Alabama: R. B. Baker, Noah B. Cloud, James F. Dowdell, John Forsyth, L. L. Nabors, William F. Samford, D. S. Troy, John W. Womack, William L. Yancey.

Arkansas: Joseph Armour.

Georgia: Alexander S. Atkinson, Harvey L. Byrd, Martin J. Crawford, L. S. DeLyon, William B. Goulden, John A. Jones, C. A. L. Lamar, Daniel Lee, Stanley L. Moore, Waring Russell, James L. Seward, Daniel H. Stewart, W. T. Thompson, Hiram Warner, William B. Williams.

Louisiana: James H. Brigham, James D. B. De Bow, Edward Delony, W. M. Kidd, J. W. P. McGimsey, Henry St. Paul.

Mississippi: Richard T. Archer, Ethelbert Barksdale, H. S. Bennett, J. A. P. Campbell, P. S. Catchings, Charles Clarke, John Cowden, J. W. Crump, I. N. Davis, G. W. Ellis, W. S. Eskridge, Samuel J. Gholson, D. C. Graham, M. B. Harris, Henry Hughes, G. W. Humphreys, John Humphreys, John J. McRae, W. T. Magruder, D. S. Pattison, H. Tisdale, D. R. Walsh, Thomas Walton.

South Carolina: James Adams, J. D. Allen, Edward Bryan, J. A. Calhoun, G. P. Elliott, Maxcy Gregg, M. C. M. Hammond, J. R. Mathews, Alexander Mazyck, John I. Middleton, William Middleton, C. W. Miller, W. S. Mullins, John S. Palmer, C. J. Prentiss, R. B. Rhett, F. D. Richardson, C. M. Rivers, L. W. Spratt, John Townsend, William Whaley, I. J. Witsell.

Tennessee: John Mitchel, J. G. M. Ramsey, William Swan.

Texas: John H. Brown, F. B. Chilton, E. H. Cushing, C. C. Herbert, P. W. Kittrell, F. R. Lubbock, John Marshall, William H. Parsons, Willard Richardson, H. R. Runnels, F. S. Stockdale, Louis T. Wigfall, A. P. Wiley.

Virginia: George Fitzhugh, L. J. Gogerty, Edward Pollard, Edmund Ruffin, A. L. Scott.

Southern Citizen, a publication almost exclusively devoted to the promotion of the African slave trade, noted this pattern. In a May 1859 letter to Edmund Ruffin, he wrote: "The circulation of the *Citizen* is not yet more than 300—but that it goes all over the South, throughout every State more or less, but its largest circulation is in S. Carolina, Georgia, Ala. & Miss."[3] Except for Irish patriot John Mitchel, all of the 41 advocates sampled for place of birth were born in the United States. Six were born in Georgia, one in Kentucky, two in Massachusetts, two in Mississippi, one in North Carolina, one in Ohio, nineteen in South Carolina, three in Tennessee, four in Virginia, and one in Vermont. The Southern-born advocates came from all sections of the South, but more were born in South Carolina than in any other state. James Adams, Edward Bryan, and Leonidas W. Spratt of South Carolina, as well as Harvey L. Byrd of Georgia, Noah B. Cloud of Alabama, J. A. P. Campbell of Mississippi, James De Bow of Louisiana, and Francis R. Lubbock and Louis T. Wigfall of Texas, were sons of the Palmetto State.

An analysis of the occupations of 54 advocates shows that they were chiefly lawyers, editors, and planters.[4] Many of the planters were extremely large slaveholders. Richard T. Archer owned 221 slaves; A. S. Atkinson, 68 slaves; P. S. Catchings, 42 slaves; John A. Jones, 43 slaves; C. C. Herbert, 47 slaves; John Townsend, 272 slaves; R. B. Rhett, 190 slaves; John S. Palmer, 200 slaves; J. A. Calhoun, 135 slaves; James H. Adams, 197 slaves; and John I. Middleton, 318 slaves.[5] No doubt many

---

[3] Mitchel to Ruffin, May 15, 1859, Ruffin Papers, University of North Carolina Library.

[4] Forty-four of the 54 advocates were lawyers, editors, and planters. The others were a minister, doctor, physician-banker, merchants, writers, and sociologists.

[5] United States Census Bureau, 1850 Census Population Schedules, South Carolina Slave Schedules, St. John's Collection, MSS. (microfilm copy in the University of North Carolina Library), pp. 332–333; South Carolina Slave Schedules, Richland, pp. 186–193; 1860 Census Population Schedules, Mississippi Slave Schedules, Claiborne, pp. 140–143; Mississippi Slave Schedules, Copiah, p. 95; Texas Slave Schedules, Colorado, p. 38; Georgia Slave Schedules, Camden, pp. 33–34; Georgia Slave Schedules, Polk, p. 22; May and Reynolds, *South Carolina Secedes*, pp. 121, 122, 185, 191, 192, 199, 200, 220, 221.

critics of the African slave-trade agitation also held numerous
slaves: Hershel V. Johnson owned 113 slaves; W. L. Sharkey,
65 slaves; and James Hammond, more than 300 slaves. Nevertheless, as the Mobile *Daily Register* correctly observed in 1859,
"among the advocates of the re-opening of the slave trade are
some of the largest slaveholders in the country. . . ."[6] Since
slaveholding was the basis of their wealth and prestige, these
men had definite vested interests in the peculiar institution.
Some important African slave-trade advocates like Spratt owned
no slaves. But as lawyers, writers, and editors, and as members
of a professional class, they identified themselves with slaveholders, especially the planter class—the possessor of status and
power. As Southern writers and editors, they felt a special
responsibility to formulate an ideological defense of Southern
society and the institution of slavery. To an important extent,
therefore, the agitation to reopen the African slave trade was
composed of wealthy, literate, and professional men.

The agitation to reopen the African slave trade also had
political leadership. At least 43 of the 97 advocates were political
officeholders. A breakdown according to state and federal offices
reveals that at one time or another 39 of them were members
of state legislatures, 3 were governors, 8 were United States
Congressmen, and 3 were United States Senators. A survey of
21 advocates whose party affiliations have been identified shows
that with one exception—F. D. Richardson who was a Know
Nothing—these advocates were Democrats. And of the 20 Demo-

[6] Mobile *Daily Register*, in Savannah *Morning News*, September 6,
1857. Other opponents holding numerous slaves: W. C. Smedes, 58
slaves; T. S. Dabney, 200 slaves; A. M. Clayton, 140 slaves; Wade Hampton III, 229 slaves. United States Census Bureau, 1860 Census Population Schedules, Jefferson County, MSS. (microfilm copy in the University
of North Carolina Library), pp. 16–18; Mississippi Slave Schedules, Marshall County, pp. 32–34; Mississippi Slave Schedules, Hinds County, pp.
218–220; Mississippi Slave Schedules, Claiborne County, pp. 69–70; Mississippi Slave Schedules, Warren County, pp. 51, 141–142; 1850 Census
Population Schedules, South Carolina Slave Schedules, Richland, pp. 381–
387; Elizabeth Merritt, *James Henry Hammond, 1807–1864* (Baltimore:
Johns Hopkins University Press, 1923), p. 116; James Hammond plantation records, Hammond papers, Vol. 21, Library of Congress.

crats, at least 19, including James Adams, Edward Bryan, Edward Delony, J. F. Dowdell, Maxcy Gregg, John McRae, and L. W. Spratt, were States Rights or Southern Rights Democrats. Furthermore, James Adams, Robert B. Rhett, and John I. Middleton had been nullifiers in 1832; Rhett and Louis T. Wigfall had been leaders of the secessionist Bluffton movement of 1844; and Adams, Rhett, Middleton, M. J. Crawford, Maxcy Gregg, J. L. Seward, and William Yancey had rejected the Compromise of 1850. These leaders brought the politics of pro-slavery radicalism to the agitation to reopen the African slave trade.

The youthfulness of the African slave-trade advocates was most striking. Of the 41 advocates whose birthdates were ascertained, 25 were born between 1810 and 1832. In 1832 during the South Carolina nullification crisis, 9 of these Southerners were in their thirties, 11 in their twenties, and 21 were teenagers or children. In 1853, the year Leonidas W. Spratt had begun the agitation to reopen the African slave trade, 9 men were in their fifties, 13 in their forties, 11 in their thirties, and 8 in their twenties. A survey of important advocates reveals that Leonidas W. Spratt was 35; William Yancey, 39; Edmund Ruffin, 59; James Adams, 41; Henry Hughes, 24; Edward H. Cushing, 24; Ethelbert Barksdale, 29; Edward Bryan, 27; George Fitzhugh, 47; Edward Pollard, 22; James De Bow, 35; and Charles A. L. Lamar, 29. Clearly many of them were young men of the South.[7]

We must, however, be careful here. Our analysis does not clearly show that pro-slavery radicals tended to be youthful, though more extensive studies of them may support such a conclusion. And certainly it does not show that young men were pro-slavery radicals. But our study does indicate that an important group of radicals—the African slave-trade advocates —included many young men. Southern Unionist opponents of the African slave-trade proposal, on the other hand, seemed to

[7] For a suggestive analysis of youth and the American Revolution, see Eric McKitrick and Stanley Elkins, "Young Men of the Revolution," *Political Science Quarterly*, LXXVI (June, 1961), no. 2, pp. 181–216.

have been older men. A survey of 19 Southern Unionists who criticized the African slave-trade agitation reveals that 2 were in their sixties, 7 in their fifties, 6 in their forties, 3 in their thirties, and 1 was in his twenties. Compared to these Southern Unionists, the advocates of the African slave trade tended to be younger men.

These young Southerners had extremely energetic life styles. Representative of this activism was James De Bow, the pro-slavery magazinist of the Old South. As editor of *De Bow's Review* and *De Bow's Agricultural Journal,* he solicited articles from writers like Ruffin, Fitzhugh, and Simms; wrote editorials and essays; and corrected pageproofs as he travelled throughout the South selling magazine subscriptions. As superintendent of the 1850 census, De Bow reorganized the census office and introduced new methods of census-taking and statistical analysis. In 1854 he published a weighty volume of statistical information; the title was most appropriate: *Encyclopaedia of the Trade and Commerce of the United States, more particularly of the southern and western states: giving a view of the commerce, agriculture, manufacturers, internal improvements, slave and free labour, slavery institutions, products, etc.* During the 1850's, De Bow was involved in an incredible number of activities. He taught economics at the University of Louisiana, and promoted school reform and the establishment of public libraries. He was vice-president of the United States Agricultural Society, an enthusiastic member of the New Orleans Academy of Science, president of the 1857 Knoxville Southern Commercial Convention, and president of the African Labor Supply Association. During this time, De Bow also had a busy private life. He married Caroline Poe in 1854 and was the father of a daughter and son within two years. His son died in 1857, and his wife became ill and died the following year. Much of De Bow's attention and energy was directed to women. De Bow, as his biographer has observed, "was unable to remain indifferent to the 'raven or golden tresses' that waved in the breezes at the springs of Virginia." His concerned relatives urged him to marry and quit "flirting about all the time." [8] In 1860, after a year of ardent courtship, he married the daughter of a prominent Nashville planter family, and took her on a honeymoon trip to Washington, Philadelphia, and New York. The editor must have taken along pageproofs of articles on slavery and secession to be published in the next issue of his *Review*. De Bow represented the youth and activity of many slave-trade advocates. Young men like Spratt, Hughes, and Barksdale were courting women or raising families, writing books and articles, editing newspapers, traveling to commercial and political conventions, campaigning for and holding political offices, organizing African slave-trade public meetings, and giving speeches on the importation of African slaves.

But the youthfulness of African slave-trade advocates involved more than energy. Unlike older Southerners, these young men had few vital common experiences with Northerners; they had not participated in nation-building. They had not taken part in the American Revolution. During the Revolution "the corridors of history converged and Cavalier and Yankee had stood and fought shoulder to shoulder." [9] Young men like Lamar, Pollard, and De Bow had no direct attachments to the nationalism of the War of 1812. Born after the battle of New Orleans, they could not have felt to the same extent as older men the thrilling patriotic emotions expressed in "The Hunters of Kentucky," a popular song about General Jackson's "glorious" victory. For De Bow, the War of 1812 was something he had read about in a history book as a teenager. [10] These young men did not have the tensions of international war and fierce Anglo-American hostilities to provoke feelings of indignant nationalism in their souls. Since the Lion became less threatening and annoying to the United States after the second war of independence, these young Southerners were more concerned about

8 Skipper, *De Bow*, p. 109.
9 William Taylor, *Cavalier & Yankee: The Old South and American National Character* (New York: Doubleday, 1963), p. 243.
10 Skipper, *De Bow*, p. 5. For a discussion on "The Hunters of Kentucky," see John William Ward, *Andrew Jackson—Symbol for an Age* (New York: Oxford, 1962), pp. 3–30.

sectional rather than national survival and more concerned about the defense of their interests as Southerners rather than as Americans. No doubt Northerners and Southerners fought side by side in the war against Mexico during the 1840's. But this common experience was a disaster for national unity. Despite the rhetoric of manifest destiny, the Mexican-American War intensified the angry debate over the extension of slavery into the territories and left Northerners and Southerners bitterly divided. The generational experience of these young men drove them in the direction of a Southern identity.

These young Southerners had come of age after William Lloyd Garrison had opened his attack on the South, after the terrifying Nat Turner slave insurrection of 1831, after the nullification crisis, after the era when Southerners had been willing to admit publicly that slavery was "a necessary evil." They grew up in a society sensitive and intolerant toward Northern abolitionist criticisms and Southern doubts about slavery, in a society lashing out at the tariff in order to exorcise the dreadful spectre of Garrison and demanding the "Gag Rule" in Congress and the suppression of abolitionist literature in Southern post offices. They grew up in a society almost hysterically afraid of slave revolts. Nat Turner's violent and bloody strike against slavery was a trauma for the entire white South. Southerners were horrified. Unlike Gabriel Prosser in 1800 and Denmark Vesey in 1822, Nat Turner and his slave rebels killed Southern whites: they slew nearly 60 whites, including women and children. Southerners were suspicious, a Virginian explained, "that a Nat Turner might be in every family, that the same bloody deed could be acted over at any time and in any place. . . ." The revolt set off waves of hysteria and rippled the consciousness of frightened white children. During the 1850's, a white Southerner told Olmsted about his fearful childhood days. "I remember when I was a boy—mus ha' been about twenty years ago—folks was dreadful frightened about the niggers. I remember they built pens in the woods where they could hide, and Christmas time they went and got into the pens 'fraid the niggers was rising." [11] Thomas R. Gray, the recorder of Turner's confessions, observed that the revolt would "long be remembered in the annals of our country, and many a mother as she presses her infant darling to her bosom, will shudder at the recollection of Nat Turner. . . ." [12] The young advocates of the African slave trade in the 1850's had been children during this time of intense Southern anxiety.

These young men of the South were raised in a society seeking refuge from fears of abolitionism and slave revolts in the security of a Cavalier mythology. The eighteen thirties, as William Taylor has observed in his brilliant study of *Cavalier & Yankee*, was "the most active period of Southern myth-making. . . ." Southern novelists like Nathaniel Beverley Tucker were busily spinning out stories about genteel and paternalistic planters and their respectful and happy slaves. Southern culture during this time was immersed in the romantic fantasies of Sir Walter Scott. Scott's novels about gallant gentlemen and fair ladies enchanted antebellum Southerners. The Southern fascination for Scott's romances was so great that Mark Twain later called it the "Sir Walter disease." "Before 1850 it was good form for Southern gentlemen to place Sir Walter Scott's novels on their library shelves and for all Southern boys and girls to read these books as the great models of life and good breeding." Southern children were taught to cherish notions about chivalry and honor. A Southern father had conditioned his son to "resent the smallest indignity of another boy. . . ." Little wonder many of the young fire-eaters, who clamored for the reopening of the African slave trade, were extremely sensitive about their honor and quick to defend their integrity. [13]

[11] For an excellent analysis of the Nullification Crisis, see Freehling, *Prelude to Civil War;* Jesse B. Harrison, quoted in Clement Eaton, *The Freedom of Thought Struggle in the Old South* (New York: Harper, 1964), p. 109; Olmsted, *A Journey in the Back Country,* p. 203.

[12] T. R. Gray, *The Confessions of Nat Turner,* in appendix of Herbert Aptheker, *Nat Turner's Slave Rebellion* (New York: Grove, 1968), pp. 130–131.

[13] William Taylor, *Cavalier & Yankee* (New York: Doubleday, 1963), pp. 43, 281–287; Mark Twain and William Dodd, quoted in Rollin G.

The Young Fire-Eaters

Educated in sectionalist-oriented schools like the College of South Carolina, many of these youthful African slave-trade advocates had been trained in pro-slavery polemicism. The biographies of 28 advocates indicate that they had attended or received degrees from institutions of higher learning. Several important ones, including James Adams, Alexander Mazyck, E. H. Cushing, and William Yancey had gone to Northern colleges like Dartmouth and Princeton, but most of the advocates were educated in the South. Many of them had graduated from the College of South Carolina—an institution dominated by the states-rights and pro-slavery philosophy of President Thomas Cooper.[14] Among the alumni of South Carolina College were Maxcy Gregg, John Townsend, Louis T. Wigfall, Willard Richardson, and Leonidas W. Spratt. These young Southerners were graduates of a training school for fire-eaters. Many South Carolina College students were the Southern counterparts of the Lane Seminary student rebels: they were pro-slavery activists. "The students of the South Carolina College repudiate old Clay and all his principles," declared a student of the Palmetto school in 1851. "Free soilism and abolitionism cannot flourish on the soil irradiated by the genious of Calhoun . . . and should South Carolina secede, her college claims a place in the picture near the 'flashing of her guns.' " [15] Indeed, when South Carolina moved to disrupt the Union, 68 of the 168 delegates to the state's secession convention were South Carolina College alumni.[16] The relationship between pro-slavery radicalism and the College of South Carolina was clear to one traveler in the South many years before secession. During his visit to the college in 1835, he noticed "the total want of caution

Osterweis, *Romanticism and Nationalism in the Old South* (Baton Rouge: Louisiana State University Press, 1967), pp. 41–53; Clement Eaton, *The Growth of Southern Civilization, 1790–1860* (New York: Harper, 1965), p. 297.

14 For a discussion on the College of South Carolina as a training ground for Southern extremists, see Hollis, *University of South Carolina,* I, pp. 76, 104, 266–267; and Schultz, *Nationalism and Sectionalism,* p. 8.

15 Quoted in Hollis, I, p. 267.

16 *Ibid.,* p. 266.

and reserve in the ultra opinions" professors expressed about politics. "If the children of these Nullifiers," he added, "are brought up on the same opinions, which they are likely to be, here are fine elements for future dissension. . . ." [17]

Significantly these young men launched themselves into careers as editors, writers, and politicians during a time of Southern insecurity over slavery, and their careers were closely identified with the aggressive defense of the peculiar institution. They won literary recognition and political power in the South as pro-slavery defenders. Henry Hughes, an ambitious Mississippi scholar, published his pro-slavery *Treatise on Sociology* in 1854 at the age of twenty-five and was sent to the state senate in 1856. In 1854 thirty-year-old Ethelbert Barksdale became editor of the Jackson *Mississippian,* an influential pro-slavery newspaper. Twenty-four-year-old Edward Bryan published his secessionist *The Rightful Remedy* in 1850, and was elected to the South Carolina legislature four years later. James De Bow began his career as a writer in 1844 when the *Southern Quarterly Review* published his essay, "The Characteristics of the Statesman," a condemnation of the protective tariff and the Northern violation of the fugitive slave law. Two years later, at the age of twenty-six, he established *De Bow's Review.* As the editor of the *Review,* he relentlessly defended Southern interests and earned the applause of his readers. As editor of the Charleston *Standard* and the leader of the African slave-trade agitation, thirty-five-year-old Leonidas W. Spratt became widely known throughout the South. Young Southerners like Hughes, De Bow, and Spratt could see the relationship between their careers and their defense of slavery. In his effort to recruit Southerners into the agitation, Spratt privately informed a rising young South Carolina politician: "I would be glad [if] I could persuade you to favor the proposition to remove the restrictions from the slave trade. I think we will certainly come to defend slavery

[17] Quoted in Rollin G. Osterweis, *Romanticism and Nationalism in the Old South* (Baton Rouge: Louisiana State University Press, 1967), p. 141.

in its integrity and I think it would be well for *a young man* to have no record upon the subject to be expunged." [18]

Since slave prices were extremely high in the 1850's and since slaveholding social mobility was diminishing as the Civil War approached, the defense of slavery was an important route to prestige and power for many of these young men of the South. The pro-slavery rhetoric of nonslaveholding fire-eaters like Spratt was a key to the parlours of the planter class. Committed to the defense of slave property, they were identified politically with the planter class; furthermore, they had a social relationship with the Southern elite. Young men like De Bow could even marry into the planter class. Their pro-slavery aggressiveness may have functioned as a substitute for the actual basis of status—large slaveholding assets. But their concerns went beyond status. As advocates of a proposal often regarded as too "ultra" in Southern society, many of them were actually risking their careers.[19] Perhaps they truly believed that they would be able to persuade the South "to defend slavery in its integrity," and that it would be well for them as young men to have an unblemished record on the African slave-trade question.

Above all, however, advocates like Spratt and Hughes were pro-slavery moralists, aggressively avowing their belief in the rightness of slavery. Their anxiety about slavery as a moral question was related to their youthfulness. As young men growing up and maturing in an era of crisis, they faced the greater part of a lifetime ahead of them and worried about the destiny of the slave states. Concerned about Northern moral criticisms and Southern moral doubts towards slavery, they felt an overriding sense of urgency to confront and resolve the vexatious moral dilemmas of their besieged slaveholding society. Unlike Southern men of an earlier era, they could not declare, as did Hezekiah Niles of Maryland in 1830, that the question of slavery "*must* be met sometime, though probably not in our

[18] Spratt to J. J. Pettigrew, November 29, 1856, Pettigrew Papers, North Carolina Archives. Italics added.
[19] Milledgeville *Federal Union*, August 23, 1859.

day." [20] The time had come, as the famous Walrus said and as these young men could see, to talk of many things.

The agitation to reopen the African slave trade was to an important extent a revolt of young men. One of them was described by a contemporary observer as "a fast young Southern . . . looked upon as a pattern man by the rising youth." [21] Of course there were old Southern fire-eaters and young Southern Unionists. But the generational experience of many young men of the South made it possible for them and helped to compel them to come to radical conclusions about the defense of slavery and the destruction of the Union. Born after the nationalistic American Revolution and the War of 1812, raised in an age of sectional crisis, educated in pro-slavery thought, anxious about the future of Southern society, these youthful and energetic Southerners were prepared to lead a pro-slavery crusade. They had been "the children of . . . Nullifiers"; their childhood memories were not about the battle at New Orleans but the slave insurrection at Southampton. Unlike earlier Southerners like George Washington and Thomas Jefferson, their career patterns were related to section- rather than nation-building. As young men of the South, they were ready to agitate for the reopening of the African slave trade in defiance of the anti-slavery sentiments of western civilization.

[20] Niles, quoted in Herbert Aptheker, *American Negro Slave Revolts* (New York: International Publishers, 1963), p. 292.

[21] New York *Tribune,* April 1, 1859. A correspondent's description of C. A. L. Lamar, an advocate of the African slave trade.

THREE

THE PRO-AFRICAN
SLAVE-TRADE
ARGUMENT

the pro-African slave-trade argument was undoubtedly the most extreme and aggressive ideological defense of slavery. In newspapers, magazines, letters, speeches, public meetings, Southern Commercial Conventions, political conventions, election campaigns, and state legislatures, hundreds of Southerners were advocating the African slave trade. In their defense of the African slave trade, they were expressing and revealing their deepest concerns and anxieties about themselves and their slaveholding society. The pro-African slave-trade argument was a mirror of the Old South in profound crisis.

After the admission of California as a free state in 1850, Southerners felt a new sense of powerlessness. They knew the North had a majority in both houses of Congress, and they worried about this new loss of Southern influence in the federal government. A few years later in the election of 1856, they watched the newly organized Republican Party make its national debut. But the anti-slavery party failed to capture the Presidency, and the editor of the Richmond *Enquirer* hailed the Democratic victory: "The Union is safe. The Star Spangled Banner yet waves in undiminished splendor in the atmosphere of a Democratic republic. . . . Let the hearts of desponding patriots take wing, in the hope that the country and its institutions are safe in the haven of Democracy." [1] But for many Southerners the election of 1856 represented a Pyrrhic victory—a success more disturbing than comforting. They saw their illusions shattered. They saw the ominous narrowness of the Buchanan margin. They saw that the Republican Party was no Liberty Party, no Free Soil Party—anti-slavery parties that could attract little support. They saw it as a vital, powerful, and therefore dangerous subversive organization which could destroy their peculiar institution. Representative William Barksdale of Mississippi pessimistically commented that the anti-slavery sentiment was at first "a mere speck upon the political horizon; now it overspreads the whole political skies." [2] And the Galveston *Weekly News,* which would soon become a propaganda engine for the African slave trade, expressed the view of many upset Southerners: "We have but just been awakened from this dream of fancied security—to find the entire North, and a large majority of the West, voting in solid columns against us, on questions vital to our very existence." [3] An Englishman touring the South

[1] Richmond *Enquirer,* November 7, 1856.

[2] William Barksdale, speech, in appendix to the *Congressional Globe,* 36 Congress, 1st session, p. 170.

[3] Galveston *Weekly News,* January 24, 1857. For further evidence, see John Mc Rae, "Governor's Message," in *Journal of the Senate of the State of Mississippi, 1856,* (Jackson: E. Barksdale, 1856), pp. 9–10; Charleston *Mercury,* November 20, 1856; Mobile *Tribune,* in Charleston *Mercury,* April 16, 1857; John A. Winston, "Governor's Message," *Journal of the*

shortly after the election, observed a deep uneasiness among Southerners, who, he said, had seen the handwriting on the wall.[4] The election had confirmed their apprehensions about the recent political powerlessness of the South.

After the election of 1856, many of these Southerners advocated the reopening of the African slave trade. But some of the advocates occasionally insisted that their aim was to save the Union.[5] They argued that the cause of the decline of Southern power in the national government was the federal prohibition of the African slave trade. As a result of this prohibition, Southern population did not increase as rapidly as Northern population, swelled by the flow of European immigrants. While Northern representation in Congress steadily increased, Southern representation lagged. While the North expanded into the territories, the South lacked the slave resources for territorial expansion. But the African slave trade, Spratt and his associates guaranteed, would reverse this dangerous trend and contribute directly to the political power of the South. Every 50,000 slaves that came would give their section the right to 30,000 votes in federal representation.[6] One of the resolutions introduced at an African slave-trade meeting at Mount Pleasant, South Carolina, asserted that only the importation of Africans could give the South sufficient political power to defend its rights within the Union.[7] Henry Hughes of Mississippi, a sociolo-

Sixth Biennial Session of the Senate of the State of Alabama, Session of 1857–58 (Montgomery: N. B. Cloud, 1858), p. 24; Jackson *Semi-Weekly Mississippian,* November 28, 1856; New Orleans *Bulletin,* in Charleston *Mercury,* November 20, 1856.

[4] James Stirling, *Letters from the Slave States* (London: John W. Parker and Son, 1857), pp. 92–93.

[5] Fitzhugh, "Wealth of the North and the South," *De Bow's Review,* XXIII (December 1857), p. 593; Fitzhugh, "The Administration and the Slave Trade," *De Bow's Review,* XXVI (1859), p. 145. For additional evidence, see Pollard, *A New Southern Policy,* p. 7; Galveston *Weekly News,* May 28, 1859; Charleston *Mercury,* July 12, 1859; Spratt, "Report, Montgomery," *De Bow's Review,* XXIV (June, 1858), p. 491; Richmond *Whig,* June 8, 1858.

[6] J. A. Calhoun, in *De Bow's Review,* XXII (January, 1857), p. 221; New Orleans *Delta,* in Charleston *Mercury,* November 6, 1856; Spratt, *Foreign Slave Trade,* p. 4.

[7] Charleston *Mercury,* October 22, 1859.

gist and state senator, suggested that if Mississippi promptly reopened the trade, the new African population would entitle his state to nine instead of five Congressmen in 1860.[8]

Furthermore the African slave trade could provide a supply of slaves for Southern expansion into the territories. The Kansas-Nebraska Act and the Dred Scott Decision had opened the territories to slavery, but where were the slaves to occupy these new lands, these potential slave states? "Why," asked a writer to the Edgefield *Advertiser,* "contend for the abstract right to extend the area of slavery in Kansas, California and in other localities without furnishing the Africans necessary to accomplish it?"[9] After the voters of Kansas had rejected the pro-slavery Lecompton Constitution in 1858, Spratt pointed to the Kansas disappointment and declared: "Ten thousand masters have failed to take Kansas, but so would not have failed ten thousand slaves. Ten thousand of the rudest Africans . . . would have swept the free soil party from the land." [10] The horizon of Southern expansionist dreams, however, was not limited to Kansas but extended to Mexico, Cuba, and South America. The South needed Africans to cultivate "all these beautiful rich prairie plains, not only here where the Eagle already floats—but if it be our destiny in the Providence of God—over the fallen Empire of the Astec [*sic*], and Central America, and even to the rich valley of the Amizon [*sic*]." [11] Thus Southerners like Spratt and Hughes concluded

[8] Jackson *Semi-Weekly Mississippian,* January 12, 1858. See also Spratt, "Report, Montgomery," *De Bow's Review,* XXIV (June, 1858), p. 481; Spratt, speech, in Boston *Liberator,* August 12, 1859; Charleston *Mercury,* July 24, 1858; Mississippi *Cross City,* in Boston *Liberator,* October 14, 1859; New Orleans *Daily Delta,* October 1, 1858.

[9] Edgefield *Advertiser,* March 30, 1859. For further evidence, see Richmond *Whig,* May 21, 1858; Knoxville *Southern Citizen,* in Jackson *Semi-Weekly Mississippian,* January 12, 1858; Charleston *Mercury,* July 14, 1859; Spratt, *Foreign Slave Trade,* p. 5; Fitzhugh, "Missionary Failures," *De Bow's Review,* XXVII (October, 1859), p. 385; Mobile *Register,* in Richmond *Enquirer,* September 20, 1859; Savannah *Daily News,* September 27, 1858; Bryan, *Report,* p. 27; Henry S. Foote, *War of the Rebellion* (New York: Harper, 1866), pp. 254–255.

[10] Spratt, speech, in Boston *Liberator,* August 12, 1859.

[11] *American Cotton Planter,* II, No. 11 (November, 1858), p. 381; letter signed "Scipio," in Edgefield *Advertiser,* March 23, 1859; Natchez

that the South needed population, and that the influx of Africans would restore Southern power and permit the South to protect and preserve Southern rights within the Union.[12]

Of course this policy would work only if the North accepted the proposal to renew the African slave trade. But even if the North rejected the proposal, the issue could still be used to defend Southern rights, for it could help to bring about secession. This either-or-strategy was set forth clearly by Spratt. "If permitted," he argued, "it will lead the South to power and fortune within this Union; if not permitted, but yet approved of Southern sentiment, it will lead the South to independence out of it. This, therefore, is the only, the real and efficient measure."[13] Spratt was well aware that the first program—Northern acceptance of the African slave trade and the protection of slavery within the Union—was not possible, and that his real goal was secession.

Not all advocates agreed with Spratt on this point. George Fitzhugh of Virginia and William Goulden of Georgia seemed to have honestly turned to the trade to save the South and the Union. Dubious about secession, Fitzhugh praised the African slave-trade advocates as "patriots" ready to make great sacrifices to preserve peace and Union, and he warned that no other measure could save the Union from dissolution.[14] Dedicated to

Free Trader, February 5, 1859; in Rainwater, *Mississippi, Storm Center of Secession, 1856–1861,* pp. 76–77; *De Bow's Review,* XXIII (September, 1857), p. 237; New Orleans *Delta,* in Charleston *Mercury,* November 25, 1856.

[12] Spratt, "Report, Montgomery," *De Bow's Review,* XXIV (June, 1858), p. 481; John McRae, in New Orleans *Daily Delta,* October 1, 1858; Port Gibson *Southern Reveille,* December 26, 1857, in Henry Hughes Scrapbook, Hughes Papers, Mississippi State Archives, Jackson, Mississippi; Spratt, speech, in Boston *Liberator,* August 12, 1859; New Orleans *Daily Delta,* March 31, 1858.

[13] Spratt, "Report, Montgomery," in *De Bow's Review,* XXVII (June 1859), p. 209. See also C. W. Miller, *Address on Re-opening the Slave Trade,* p. 10; Fitzhugh, "Wealth of the North and the South," *De Bow's Review,* XXIII (December, 1857), p. 595.

[14] Fitzhugh, "Wealth of the North and the South," *De Bow's Review,* XXIII (December, 1857), p. 593; Fitzhugh, "The Administration and the Slave Trade," *De Bow's Review,* XXVI (1859), p. 145; see also C. Van Woodward, "Preface," to George Fitzhugh, *Cannibals All! or Slaves with-*

the African slave trade, Goulden was nonetheless a Unionist. In 1860 he opposed the Southern bolt from the National Democratic Convention at Charleston and campaigned for Stephen A. Douglas in the presidential election.[15] Fitzhugh and Goulden supported both the Union and the African slave trade.

But most advocates, even those who talked about the trade as a Unionist program, were actually seeking to destroy the Union through the African slave-trade agitation. In their rhetorical appeal to Unionism, they sought to involve the South in a movement for an impossible demand, and to force the frustrated South into secession. They knew Congress would never repeal the federal laws against the trade. One of the advocates, Colonel Shepherd of Alabama, frankly admitted that he did not believe those laws could be repealed, and that his position on the African slave trade would lead to disunion.[16] The efforts of many advocates to repeal these laws were designed to *agitate* an issue rather than actually to remove the prohibition. In a private letter to Representative William P. Miles, Spratt urged that Southern Congressmen continue fighting for the repeal, "not to triumph. . . . Our only object is to render the South *Sui Juris* upon the subject of domestic slavery and the war in Congress if it shall not end in victory on that field will gain as much by demonstrating the fact that the Union is inconsistent with our objects."[17]

The demand for the African slave trade could hardly have been a Unionist program because with rare exceptions the advocates were secessionists. William Yancey and Edmund Ruffin

out Masters, edited by Woodward (Cambridge, Mass.: Belknap Press, 1960), p. xxx; Harvey Wish (ed.), "Introduction," *Ante-Bellum Writings of George Fitzhugh and Hinton Rowan Helper on Slavery* (New York: Putnam's, 1960), p. 15.

15 W. Goulden, speech, in *The Rebuke of Secession Doctrines by Southern Statesmen* (Philadelphia, 1863), p. 14; Washington *National Intelligencer,* May 5, 1860; Milledgeville *Federal Union,* September 11, 1860.

16 Colonel Shepherd, in Galveston *Civilian,* July 19, 1859; Ruffin, Diary, December 24, 1857, Library of Congress.

17 Spratt to Miles, February 12, 1859, Miles Papers, University of North Carolina Library. See also New Orleans *Delta,* in Boston *Liberator,* November 14, 1856; William Yancey, in *De Bow's Review,* XXIV (June, 1858), p. 587.

were the chief founders of the League of United Southerners, whose aim, according to Yancey, was to *"fire the Southern heart, instruct the Southern mind . . . and at the proper moment, by one organized, concerted action . . . precipitate the cotton States into a revolution."* [18] Most advocates were convinced that the South could never remain in the Union and at the same time preserve slavery. "We must separate," Edmund Ruffin bluntly informed a fellow Southerner. Dr. J. G. M. Ramsey of Tennessee concealed from no one his deep conviction that the days of the Union were numbered. For William Middleton of South Carolina, the chief question was not the destruction of the Union but the means to destroy it. South Carolina State Senator Edward Bryan announced loudly: "THE POLITICAL INDEPENDENCE OF THE SOUTH, *in this Union,* IS DEAD." [19] On June 19, 1856, the editor of the Charleston *Mercury* fatalistically prophecized that the entry of the slavery issue into national politics had sealed the doom of the Union, and that the South must secede from or be destroyed by the Union.[20]

Many African slave-trade advocates themselves, moreover,

[18] William Yancey, letter to Mr. Slaughter, in Richmond *Whig,* July 21, 1960. For further information about the League of United Southerners, see Ruffin, Diary, May 27, 1858, August 11, 1858, and August 31, 1858, Library of Congress; Richmond *Enquirer,* August 2, 1858, and September 21, 1858, Charleston *Mercury,* July 26, 1858, and August 2, 1858; Milledgeville *Federal Union,* August 10, 1858; Montgomery *Confederation,* in New York *Anti-Slavery Standard,* August 7, 1858.

[19] Ruffin to C. C. Clay, February 2, 1857, C. C. Clay Papers, Duke University Library; Ramsey to Spratt, April 29, 1858, Ramsey Papers, University of North Carolina Library; William Middleton, "Black Republican Success and a Southern Union," *De Bow's Review,* XXVIII (January, 1860), pp. 17–18; Edward Bryan, *The Disunionist: or, Secession, The Rightful Remedy* (Charleston: 1850), in Bryan, Scrap Book, IV (n.p. n.d.), p. 140, University of North Carolina Library.

[20] Charleston *Mercury,* June 19, 1856. For additional evidence, see Charleston *Mercury,* October 29, 1856, August 13, 1858; John Townsend, *The Southern States, Their Present Peril* (Charleston: E. C. Councell, 1850), p. 28; Dillon, *Life of John Mitchel,* 11, p. 107; R. T. Archer, in Charleston *Mercury,* October 23, 1856; R. B. Rhett, letter to J. Adams, in Charleston *Mercury,* November 7, 1856; A. P. Calhoun, in *De Bow's Review,* XXVI (April, 1859), p. 476; New Orleans *Delta,* in Charleston *Mercury,* March 2, 1858; New Orleans *Crescent,* in Charleston *Mercury,* May 6, 1857.

openly confessed that their proposal would deepen the sectional antagonism and hasten the conflict. Spratt boldly challenged: "Is it that it would precipitate an issue? That is to be wished for. The contest is inevitable. The power is with the North and the purpose of aggression is declared."[21] After his visit to Charleston in 1857, Ruffin recorded in his diary that the renewal of the trade was impossible but that the proposal would operate strongly to promote secession.[22] During an 1859 Fourth of July celebration in South Carolina, the people toasted: *"The African Slave Trade.*—Regarded by some as a step towards dissolution. If it be that thus the Union will be dissolved, in God's name, let the step be taken." [23]

This relationship between the African slave-trade agitation and disunion involved the disruption of the National Democratic Party. Aware that the National Democracy was, in William Yancey's words, "the only ligament that united the North and the South," advocates of the African slave trade knew their issue could split the party and thereby clear the path to secession.[24] They had seen the Etheridge Congressional resolution divide the National Democratic Party in December 1856. They did not openly confess that their purpose was to break the Democracy, yet they privately expressed hopes for the destruction of the party. In his diary, Ruffin wrote that he heartily desired an open break between the Southern and Northern Democrats, and the end of the National Democratic Party. "Still better if this 'national' democratic party, shall then be defeated and ruptured, and an abolitionist elected. Then perhaps the South may act for its defence and only salvation." [25] In addition

21 Spratt, speech, in Jackson *Semi-Weekly Mississippian*, May 20, 1859. See also Spratt, *Foreign Slave Trade*, p. 29.

22 Ruffin, Diary, May 15, 1857, Library of Congress.

23 Savannah *Morning News*, July 14, 1859. For further evidence, see Galveston *Weekly News*, March 9, 1858; Charleston *Mercury*, August 13, 1858; Spratt, *Foreign Slave Trade*, pp. 9, 29; New Orleans *Delta*, in Boston *Liberator*, November 14, 1856.

24 Yancey, quoted by Roger Pryor, speech, Montgomery Convention, in *De Bow's Review*, XXIV (June, 1858), p. 582.

25 Ruffin, Diary, April 25, 1859, August 14, 1858, August 15, 1858, Library of Congress.

The Pro-African Slave-Trade Argument

they publicly expressed their distrust of the national party. State Representative John Izard Middleton, an advocate from South Carolina, asked the readers of the Charleston *Mercury:* "Is not the northern wing hopelessly abolitionized?" John Mitchel of the *Southern Citizen* charged that the most effective allies of William Seward and the North were the Southern National Democrats. In his speech in the United States Senate on February 24, 1851, Robert Barnwell Rhett saw no hope for cooperation with the Northern Democrats: "At the last session of Congress they surrendered to their enemies; they went over in the free States to the consolidationists, in order that together they might spoil the South." [26] The connection between pro-slave-trade and anti-Democratic sentiments may be seen in a letter signed "H" in the Edgefield *Advertiser* of September 15, 1858. While urging the renewal of the trade and Southern secession, this writer assailed the National Democratic Party. "The more we become Nationalized, or affiliate with National Democracy," he argued, "the worse it will be for the South."

Contemporary observers often noted this relationship between the African slave-trade agitation and secession. Frederick Law Olmsted, the ubiquitous traveler in the South, viewed the issue as a logical step towards disunion. "Is dissolution or the slave trade," he asked, "to be the next alternative presented to us by the politicians of the South?" [27] William H. Trescot, who thoughtfully probed the nature of the trade question, came to a similar inescapable conclusion. "I am brought to the conclusion," he wrote to William Porcher Miles, "that in the Union there is no room for the discussion of these questions and if they are so earnest . . . as Southern men would represent—then dissolution is absolutely necessary." [28]

[26] John Middleton, Letter, in Charleston *Mercury*, February 22, 1856; Knoxville *Southern Citizen*, in Richmond *Whig*, May 25, 1859; Rhett, in Edgefield *Advertiser*, March 13, 1851. For additional evidence, see Charleston *Mercury*, December 5, 1854, May 11, 1857; New Orleans *Delta*, in Charleston *Mercury*, November 25, 1856, May 11, 1857; J. H. Adams, in Galveston *Weekly News*, October 26, 1858.

[27] Olmsted, *A Journey in the Back Country*, p. 372.

[28] Trescot to Miles, February 8, 1859, Miles Papers, University of

Clearly the African slave-trade agitation had a secessionist function. But the advocates were divided over an important question: should the South actually reopen the African slave trade? Advocates like Georgia businessman C. A. L. Lamar thought the agitation should involve the actual importation of African slaves. Such boldness would certainly hasten the end of the Union. But advocates like William Yancey made a distinction between the demand for the repeal of the federal laws against the trade and the demand for the actual reopening of the trade. In his report to the 1858 Montgomery Southern Commercial Convention, Yancey argued that the laws prohibiting the foreign slave trade not only violated the spirit of the Constitution but were also unjust and insulting to the South. He asked the convention to adopt a resolution calling for the repeal of those laws.[29] But unlike Lamar, Yancey did not advocate the reopening of the trade. In a letter to Thomas J. Orme, Yancey explained that a reading of his report would show that he did not recommend the reopening of the African slave trade. "What I did recommend was simply *the repeal* of the laws of Congress making the foreign trade in slaves piracy." Yancey added that his real interest was "to strip the Southern ship of State for battle. . . ."[30] Thus Lamar and Yancey had different views about the actual importation of African slaves. But they both hoped their agitation would help them realize their wildest dreams of a Southern Confederacy.

The agitation to reopen the African slave trade was designed to protect the South against the emergence of political anti-slavery in the North. But the agitation was much more than a

North Carolina Library. See also the Cincinnati *Gazette*, in the Washington *National Intelligencer*, January 23, 1861; *Republican Banner and Nashville Whig*, December 28, 1856; Wade Hampton to J. J. Pettigrew, May 28, 1858, Pettigrew Papers, North Carolina Archives.

[29] Yancey, in Jackson *Semi-Weekly Mississippian*, May 28, 1858.

[30] Yancey to Orme, in John W. Du Bose, *The Life and Times of William Lowndes Yancey*, 2 Vols. (New York: Peter Smith, 1942), I, p. 367. See also *ibid.*, I, p. 359; Yancey, speech, *De Bow's Review*, XXIV (June, 1858), p. 587.

revolution to achieve Southern political independence from a Northern-controlled Union. Consequently what concerns us more deeply in our analysis is the question: how was the African slave-trade radicalism a response to the internal crisis of the Old South?

The internal crisis was related to the economic threat of the scarcity of slave labor. During the 1850's many advocates of the African slave trade shared an uneasy fear of foreign cotton competition. They were anxiously aware of reports describing the successful cultivation of cotton in India and Africa. In February 1854, the *American Cotton Planter* published Alexander Mackay's report that the South might find India a formidable competitor in reduced-price cotton.[31] A few years later the *Southern Planter* informed its readers that Great Britain had imported 654,758,008 pounds of cotton from the South and 250,338,144 pounds from India in 1857. But Africa, too, loomed as a potential competitor. According to an article reprinted in the Charleston *Mercury*, Africa was suitable for cotton cultivation and was already marketing raw cotton.[32]

Ironically this new threat of foreign cotton cultivation was due largely to the rise in cotton prices. Throughout the 1840's the South had been in a severe depression caused chiefly by the collapse of cotton prices. The average price of cotton for that decade was about 8 cents per pound, a significant drop from the 12.6 cents average price of the 1830's. In 1845 cotton hit a disastrous low of 5¾ cents per pound.[33] "At no period of

[31] Alexander Mackay, "The Growth of Cotton in India," *American Cotton Planter*, II, No. 2 (February, 1854), p. 46. See also the *Southern Planter*, XVIII, No. 9 (September, 1858), p. 524; London *Economist*, February 12, 1859, in E. N. Elliott (ed.), *Cotton Is King* (Augusta: Pritchard, 1860), p. 104.

[32] *The Southern Planter*, XX, No. 1 (January, 1860), p. 14; Charleston *Mercury*, November 1, 1858. According to James Adams, in his 1856 message to the legislature, the United States in 1855 sent 679 million pounds of cotton to Britain, while the East Indies, Egypt, and Brazil sent 202 million pounds. Adams, "Message," reprinted in Bryan, *Report*, p. 47. See also New Orleans *Daily Delta*, October 6, 1858; *De Bow's Review*, XXIII (December, 1857), pp. 624–639.

[33] Russel, *Economic Aspects of Southern Sectionalism*, p. 33; *De Bow's Review*, XXII (1857), p. 475; Phillips, *Life and Labor in the Old*

our history from the year 1781," wrote a contributor to the *Southern Quarterly Review* of July 1845, "has a greater gloom been cast over the agricultural prospects of South Carolina, than at the present time." [34] Four years later, however, the price of cotton shot up to 11½ cents a pound, and the South entered into a decade of economic prosperity.[35] But it was this very rise in cotton prices that stimulated the production of cotton in Africa and India.

Advocates of the African slave trade undoubtedly welcomed the new price rise, but they were also extremely apprehensive that the development of foreign cotton competition would jeopardize the Southern cotton monopoly. They noticed that the European demand for cotton was increasing rapidly but that the Southern capacity to keep pace with the demand was handicapped by its limited supply of labor. They knew only too well that the closing of the African slave trade had transformed slavery into an inflexible system of labor—a system dependent on natural increase for new laborers.

And they could clearly see the dangerous consequences of this weakness. Louisiana State Senator Edward Delony observed that the Southern cotton production in 1856 was only 3 million bales, the same as the Southern cotton output of 1851. European cotton consumption, on the other hand, was rising. Unless the South found a means to increase her production of cotton, Delony concluded, Europe would be forced to look elsewhere for it.[36] In his 1856 message to the South Carolina legislature, Governor James H. Adams warned that high cotton prices would encourage foreign countries to cultivate more cotton, and this competition would lead to the destruction of the Southern cotton monopoly. The loss of this monopoly would be a disaster for

South, p. 177; F. W. Sargent, *England, the United States and the Southern Confederacy* (London: Hamilton, Adams and Company, 1864), pp. 68–69.

[34] *Southern Quarterly Review*, VIII (July, 1845), p. 118, quoted in Russel, p. 34.

[35] Phillips, *Life and Labor*, p. 177; Russel, *Economic Aspects of Southern Sectionalism*, p. 35; Edgefield *Advertiser*, June 13, 1855.

[36] Edward Delony, "The South Demands More Negro Labor," *De Bow's Review*, XXV (1858), pp. 496–497.

the South. "Whenever England and the continent can procure
their supply of raw material elsewhere than from us, and the
cotton states are limited to the home market, then will our
doom be sealed. Destroy the value of slave labor, and emancipation follows immediately." [37] Thus, in order to meet the
demand for cotton, crush the new African and Indian competitors in cotton cultivation, and preserve slavery, Governor
Adams recommended the reopening of the African slave trade.[38]

The high cotton prices of the 1850's noticeably boosted
the price of slaves. The price of a prime field hand in the New
Orleans market skyrocketed from $700 in 1845 to $1,000 in 1850
to $1,800 in 1860, and the slave prices in the Virginia, Georgia,
and Charleston markets followed the same pattern.[39] In 1859
Edmund Ruffin estimated that slave prices had doubled since
1844 and that the escalation would continue. A Southerner told
Frederick Olmsted "a nigger that wouldn't bring over $300,
seven years ago, will fetch $1,000, cash, quick, this year."
Southern newspapers throughout the fifties reported the new
slave prices with great excitement. In 1854 the New Orleans
Delta, for example, announced that at a recent sale slave prices
were "extraordinary," and that one man commanded $3,000,
another $1,970, others $1,600 and $1,700.[40]

[37] Adams, "Message," in Bryan, *Report on the Message of Governor
Adams*, pp. 46–47.

[38] For this argument, see also Charleston *Mercury*, August 3, 1858;
George Fitzhugh, "The Administration and the Slave Trade," *De Bow's
Review*, XXVI (1856), p. 145; Fitzhugh, "Wealth of the North and the
South," *De Bow's Review*, XXIII (December, 1857), pp. 592–593; Bryan,
Report on the Message of Governor Adams, p. 19; James De Bow, letter
to William Yancey, in *De Bow's Review*, XXVII, (August, 1859), p. 234;
and Mobile *Daily Register*, in Jackson *Semi-Weekly Mississippian*, August
12, 1859.

[39] Phillips, *American Negro Slavery*, p. 370. See also Lewis C. Gray,
History of Agriculture in the Southern United States to 1860, 2 Vols.
(Washington: Waverly Press, 1933), Vol. II, p. 666.

[40] Bancroft, *Slave Trading*, p. 342; Olmsted, *A Journey in the Back
Country*, p. 226; New Orleans *Delta* in Milledgeville *Federal Union*,
February 28, 1854. See also Newbern (North Carolina) *Daily Progress*,
January 8, 1859; Huntsville *Texas Beacon*, in *Republican Banner and
Nashville Whig*, May 22, 1858; Richmond *Dispatch*, in Charleston *Mer-
cury*, February 2, 1856; New Orleans *Picayune*, January 20, 1860; Jack-

Many Southerners were worried because the new high prices departed from the old rule of pricing a slave by the price of a pound of cotton. According to this rule, if cotton were worth twelve cents, a slave was worth $1,200. But, as the above prices show, this ratio was hardly the case in the 1850's. While cotton prices had doubled, slave prices had tripled. The editor of the Montgomery *Journal* reported the slave prices at an auction in 1854. "These are the highest prices," he commented, "which we have ever noticed paid for negroes of this description." While Southerners could view the high prices as an indication of the abiding confidence in the prosperity of the planting interest, they also feared that prices were ranging "far above their legitimate point" and were not justified by the ruling rates for the value of cotton.[41]

Some Southerners blamed speculation for this discrepancy between cotton and slave prices. A domestic slave trader told Olmsted there was a passion among Louisiana planters to buy slaves. The editor of the Milledgeville *Federal Union* observed that there was "a perfect fever raging in Georgia now on the subject of buying negroes. . . . Men are borrowing money at exorbitant prices. . . . Men are demented on the subject." [42] But many Southerners emphasized the scarcity of slave labor as the explanation for the unreasonable rise in slave prices. P. A. Morse of Louisiana calculated that the natural increase of slaves could not supply the number of slaves necessary to produce enough cotton to satisfy the demand for cotton in 1860. Thus the cotton planters were forced to buy slaves at excessive rates.[43] J. M.

son *Semi-Weekly Mississippian,* January 14, 1859, and May 6, 1859; Nashville *Union,* December 13, 1856, and February 8, 1859; Montgomery (Alabama) *Journal,* in *Hunt's Merchant Magazine,* XXX (April, 1854), p. 500.

[41] Montgomery Journal, in *Hunt's Merchant Magazine,* III (April, 1854), p. 500.

[42] Frederick Law Olmsted, *A Journey in the Seaboard Slave States in the Years 1853–1854 with Remarks on their Economy,* 2 Vols. (New York: G. P. Putnam's Sons, 1904), Vol. II, pp. 308–309; Milledgeville *Federal Union,* January 17, 1860. See also, Bancroft, *Slave Trading in the Old South,* p. 340.

[43] P. A. Morse, "Southern Slavery and the Cotton Trade," *De Bow's Review,* XXIII (November, 1857), pp. 479–480.

Cardoza of Charleston pointed out that while the cotton demand had increased, the labor supply had been limited, and thus the price of field hands had risen nearly 100 per cent in five years. The editor of the Charleston *Mercury* explained that the doubling of prices was due to "the *scarcity of,* as compared with the multiplying *demands for labor.*" [44]

And what was the cause of the scarcity of slave labor? The advocates blamed the federal prohibition of the African slave trade. "All the southern states," complained Edmund Ruffin, "suffer greatly from the scarcity and high price of labor. They can obtain no supply from abroad, because the only available and useful supply, of negroes, is prohibited by law." Concerned about the limited resources of slave labor and the consequent high prices of slaves, the editor of the *American Cotton Planter* demanded the reopening of the African slave trade. [45]

The fresh supply of Africans, advocates promised, would reduce the cost of production and increase profits. [46] This point had a special interest for Edmund Ruffin, Virginia's leading agriculturalist. In "The Effects of High Prices of Slaves," published in *De Bow's Review,* he asserted that the prices for slaves had already exceeded the profits of their labor in Virginia, and he implied that the African slave trade would correct this dangerous situation. [47] In a private letter to Ruffin, dated June 29, 1859, editor James De Bow wrote: "Your article in June No. is capital. It is exactly to our purpose and proves *we must have*

[44] J. M. Cardoza, "Growth and Consumption of Cotton," *De Bow's Review,* XXI (August, 1856), 158; Charleston *Mercury,* reprinted in Edgefield *Advertiser,* November 16, 1854.

[45] Ruffin, Diary, May 15, 1857, Library of Congress. For additional evidence, see Daniel Lee, "Laborers for the South," *Southern Cultivator,* XVI, No. 8 (August, 1858), p. 234; Richmond *Whig,* in Savannah *Morning News,* September 26, 1857; *American Cotton Planter,* II, No. 10 (October, 1858), p. 325; Charleston *Mercury,* in Edgefield *Advertiser,* November 16, 1854; Jackson *Semi-Weekly Mississippian,* April 12, 1859; *De Bow's Review,* XXVI, p. 145.

[46] Spratt, "Report on the Slave Trade Made to the Southern Convention at Montgomery, Alabama," *De Bow's Review,* XXIV (June, 1858), pp. 484–485.

[47] Edmund Ruffin, "The Effects of High Prices of Slaves," *De Bow's Review,* reprinted in the *Southern Planter,* XIX, No. 7 (July, 1859), p. 473.

Africans."[48] Many planters, however, feared that the cheap Africans would diminish the value of the slaves they already owned. But a writer to the Charleston *Mercury* reminded them that the slave's intrinsic value was his ability to produce and to improve his master's land. And State Senator I. N. Davis, a fiery advocate from Panola, Mississippi, argued that reduced slave prices would permit the planter to buy with the same annual income twenty rather than ten fieldhands.[49] Furthermore, the advocates pointed out, the new Africans could be used to restore exhausted lands, to cultivate new lands, and to improve the millions of acres of impoverished lands. If the planter spent less on labor, they added, he would be able to spend more on fertilizing the land. In a letter to Spratt, J. G. M. Ramsey, a Tennessee physician, explained that the African slave trade would allow the South to expand the area of agricultural production.[50] But could these newly imported Africans be easily and quickly trained for agricultural labor? African slave-trade radicals proposed the "couple-working system" to facilitate the training of Africans. In this system, the African "savage" would be placed under the tutelage of a "civilized negro." "Education thus becomes imitation, and imitation is the African's talent; he watches his partner and duly learns to plow" the fields and to pick the cotton. The African slave trade and the "couple-working system" would

[48] De Bow to Ruffin, Ruffin Papers, University of North Carolina Library. Alexander Mazyck also made this point. See Las Casas (pseudonym for Alexander Mazyck), *The Charleston Courier and the African Slave Trade* (1858), p. 9.

[49] Letter signed "South," Charleston *Mercury*, August 11, 1858; letter signed "Barnwell," Charleston *Mercury*, August 6, 1858; I. N. Davis, in Jackson *Semi-Weekly Mississippian*, April 26, 1859.

[50] August *Constitutionalist*, in Charleston *Mercury*, February 12, 1858; Jackson *Semi-Weekly Mississippian*, April 24, 1860; Daniel Lee, "Laborers for the South," *Southern Cultivator*, XVI, No. 8 (August, 1858), p. 236; J. G. M. Ramsey to Spratt, April 13, 1858; J. G. M. Ramsey Papers, University of North Carolina Library. For further evidence, see Bryan, *Report on the Message of Gov. Adams*, pp. 19–20; C. W. Miller, *Address on Re-opening the Slave Trade . . . to the Citizens of Barnwell at Wylde-Moore* (Columbia, 1857), p. 3; Edward Pollard, *A New Southern Policy, or the Slave Trade as Meaning Union and Conservatism.* (n.p. 185?), p. 5; Galveston *Weekly News*, June 20, 1857, and September 14, 1858.

provide the South with thousands of trained cultivators of the soil.[51]

But, for many Southerners, more important than the cultivation of new fields was the construction of new factories. "The South can manufacture for the world. . . . Manufactures contiguous to the cotton fields have already proved more profitable than cotton culture itself. . . . The smoke of the steam engine should begin to float over the cotton fields, and the hum of spindles and the click of looms make music on all our mountain streams." [52] Clearly these words remind us of the spirit of Henry W. Grady and the "New South" of the 1880's. They were written, however, by the editor of the New Orleans *Picayune* in September 1858, and they expressed a new and exciting Southern ferment to industrialize. This enthusiasm for the development of Southern manufacturing could be found in the essays and speeches of the Southern industrialist William Gregg, in the Southern newspapers announcing and applauding the establishment of factories, in the widely read *De Bow's Review,* in the messages of governors, in the legislative reports, and in the Southern Commercial Conventions. Unlike the latter-day Frank L. Owsley and his band of agrarian sentimentalists, these antebellum Southerners were not rigidly attached to an agrarian ideal.[53]

Neither were they really concerned about the contradiction between the Southern drive for an industrial society and the Southern pride in a cavalier society. Surely a Southern gentleman should feel uncomfortable in the alien and busy world of factories and cities. Yet these antebellum Gradys were willing to "out-Yankee the Yankee" in manufacturing. And like the "New South" of Grady, the quest for Southern industrialism in

[51] New Orleans *Delta,* February 14, 1858.

[52] New Orleans *Picayune,* September 4, 1858. The editor of the *Picayune* was not an advocate of the African slave trade; but, as we shall see, his enthusiasm for industrialization was shared with many advocates.

[53] See Frank Lawrence Owsley, "The Irrepressible Conflict," in *I'll Take My Stand: The South and the Agrarian Tradition* (New York: Harper & Brothers, 1962), pp. 61–91.

the 1850's was not motivated simply by a love for progress but also by a deep hatred for Southern economic dependence upon the North. Southerners were jealously aware of their inferior economic status. They saw the obvious economic differences between the two sections in the tables of the 1850 Census published in *De Bow's Review,* and they were reminded about this dependence again and again by Southern newspapers. The editor of an Alabama newspaper, for example, observed:

> At present, the North fattens and grows rich upon the South. We purchase all our luxuries and necessaries from the North. . . . With us, every branch and pursuit in life . . . is dependent upon the North. . . . The slaveholder dresses in Northern goods, rides in a Northern saddle . . . sports his Northern carriage, patronizes Northern newspapers, drinks Northern liquors. . . . The aggressive acts upon his rights and his property arouse his resentment—and on Northern-made paper, with a Northern pen, with Northern ink, he resolves and re-resolves in regard to his rights! [54]

One of the chief objectives of the sound and fury of Southern industrialism in the 1850's was the overthrow of this despised economic dependence on the North in order to fortify Southern political defenses against Northern abolitionism. W. Sykes advocated the construction of railroads and factories as "the Best Guaranty for the Protection of Southern Rights." In *Sociology for the South,* Fitzhugh proclaimed manufacturing as the road to Southern independence. A writer to the Augusta *Constitutionalist* explained that the introduction of slaves into factories and the industrial development of the South would

[54] Quoted in F. A. P. Barnard, *An Oration Delivered before the Citizens of Tuscaloosa, Alabama, July 4, 1851,* p. 12, requoted by Russel, *Economic Aspects of Southern Sectionalism,* p. 48. For additional evidence, see New Orleans *Daily Crescent,* July 20, 1855, in Avery Craven, *The Growth of Southern Nationalism, 1848–1861* (Baton Rouge: Louisiana State University Press, 1953), pp. 248–249; Lynchburg *Virginian,* quoted in Olmsted, *A Journey in the Seaboard Slave States,* Vol. II, p. 185; *De Bow's Review,* XVI (January, 1854), pp. 81–96.

The Pro-African Slave-Trade Argument

effectively "counteract the incessant and vexatious attacks of the North." [55]

Many advocates of the African slave trade shared this passion for Southern industrialism and economic independence, but they saw that Southern industrial progress was handicapped by the lack of laborers to fill the factories. In a letter to the Jackson *Daily Mississippian,* Henry Hughes asked how the South could develop manufacturing when it did not have enough slaves for agriculture. John Mitchel of the Knoxville *Southern Citizen* put it this way: "What hinders the South from manufacturing her own cotton? Want of labor." Obviously Southern industrialism was impossible without the reopening of the African slave trade.[56] But if the South could reopen her gates to African slaves, industrialism would become a reality. "Give us, then," they promised, "more and cheap operatives, and we would not only have the will, but be enabled to diversify our labor, and improve our country. We would build our own vessels and steamboats, railroads . . . erect manufactories and foundries, build our levees and dikes. . . ." [57] Dr. Daniel Lee, editor of the *Southern Cultivator,* noted the value of Africans for

[55] W. Sykes, "The Development of Southern Resources the Best Guaranty for the Protection of Southern Rights," *De Bow's Review,* XII (May, 1852), pp. 540–542; George Fitzhugh, *Sociology for the South, or the Failure of Free Society* (Richmond: A. Morris, 1854), pp. 93–94; Augusta *Constitutionalist,* reprinted in *De Bow's Review,* VIII (January, 1850), pp. 75–76. For further evidence, see New Orleans *Picayune,* May 27, 1858, and April 27, 1859; John Forsyth, "The North and the South," *De Bow's Review,* XVII (October, 1854), p. 376.

[56] Jackson *Daily Mississippian,* February 7, 1860; Knoxville *Southern Citizen,* in Jackson *Semi-Weekly Mississippian,* January 12, 1858; Jackson *Semi-Weekly Mississippian,* May 20, 1859; February 3, 1860; Fitzhugh, "Missionary Failures," *De Bow's Review,* XXVII (October, 1859), p. 385; Spratt, "Report, Montgomery," in *De Bow's Review,* XXVII (August, 1859), p. 207; Spratt, Speech in the Hall of Representatives, Jackson, Mississippi, Jackson *Semi-Weekly Mississippian,* May 20, 1859.

[57] I. N. Davis, in Jackson *Semi-Weekly Mississippian,* April 26, 1859. For further evidence of the advocacy of the use of Africans to build internal improvements, see *De Bow's Review,* XXVII (September 1859), p. 364; Richmond *Enquirer,* October 29, 1858; Richmond *Whig,* June 8, 1858; Jackson *Semi-Weekly Mississippian,* June 17, 1859; Edward Delony, "Louisiana Senate Report on the African Apprentice System," *De Bow's Review,* XXIV (May, 1858), p. 423.

the mining industry. The editor of the Jackson *Semi-Weekly Mississippian* asserted that the Africans could be used in cotton factories located amidst the fields.[58]

But could the Negro, some Southerners asked, be used as an industrial worker? Did he not have "limited mental capacities," and was he not "unfit for anything save the plantation and menial services?" [59] While African slave-trade radicals agreed that the Negro had an inferior intelligence, they argued that he was well qualified to operate machines. "The negro," Spratt remarked, "in his common absence from reflection, is, perhaps, the best manipulist in the world." [60] The advocates could also point to the thousands of slaves already employed in the iron and tobacco industries of Virginia, the hemp factories of Kentucky, the cotton textile mills of South Carolina and Tennessee, the sawmills of Alabama, the distilleries of Louisiana, and the flour mills of Georgia.[61] To Southerners who doubted the feasi-

[58] Daniel Lee, in Savannah *Daily News*, February 15, 1859; Jackson *Semi-Weekly Mississippian*, June 14, 1859. For additional evidence, see Jackson *Daily Mississippian*, February 3, 1860; Jackson *Semi-Weekly Mississippian*, May 23, 1859; C. W. Miller, *Reopening*, p. 8; Spratt, "Report, Montgomery," *De Bow's Review*, XXIV (June, 1858), p. 484; Houston *State Gazette*, April 14, 1860, in Anna I. Sandbo, "First Session of the Secession Convention in Texas," *The Southwestern Historical Quarterly*, XVIII, No. 2 (October, 1914), p. 165; Charleston *Mercury*, November 17, 1858; J. H. Adams, "Message, 1856," in Bryan, *Report*, p. 48; J. S. Palmer of South Carolina, in New York *Times*, November 17, 1859.

[59] *Republican Banner and Nashville Whig*, June 17, 1858; Lagrange *Reporter*, in *Republican Banner and Nashville Whig*, June 12, 1858.

[60] Spratt, in *De Bow's Review*, XXIV (June, 1858), p. 484; article signed "South," in Charleston *Mercury*, November 17, 1858.

[61] New Orleans *Picayune*, October 16, and November 12, 1858, January 13, and April 27, 1859; Nashville *Union and American*, February 6, and February 20, 1858; Kathleen Bruce, *Virginia Iron Manufacture in the Slave Era* (New York: Century, 1931); *De Bow's Review*, VI (October and November, 1848), p. 291, VII (October, 1849), p. 458, VIII (January, 1850), pp. 75–76, XIV (June, 1853), p. 623, XVIII (April, 1855), p. 530, XIX (August, 1855), p. 194, XXV (December, 1858), p. 717, XXVI (March, 1859), p. 319; Olmsted, *Seaboard*, I, pp. 183–184, II, p. 53; Frederick Law Olmsted, *A Journey Through Texas* (New York: Dix, 1857), pp. 19, 32; Frederika Bremer, *The Homes of the New World: Impressions of America*, 3 Vols. (London: Hall, 1853), III, p. 315; Sterling, *Letters*, p. 296; Charleston *Mercury*, February 26, and October 21, 1858; E. A. Blanch to George Yerger, August 25, 1857,

bility of employing "uncivilized" Africans in manufacturing, Spratt suggested that the Africans could be used in the fields while the civilized slaves could be directed into the factories. In 1859 several Mississippians purchased ten African slaves imported illegally and followed Spratt's advice. According to the Vicksburg *Sun*, "Ten Africans were sold in Vicksburg varying in price from four hundred to one thousand dollars each. . . . these gentlemen wish to establish a manufactory and place their Mississippi born negroes under an overseer, who will learn them to spin, weave and attend the machinery, while they make the Africans cultivate their crops, help to build levees and construct railroads. This arrangement would enable the South to manufacture its own cotton into cloth, and be independent of the North." [62] Obviously the African slave-trade radicals had a more informed and sophisticated understanding of the versatility of slavery as a labor system than certain twentieth century historians. The radicals knew black workers could be used not only in agriculture but also in industry. The expansion of slavery, they could see, had no "natural limits," and an industrial society could be based on the labor of black slaves.[63]

Of course, the South could have attempted to base its industrialization on white labor. But the African slave-trade radicals abhorred such a development, for they were extremely worried about the internal threat of the nonslaveholders of the South. Southern industrialization, these radicals argued, would

T. B. King Papers, University of North Carolina Library; Newbern (North Carolina) *Daily Progress*, January 12, 1859.

[62] Spratt, in Herbert Wender, *The Southern Commercial Conventions* (Baltimore: Johns Hopkins, University Press, 1930), p. 215; Vicksburg *Sun*, in Jackson *Semi-Weekly Mississippian*, May 23, 1859.

[63] Article signed "South," in Charleston *Mercury*, November 17, 1858. For the "Natural Limits" thesis, see Charles W. Ramsdell, "The Natural Limits of Slavery Expansion," *Mississippi Valley Historical Review*, XVI (1929), pp. 151–171. For more evidence on the use of slaves in industry, see Richard C. Wade, *Slavery in the Cities: The South, 1820–1860* (New York: Oxford University Press, 1964), and Robert Starobin, "Industrial Slavery in the Old South, 1790–1861," unpublished Ph. D. thesis, University of California, Berkeley, 1968.

require a large labor supply. The supply of Southern slaves, however, was already limited. Unless the African slave trade were reopened, the industrial workers of the South would have to be white and these white workers in the South would constitute a force hostile to slavery. Thus Southern industrialization and economic independence from the North without the African slave trade would not offer security to the institution of slavery and the South.

Economic competition between white laborers and slaves had existed in the South for a long time. In South Carolina, even as early as 1720, slave labor drove white artisans from the colony; and in 1742, a grand jury, concerned for the interests of white workingmen, demanded a law to prevent the hiring out of slave tradesmen. "I hear the Negroes in Carolina," a Georgian declared, "learn all Sorts of trade, which takes away the bread of a poor white trades'man Likewise." [64] Similar sentiments were expressed about a century later during the famous slavery debate in the Virginia legislature of 1831–32. Slavery, declared Charles James Faulkner, "banishes free white labor, exterminates the mechanic, the artisan, the manufacturer. It deprives them of occupation. It deprives them of bread. . . . Shall all interests be subservient to one—all rights subordinate to those of the slaveholder? Has not the mechanic, have not the middle classes their rights—rights incompatible with the existence of slavery?" [65] In New Orleans, white mechanics declared they would never train slaves; and in Baltimore, the white shipyard apprentices brutally attacked Frederick Douglass, a young slave worker.[66]

A decade later the competition between the white and

[64] U. B. Phillips, "The Slave Labor Problem in the Charleston District," *Political Science Quarterly*, XXII (September, 1907), p. 423; Reverend John M. Bolizius, quoted in Davis, *Slavery*, p. 149.

[65] Quoted in Hinton R. Helper, *The Impending Crisis of the South: How to Meet It* (New York: Burdick Bros., 1857), p. 177; also Olmsted, *A Journey in the Seaboard States*, Vol. I, p. 320.

[66] Ambrose C. Fulton, *A Life's Voyage, A Diary of a Sailor on Sea and Land, Jotted Down During a Seventy Years' Voyage* (New York: Fulton, 1898), p. 107; Frederick Douglass, *Life and Times of Frederick Douglass* (New York: Collier, 1962), p. 179.

The Pro-African Slave-Trade Argument

slave laborers increased. During the 1840's, partly due to the collapse of cotton prices and the consequent surplus of slave labor, many planters diverted their slaves into the mechanic trades. The white workers protested. In Mississippi white mechanics forced the enactment of municipal ordinances prohibiting slaves from hiring their own time.[67] South Carolina grand jury presentments between 1849 and 1851 demanded the enforcement of the law against Negro competition.[68] In 1845 Georgia passed an act that prohibited the hiring of slaves and free Negroes as mechanics and provided that violators be fined. Sir Charles Lyell, visiting Georgia at the time, observed that Georgia white mechanics were using their political power to pass disabling statutes against the black workers, and that such actions would forward the substitution of white for black labor and might hasten the era of general emancipation.[69]

In the 1850's slaveholders continued to pit their slaves directly against white workers. In Texas slaveholders underbid the German laborers for the contract to construct the state capitol building, and in Savannah shipping merchants used slaves to break a white labor strike in 1856. Southern white workers resented this competition. At Wilmington, North Carolina, in 1857, the framework of a new building erected by Negro carpenters was destroyed as a protest against the use of Negro labor in the construction trade. In New Orleans a white mechanic observed that the white workingmen were rapidly displacing the slaves, and he hoped and believed that soon every Negro would be driven out of the town.[70] A slave told Olmsted

[67] Russel, *Economic Aspects of Southern Sectionalism*, p. 210; S. R. Cockrill, "Manufacture of Cotton by Its Producers," *De Bow's Review*, VII (October, 1849), pp. 488–489; Charles S. Sydnor, *Slavery in Mississippi* (New York: D. Appleton-Century, 1933), p. 180.

[68] *Journal of the House of Representatives of South Carolina, 1849* (Columbia: 1849), pp. 48, 83; *South Carolina House Journal, 1851* (Columbia, 1851), p. 28.

[69] Charles Lyell, *A Second Visit to the United States*, 2 Vols. (London: J. Murray, 1855), Vol. II, pp. 82–83. See also *ibid.*, Vol. II, pp. 160–161; Flanders, *Plantation Slavery in Georgia*, p. 205.

[70] Frederick Law Olmsted, *A Journey Through Texas* (New York: Dix, Edwards, 1857), p. 114; New Orleans *Picayune*, December 11, 1856; Olmsted, *A Journey in the Back Country*, pp. 180–181.

that he had been forced to leave San Antonio because "they made a law that no nigger shouldn't hire his time in San Antone, so I had to cl'ar out, and mass'r wanted me, so I come back to him." [71] In a petition presented to the Atlanta city council, 200 white mechanics and laborers complained that slave mechanics were underbidding them. The Mechanical Association of Jackson, Mississippi, resolved that the practice of making public mechanics of slaves should be suppressed.[72] The Mechanics Institute of Little Rock demanded the enactment of state legislation to suppress Negro mechanics, and refused to instruct Negroes in the mechanic arts, to employ Negro mechanics, and to work with them. Between 1854 and 1860 organizations like the Charleston Mechanics Association and the South Carolina Mechanics Association of Charleston sent the state legislature no fewer than ten petitions and memorials demanding the prohibition of slave hiring and the removal of slave competition. In 1859 a resolution to consider the enactment of a law prohibiting slave competition was introduced in the Alabama House, and a bill forbidding slaves to be public craftsmen was introduced in the Mississippi House.[73] "The white *canaille* of the South," an English visitor observed, "regard the slaves as interfering with

[71] Olmsted, *A Journey in the Seaboard States*, Vol. II, p. 237; Olmsted, *Texas*, p. 230.

[72] Ulrich B. Phillips (ed.), *Plantation and Frontier Documents: 1649–1863*, 2 Vols. (Cleveland: Arthur H. Clark, 1909), Vol. II, pp. 367–368; Jackson *Semi-Weekly Mississippian*, January 7, 1859.

[73] Little Rock *Gazette and Democrat*, in Jackson *Eagle*, October 16, 1858, clipping, Henry Hughes Scrapbook, Hughes Papers, Mississippi State Archives, Jackson, Mississippi; *South Carolina House Journal, 1854*, pp. 156–157; *House Journal 1856*, p. 39; *House Journal, 1860*, p. 131; *South Carolina Senate Journal, 1854*, p. 110; *Senate Journal, 1858*, p. 10; *Senate Journal, 1859*, pp. 52, 97; J. Harleton Read, Jr., "Report on several memorials asking for laws prohibiting slaves from hiring their own time . . . ," *De Bow's Review*, XXVI (May, 1859), p. 600; *Journal of the Seventh Biennial Session of the House of Representatives of the State of Alabama, 1859–60* (Montgomery: Shorter and Reid, 1860), pp. 81–82; *Journal of the House of Representatives of the State of Mississippi, 1859* (Jackson: E. Barksdale, 1959), p. 123. For evidence on Louisiana see *Official Journal of the House of Representatives of the State of Louisiana, 1859* (Baton Rouge: J. M. Taylor, 1859), p. 34.

The Pro-African Slave-Trade Argument

their interests as free labourers; they detest them as rivals. . . ." [74]

"The [slaveholders'] policy of teaching negroes the various trades," a Mississippi editor declared, "instead of putting them on the plantations, where they belong, tends to make the rich richer and the poor poorer, by bringing slave labor into competition with white labor, and thus arraying capital against labor, (for the negro is capital) and this will produce a spirit of antagonism between the rich and the poor. Such a policy . . . tends to elevate the negro at the expense of the poor white man, and makes the poor mechanic at the South the enemy of the negro and of the institution of slavery." [75] A strange and unique pattern of class conflict was taking shape in the Old South—white labor versus slaveholders and their slave "capital."

The white workers' opposition to slave mechanics was motivated by racism as well as economic self-interest. White workers were concerned about their status as white laborers worthy of dignity and respect. They did not want to do jobs Negroes did. "No white man would ever do certain kinds of work . . .," a Virginian explained, "and if you should ask a white man you had hired, to do such things, he would get mad and tell you he wasn't a nigger." [76] If slaves did mechanical labor, white mechanics thought, wouldn't the white mechanic be "a nigger"? The white mechanics in competition with slaves

[74] Sterling, *Letters from the Slave States,* p. 86.

[75] Canton (Mississippi) *Citizen,* in Brunswick *Herald,* June 23, 1858; also Lagrange *Reporter,* in *Republican Banner and Nashville Whig,* June 12, 1858. For additional evidence on slave-white competition, see Helper, *Impending Crisis,* p. 165; *De Bow's Review,* XXVI (April, 1859), pp. 477–478; *ibid.,* XXVII (May, 1859), p. 102; J. H. Taylor, "Manufactures in South Carolina," *De Bow's Review,* VIII (January, 1850), pp. 25–26; M. W. Phillips, in *De Bow's Review,* XXVII (July, 1859), p. 120; Olmsted, *Texas,* p. 230; Olmsted, *A Journey in the Seaboard States,* Vol. II, pp. 30, 149, 237, 239, 332–333; Olmsted, *A Journey in the Back Country,* pp. 180–181; Galveston *News,* November 15, 1856; New Orleans *Picayune,* January 27, 1859; Spartanburg *Express,* in Boston *Liberator,* August 11, 1854; Morehouse (Louisiana) *Advocate,* in Olmsted, *Seaboard,* Vol. II, p. 238; Darlington *Flag,* in Edgefield *Advertiser,* April 6, 1859; Camden (South Carolina) *Journal,* in Southern *Cultivator,* XVIII, No. 2 (February, 1860), p. 54.

[76] In Olmsted, *Seaboard,* I, pp. 91–92.

felt a sense of degradation. A writer to *De Bow's Review* warned that the presence of slaves in the mechanic trades had degraded the trades to the condition of menial services, and that consequently "the no-property men of the South" shared "a feeling of deep-rooted *jealousy and prejudice, of painful antagonism,* if not *hostility, to the institution of negro slavery."* [77]

The use of white labor in the South threatened to become more extensive during the 1850's. Wages in the South, it was reported, were higher than wages in the North. In a detailed study of wages in American cities, a United States Senator from Tennessee showed that wages for painters, bricklayers, carpenters, and other workers were higher in Southern than in Northern cities. A Texas newspaper editor complained about the high cost of hired labor in the south *vis à vis* labor in the North. Olmsted estimated that the wages for common laborers were 25 per cent more in Virginia than in New York. The high Southern wages encouraged the migration of European and Northern workers into the South, and their presence in Southern towns and cities was noticeable. The population of Montgomery included a considerable proportion of Northern and foreign-born mechanics, and the mechanics in Mobile were mainly from the North. The major portion of tradesmen in the river and coastal towns and cities of Mississippi were Northerners or immigrants. [78]

Thus the rise in cotton prices during the 1850's along with the demand for more labor, the high slave prices, the high wages in the South, and the increasing movement of white workers into the South seemed to predict the rise of a Southern white

[77] "The Issues of 1860," by "Python," *De Bow's Review,* XXIII (February, 1960), pp. 254–255. See also Olmsted, *A Journey in the Back Country,* pp. 299–300; *De Bow's Review,* XXVI (April, 1859), pp. 477–478.

[78] In *De Bow's Review,* XXIX (September, 1860), p. 381; Houston *Telegraph,* in Galveston *Weekly News,* March 9, 1858; Olmsted, *Seaboard,* I, p. 208, II, p. 191; New York *Journal of Commerce,* in Richmond *Enquirer,* January 6, 1860; Savannah *Morning News,* September 29, 1859; Herbert Weaver, *Mississippi Farmers, 1850–1860* (Nashville: Vanderbilt University Press, 1945), p. 32.

The Pro-African Slave-Trade Argument

working class.[79] And it was this forecast that struck fear in the minds of many African slave-trade radicals. They pointed out that the increase in cotton prices and the consequent rise in the demand for labor would force the South to find some way to meet this new demand. Since the African slave trade was closed, the flow of labor would have to come from the North and Europe, and the new labor demand and the high wages in the South would attract these outside workers. Thus the ranks of free labor in the South would be augmented and slavery would be threatened. "If we cannot supply the demand for slave labor," Governor Adams warned in his message of 1856, "then we must expect to be supplied with a species of labor we do not want, and which is, from the very nature of things antagonistic to our institutions." [80]

Many advocates were indeed greatly disturbed by this antagonism. They observed that many white workingmen had emigrated to the South since the prohibition of the African slave trade, that they were struggling for subsistence in competition with slaves, and that they were "distinctly conscious" of the "difference between 'labor' and 'slave labor.'" The advocates also noticed that Negroes were no longer being employed as draymen in the large Southern cities because poor white men were unwilling to compete with slaves. They saw that foreigners, especially Irishmen, were being employed in Southern hotels, factories, steamboats, and railroads. If the South could procure a new supply of labor only from Europe, the African slave-trade

[79] For more information about wages and movement of white workers into the South, see Phillips, *American Negro Slavery*, pp. 409–410; Edgefield *Advertiser*, November 3, 1853; Charles H. Ambler, *Sectionalism in Virginia, 1776–1816* (Chicago: University of Chicago Press, 1910), p. 304, *De Bow's Review*, XIII (August, 1852), p. 196; Ella Lonn, *Foreigners in the Confederacy* (Chapel Hill: University of North Carolina Press, 1940), p. 13.

[80] Adams, "Message, 1856," in Bryan, *Report on the Message of Gov. Adams*, p. 48. See also J. F. Dowdell, speech, in William R. Smith, *History and Debates of the Convention of Alabama, 1861* (Montgomery: White, Pfister, & Co., 1861), pp. 255–256; Charleston *Standard*, in New York *National Anti-Slavery Standard*, November 8, 1856; Spratt, speech in *De Bow's Review*, XXVII (June, 1859), p. 208; article signed "Scipio," in Edgefield *Advertiser*, March 16, 1859.

advocates warned, the control of government in the South could be transferred from the "original and native population" to the enfranchised immigrant workers.[81]

Like John C. Calhoun, whom the historian Richard Hofstadter has called "The Marx of the Master Class," many African slave-trade advocates understood and admired slavery as an institution liberating the South from the dangers of class conflict.[82] "From the conservative character of the institution," observed Calhoun years before the African slave-trade agitation, "it would prevent that conflict between labor and capital, which must ever exist in populous and crowded communities, where wages are the regulator between them. . . ." In Calhoun's view, every plantation was a little community in which the interests of capital and labor were united under a master.[83] During the 1850's, African slave-trade advocates like George Fitzhugh of Virginia and Henry Hughes of Mississippi also argued that the conservatism of slavery rested on the united interests of capital and labor. Since slaveholders viewed their slaves not only as workers but also as capital assets, they had a special interest in the proper maintenance of their slaves. "In our labor system," they explained, "the laborers are capital. Capitalists are therefore economically enforced to keep them in the best possible working order, and cannot afford to let fifteen hundred dollars die by starvation." Unlike the exploited, miserable, and rebellious white workers of a free labor society, the slave workers were "comfortable." [84] Thus Southern slaveholding society did

[81] Spratt, "Report, Montgomery," *De Bow's Review*, XXIV (June, 1858), pp. 487, 602; "Scipio," in Edgefield *Advertiser*, March 16, 1859; A. L. Scott, in *De Bow's Review*, XXII (January, 1857), p. 217.

[82] Adams, "Message, 1856," in Bryan, *Report on the Message of Gov. Adams*, p. 48; Richard Hofstadter, "John C. Calhoun: Marx of the Master Class," *The American Political Tradition* (New York: Vintage 1960), pp. 68–92.

[83] Richard K. Cralle (ed.), *The Works of John C. Calhoun*, 6 Vols. (Charleston: Walker & James, 1851–1856), Vol. IV, pp. 532–533, quoted by Richard Current, *John C. Calhoun* (New York: Washington Square Press, 1963), pp. 95, 96.

[84] Henry Hughes, in Port Gibson *Southern Reveille*, July 30, 1858, clipping in Hughes Scrapbook, Hughes Papers, Mississippi State Archives, Jackson, Mississippi; New Orleans *Delta*, in Charleston *Mercury*, January

not have to worry about mobs, trade unions, strikes for higher wages, armed resistance to the law, and social revolution.

But while African slave-trade radicals echoed Calhoun's claim about the conservatism of the institution, they asserted that the crucial basis of Southern conservatism was not the united interests of capital and labor and the slavemasters' care for their slaves, but their despotic power over the slave labor class. To the 1858 Southern Commercial Convention at Montgomery, Spratt declared:

> In all democracies, and in fact, in every constitutional government, there is the right of individual action, and the citizen may meet and discuss the evils of their state, and resolve, in fact, upon the mode and measure of redress, before it shall be lawful to arrest him. And so, even in the despotism of France, they meet and chant the Marseilles, and march upon the Bostich before they encounter the force of the Empire. But not so the slave. To him there is no liberty of individual action. Hard as it may seem, he cannot move without permission of his master. To him, therefore, there can be no march, no arms, no chaunt, no meeting, even without violation of authority. The first step is an act of insubordination, upon the right to punish which there is no restraint; and whatever may be said of the hardship of that condition . . . it must be owned that it is intensely conservative of peace and order. Elsewhere it is legitimate to meet the *process* only, but here it is permitted to crush the *germ of insurrection*.[85]

Thus, in societies where labor was white and free, workers had certain political rights and could not be effectively controlled and suppressed. The South, however, had a system of labor based on the racial supremacy and the absolute power of the white master class. So long as the Southern workers were black and in bondage, the South would be an ideal conservative

17, 1856; Mobile *Daily Register*, September 18, 1857; George Fitzhugh, *Sociology for the South, or the Failure of Free Society* (Richmond: Morris, 1854), pp. 22–23, 39–40; Fitzhugh, *Cannibals*, p. 31; Townsend, *The South Alone*, p. 17.

[85] Spratt, in *De Bow's Review*, XXIV (June, 1858), p. 489.

society. In Spratt's judgment, while democracy and the "contest of classes" threatened to plunge free labor societies in the North and in Europe into revolution and anarchy, slave-labor society in the South was essentially safe from class turmoil, for the Southern black working class was enslaved and powerless.[86] But the presence and pressures of white workers in the towns and cities of the South alarmed Spratt and his associates.

Thus to meet the need for labor for the expansion of agriculture and the development of Southern industrialization, to discourage the immigration of Northern and foreign laborers into the South, to check the increase of white workers within the South, and to reduce white class conflict in their society, Southerners like Adams and Spratt demanded the reopening of the African slave trade. "We want," they insisted, "only that kind of population which will extend and secure our peculiar institutions, and there is no source but Africa." [87] Indeed, to these men, any source of white labor would only strengthen the enemy within.

But the Southern white workers probably did not represent an actual danger to slavery. If the foreigners in the South were anti-slavery,[88] the foreign-born population of the South was in-

[86] Spratt, *Foreign Slave Trade,* p. 8.

[87] Spratt, "Report, Montgomery," *De Bow's Review,* XXIV (June, 1858), p. 487.

[88] There is evidence showing that antislavery sentiments could be found among foreigners living in the South. See W. Darrell Overdyke, *The Know-Nothing Party in the South* (Baton Rouge: Louisiana State University Press, 1950), pp. 87, 153, 200; John F. Nau, *The German People of New Orleans, 1850–1900* (Leiden, Netherlands: E. J. Brill, 1858), pp. 24, 32–34; R. T. Clark, Jr., "The German Liberals in New Orleans, 1840–1860," *Louisiana Historical Quarterly,* XX, No. 1 (January, 1937), p. 995; Georgia Lee Tatum, *Disloyalty in the Confederacy* (Chapel Hill: University of North Carolina Press, 1934), pp. 45, 79–80; Roger W. Shugg, "Suffrage and Representation in Ante-Bellum Louisiana," *Louisiana Historical Quarterly,* XIX, No. 2 (April, 1936), p. 395; Ella Lonn, *Foreigners in the Confederacy* (Chapel Hill: University of North Carolina Press, 1940), p. 34; Olmsted, *Texas,* pp. 141–142, 432, 435, 501–502; Stirling, *Letters from the Slave States,* p. 318. But there is also evidence showing that many foreigners were loyal to slavery. See Anna I. Sandbo, "First Session of the Secession Convention in Texas," *The Southwestern Historical Quarterly,* XVIII (October, 1914), pp. 176–

The Pro-African Slave-Trade Argument

significant, constituting in 1850 only 4.4 per cent of the total Southern white population.[89] No doubt a few Southern states had larger ratios: Louisiana, 26.34 per cent, Maryland 12.20, Missouri 12.93, and Texas 11.44 per cent. But generally the Southern states had extremely small ratios: Alabama 1.76 per cent, Arkansas 0.90, Georgia 1.24, Mississippi 1.61, North Carolina 0.46, Virginia 2.57, South Carolina 3.10 per cent.[90] As for the white laborers in the South, it is true they did exert increasing pressure against slave competition during the 1850's. But this opposition to slave mechanics should not be interpreted as abolitionist. In their resolutions to prevent slave hiring, the Mechanical Association of Jackson, Mississippi, insisted "that our fidelity to the institution of slavery is unquestionable." [91] These white laborers simply wanted to remove the Negro from the workshop and keep him on the plantation and in slavery. Furthermore the white workers did not represent a powerful political force. Although they sent petitions to the state legislatures, these efforts were futile. In South Carolina, for example, the legislators merely directed these notices into committees and they were seen no more. Although bills and resolutions in behalf of the interest of the white workers were introduced into the state legislatures, they were quickly tabled.[92]

The African slave-trade advocates' fear of the Southern white laborers was based more on a potential than a present

177; Olmsted, *Texas,* p. 133; Overdyke, *Know-Nothing Party,* pp. 29–30; Jackson *Semi-Weekly Mississippian,* October 14, 1856.

[89] Percentage based on information from United States Bureau of Census, *Historical Statistics of the United States, Colonial Times to 1957.* (Washington: U.S. Government Printing Office, 1961), p. 12. In 1860 it was 5.9 per cent. In the North it was 23 per cent. *Ibid.,* 11–12.

[90] *De Bow's Review,* XVII (October, 1854), p. 431.

[91] Jackson *Semi-Weekly Mississippian,* January 7, 1859. For additional evidence, see Pollard, *A New Southern Policy,* p. 6; D. R. Hundley, *Social Relations in Our Southern States* (New York: Henry B. Price, 1860), p. 125; Dunbar Rowland (ed.), *Jefferson Davis, Constitutionalist: His Letters, Papers and Speeches,* 10 Vols. (Jackson, Mississippi Department of Archives, 1923), Vol. IV, p. 49.

[92] *South Carolina House Journal, 1854,* pp. 156–157; *House Journal, 1858,* p. 9; *Mississippi House Journal, 1858,* p. 123; Jackson *Daily Mississippian,* November 25, 1859; *Louisiana House Journal, 1859,* p. 34.

reality. They were afraid of a future influx of foreigners and a future threat of white laborers in the South. And, it seemed to the worried advocates, the closed African slave trade, the Southern demand for labor, and the high wages in the South would continue to encourage the expansion of white labor in the South and ultimately drive the South into a whirlwind of social revolution.

Their anxiety about the potential emergence of white labor in the South was related to certain Southern images of the free labor societies of the North and Europe. In their defense of slavery, African slave-trade radicals had investigated, criticized, and denounced the social ills of the free labor system. They had used many sources Karl Marx would later examine to expose the exploitation of free laborers in England.[93] They had called attention to the suffering and discontent of the working classes and to the explosive social disorders and upheavals in the North and Europe. Their analysis led them to an inevitable conclusion: in free society a contest was always waging between capital and labor, between rich and poor classes. The tendency of this conflict was "to make the rich richer and the poor poorer, until extremity" drove the poor "to satiate at once their vengeance and their want by slaughter and rapine." Thus free labor societies were doomed to a "continually recurring catastrophe" and to the "prostration of all law. Licentiousness will then follow with anarchy and ruin."[94] But the South could have

> perfect confidence that, when France shall reel again into the delirium of liberty—when the peerage of England shall have yielded to the masses—when democracy at the North shall hold its carnival—when all that is pure and whole shall be dragged down—when all that

[93] C. Van Woodward, "George Fitzhugh, Sui Generis," in Woodward (ed.), *Cannibals All! or Slaves without Masters,* by George Fitzhugh (Cambridge, Massachusetts: The Belknap Press, 1960), p. xxv.

[94] New Orleans *Delta,* in Charleston *Mercury,* January 17, 1856; George Fitzhugh, "Slavery Aggressions," in *De Bow's Review,* XXVIII (February, 1860), p. 139; John Townsend, *The South Alone Should Govern the South,* p. 17; J. G. M. Ramsey to Spratt, April 29, 1858; Ramsey Papers, University of North Carolina Library.

is low and vile shall have mounted to the surface—when women shall have taken the places and habiliments of men, and men shall have taken the places and habiliments of women—when Free Love Unions and phalansteries shall pervade the land—when the sexes shall consort without the restraints of marriage, and when youths and maidens, drunk at noon day, and half naked, shall reel about the market places—the South will stand, secure and erect . . . the slave will be restrained by power, the master by the trusts of a superior position; she will move on with a measured dignity of power and progress. . . .[95]

The logic and implications of their criticisms of free labor societies are highly significant. In their judgment, the social disintegration due to the conflict between labor and capital present in the North and Europe led to "licentiousness" and sexual anarchy—the confusion of male and female identities, the breakdown of marital restraints on sexuality, and the rise of "Free Love Unions." What must have concerned African slave-trade radicals was not the destruction of order and control in the North and Europe but its possibility in the South. Unlike the North and Europe, the South was a biracial society: one third of the Southern population was black. Hence the breakdown of "peace and order" in the South would have a special significance. If slave workers were not imported from Africa, if the ominous conflict between white labor and capital continued to develop within the South, and if social chaos and sexual anarchy reigned in their biracial society, Southerners would surely be living their nightmare of miscegenation.

The scarcity of slave labor and the consequent rise in slave prices plagued the advocates of the African slave trade with another problem. To the advocates, the increase of slave prices meant that fewer whites would be able to enter the slaveowning ranks, and that slavery would become the monopoly of the rich. Such a development would shatter the nonslaveholders' hope to

[95] Spratt, in *De Bow's Review*, XXVII (August, 1859), p. 210; also Fitzhugh, *Sociology for the South*, pp. 252–253.

possess slaves—the symbols of wealth and status in the slave society of the South. As Southern poet William J. Grayson remarked, "no matter how one might begin, as lawyer, physician, clergyman, mechanic, or merchant, he ended, if prosperous, as proprietor of a rice or cotton plantation." A perceptive analyst of the Southern white psychology, slave Frederick Douglass painfully knew that poor white men like Edward Covey strained "every nerve" to obtain the "first condition of wealth and respectability"—the "ownership of human property." "A plantation well stocked with hands," a settler in Mississippi observed in the 1830's, "is the *ne plus ultra* of every man's ambition who resides at the South." [96] While the increase of slave prices in the 1850's threatened to frustrate this ambition, it also intensified the slave drain from the border states to the southwest where the slave demand and slave prices were extremely high. Both the slaveholding monopoly and the slave drain, the advocates apprehensively thought, would create a large nonslaveholding population in the South—a class whose loyalty to slavery, they felt, could not be trusted.

In the past nonslaveholders had criticized the peculiar institution. During the debate on slavery in the Virginia legislature shortly after the frightening Nat Turner insurrection, the Southern critics of slavery represented the nonslaveholders of western Virginia. In their anti-slavery arguments, they expressed a concern about slave competition with white labor and the presence of a dangerous servile population.[97] Twenty-five years later Hinton R. Helper, a nonslaveholder from North Carolina, published his controversial *The Impending Crisis and How to Meet It*. Motivated by a hatred for the Negro and a love for the South, Helper argued that slavery, the source of Southern

[96] Grayson, quoted in Taylor, *Cavalier & Yankee*, p. 156; Douglass, *Life*, p. 123; J. H. Ingraham, *The Southwest by a Yankee*, 2 Vols. (New York: 1835), II, p. 84; also Joseph G. Baldwin, *The Flush Times of Alabama and Mississippi* (New York: Hill and Wang, 1967), p. 4.

[97] See Kenneth Stampp, "An Analysis of T. R. Dew's Review of the Debates in the Virginia Legislature," *Journal of Negro History*, XXVII, No. 4 (October, 1942), pp. 380–387; Robert, *The Road from Monticello*, pp. 20–22, 28, 77, 118.

economic inferiority and backwardness *vis à vis* Northern
economic superiority and progress, must be abolished, and that
Negroes must be banished from the South. He pressed racist
thought to a fiercely logical conclusion: since this should be a
white man's country, the Negro must be totally excluded. Helper
was partly echoing the exclusionist sentiments of Thomas Jefferson, who had warned that the Negro, when freed, must be removed from American society. Helper's chief concern, however,
was the welfare of the oppressed Southern nonslaveholders. In
his vitriolic protest against the poverty and powerlessness of
nonslaveholders in the South, Helper declared: "The lords of
the lash are not only absolute masters of the blacks, who are
bought and sold, and driven about like so many cattle, but they
are also the oracles and arbiters of all nonslaveholding whites,
whose freedom is merely nominal, and whose unparalleled illiter-
acy and degradation is purposely and fiendishly perpetuated."
Thus he urged his fellow nonslaveholders of the South to unite,
overthrow the planter class, and destroy slavery, "the frightful
tumor on the body politic." [98] Helper's book appalled many
Southerners. The editor of the Galveston *Weekly News,* an advocate of the African slave trade, denounced the subversive book
and charged it was impossible to read it "without feeling nau-
seated by the crude, false and unnatural sentiments expressed."
In a letter to Edmund Ruffin, William H. Harrison attacked the
"atrocious book," and warned that the incendiary work was
"calculated to do infinite injury" among the nonslaveholders of
the South. Alarmed by Helper's book, South Carolina legislators
introduced a bill prohibiting nonslaveholders to circulate and
possess books and pamphlets designed to excite prejudice against
slaveholders.[99] As the Civil War approached, slaveholders were
haunted by the spectre of Hinton Helper and his brand of
racist abolitionism within the South.

[98] Helper, *Impending Crisis,* pp. 20, 24, 25, 43, 97, 120, 155.
[99] Galveston *Weekly News,* August 1, 1857; William H. Harrison
to Ruffin, February 12, 1859, Ruffin Papers, University of North Carolina
Library; Charleston *Courier,* in Washington *National Intelligencer,* January
24, 1861.

Northern abolitionists also tried to promote conflict between nonslaveholders and slaveholders in the South. In their appeal to Southern nonslaveholders, abolitionists condemned the slaveholders as a powerful landed aristocracy, responsible for the impoverishment and ignorance of the Southern white masses. Slavery, they declared, had rendered labor disgraceful in Southern society. The destruction of slavery would mean the liberation of nonslaveholding whites from the tyranny of a self-interested Southern minority, the slaveholding aristocracy. "Without your co-operation," the Northern abolitionists concluded, "the slaveholders . . . are powerless. To you they look for . . . overseers, and drivers, and patrols. To you they look for votes to elevate them to office, and to you they too often look for aid to enforce their Lynch laws. Feel then your own power; claim your rights, and exert them for the deliverance of the slave, and consequently for your own happiness and prosperity. . . ." [100]

Like Helper and Northern abolitionists, many African slave-trade radicals viewed Southern nonslaveholders as a potential internal danger to slavery and the slaveholding class. But actually nonslaveholders were true to the South and slavery. Like Helper, many nonslaveholders despised the Negro. "I wish there warn't no niggers here," a poor white farmer told a traveler. "They are a great cuss to this country. . . ." [101] Unlike Helper, however, many nonslaveholders feared that emancipation would not mean the exclusion of Negroes from the South but economic competition with Negroes and race wars. They were reminded of the horrors of the bloody slave revolts in St. Domingo and regarded the emancipation of three million slaves in the South as a prospect of certain destruction of white society. Little wonder slave patrols were ordinarily recruited from the yeoman class. [102]

---

[100] American and Foreign Anti-Slavery Society, *Address to the Non-Slaveholders of the South, on the Social and Political Evils of Slavery,* reprinted in William H. and Jane H. Pease, *The Antislavery Argument* (Indianapolis: Bobbs-Merrill, 1965), pp. 151, 156, 162.

[101] Olmsted, *Back Country,* p. 203. See also Hundley, *Social Relations,* p. 273; Sterling, *Letters,* pp. 86, 94–95.

[102] A. G. Brown, letter, in Jackson *Semi-Weekly Mississippian,* Octo-

The nonslaveholders' worry about emancipation was partly based on their fear of the Negro man as a sexual danger to the white woman. They were warned that emancipated blacks would rape and murder Southern poor white women, and that the dreaded horror of forced miscegenation would follow the abolition of slavery. Albert G. Brown of Mississippi cautioned that freedom for the slave would mean among other things that the black man's "son shall marry the white man's daughter." If the Negro were liberated, declared Andrew Johnson of Tennessee, "blood, rape and rapine will be our portion. You can't get rid of the Negro except by holding him in slavery."[103] Hence, for many nonslaveholders, slavery was valued not as a system of labor but as a system of race control, especially the sexual control of the black man. For a long time, the image of the highly sexed black man worried whites in America. Black men, Jefferson claimed, preferred white women to black "as uniformly as is the preference of the Oran-utan for the black women over those of his own species." [104] Colonial laws not only provided for the sexual separation of the two races but also emphasized the abhorrence of sexual unions between Negro men and white women. Seventeenth-century Maryland and Virginia legislation clearly reveals that white women were being singled out for special protection and special separation from Negro men very early in the history of race relations in America. This white

ber 12, 1860; Mobile *Daily Register*, August 13, 1856. See also D. R. Hundley, letter to W. B. Figures, quoted by Clarence P. Denman, *The Secession Movement in Alabama* (Norwood, Mass., Norwood Press, 1933), p. 88; *De Bow's Review*, XXI, pp. 591–592; Olmsted, *Back Country*, p. 203; New Orleans *Delta*, in Charleston *Mercury*, October 16, 1856; Rudolph M. Lapp, "The Ante-Bellum Poor Whites of the South Atlantic States," unpublished Ph.D. Thesis, 1956, University of California, Berkeley, p. 123.

[103] Hundley to Figures, in Denman, *Secession Movement in Alabama*, p. 88; Brown, in Jackson *Semi-Weekly Mississippian*, October 12, 1860; Andrew Johnson, in E. M. Coulter, *William G. Brownlow, Fighting Parson of the Southern Highlands* (Chapel Hill: University of North Carolina Press, 1937), p. 109.

[104] Jefferson, *Notes on Virginia*, in Adrienne Koch and William Peden (eds.), *The Life and Selected Writings of Thomas Jefferson* (New York: 1944), p. 256.

male anxiety over miscegenation between Negro men and white
women must have been extreme, for a number of colonies cas-
trated Negro men guilty of sexual aggressions against white
women.[105]

During the nineteenth century, slavery continued to be a
system to keep the black man in his place socially as well as
economically. The nonslaveholders of the 1850's therefore had a
definite social stake in slavery. As one Alabama nonslaveholding
farmer told Frederick Law Olmsted:

> Well, I'll tell you what I think on it [emancipation];
> I'd like it if we could get rid of 'em to youst. I wouldn't
> like to hev 'em freed, if they was gwine to hang 'round.
> They ought to get some country and put 'em war they
> could be by themselves. It wouldn't be no good to free
> 'em, and let 'em hang 'round, because they is so mon-
> strous lazy; if they hadn't got nobody to take keer on
> 'em, you see they wouldn't do nothin' but juss nat'rally
> laze 'round, and steal, and pilfer, and no man couldn't
> live, you see, war they was—if they was free, no man
> couldn't live. And then, I've two objections; that's one
> on 'em—no man couldn't live—and this 'ere's the other:
> Now suppose they was free, you see they'd all think
> themselves just as good as we; of course they would, if
> they was free. Now, just suppose you had a family of
> children, how would you like to hev a niggar steppin'
> up to your darter? Of course you wouldn't, and that's
> the reason I wouldn't like to hev 'em free; but I tell
> you, I don't think it's right to hev 'em slaves so; that's
> the fac—taant right to keep 'em as they is.[106]

Significantly, this Alabama nonslaveholder made a moral
judgment about slavery. Slavery "taant right." It was morally
wrong to enslave Negroes. Yet his moral concern was in conflict with his social and psychological concerns. The Negro, the
Alabama farmer explained, must be kept in slavery because the
Negro was "nat'rally" lazy. Hence he must have someone to

[105] Wilbert E. Moore, "Slave Law and the Social Structure," *Journal
of Negro History*, XXVI (April, 1941), pp. 179–181; Winthrop D. Jordan,
White Over Black: American Attitudes Toward the Negro, pp. 154–158.
[106] Olmsted, *Seaboard*, II, pp. 218–219.

control him and to take care of him. Otherwise, under freedom, the Negro would not work and would steal and pilfer. He would be a criminal. An intolerable anarchy would plague the South, and the traditional caste order—especially the sexual separation of the races—would break down. If the Negro were freed, he would feel "just as good as a white man," which meant he would be "steppin' up" to the white man's "darter." And if the freed Negro and the white man's "darter" engaged in sexual intercourse, this would lead to what horrified Thomas Jefferson—"staining the blood" of the white race. White racial purity would be corrupted, and a new breed of lazy and lawless people would destroy civilization in the South. Undoubtedly the Alabama farmer would have supported Jefferson's candid warning against miscegenation. "Amalgamation with the other color," Jefferson had declared, "produces a degradation to which no lover of his country, no lover of excellence in the human character can innocently consent." [107] Thus here we have an Alabama farmer admitting slavery "taant right." Yet many Southern farmers, perhaps including our Alabama farmer, who had no vested economic interest in slavery would later go to war and be killed at Chancellorsville and other battlefields in defense of slavery—an institution that, in their eyes, protected white women and civilization in the South.

Thus slavery guaranteed *order* in the biracial society of the South. In this society, the nonslaveholder could feel he belonged to the white aristocracy, and thus all white people, according to Senator Albert G. Brown, could associate with each other on terms of perfect social equality. The presence of Negroes in the South, Jefferson Davis explained, not only raised all white men to the same general level but also dignified and exalted every white man.[108] Even the poor white, who had so little economically, had a social and psychological interest in slavery: it assigned status to his white skin. He was told that in the South "color, not money, marks the class; black is the

[107] Jefferson, quoted in Jordan, p. 547.
[108] Brown, in Jackson *Semi-Weekly Mississippian*, October 12, 1860; Davis, in Jenkins, *Pro-Slavery Thought*, p. 192.

badge of slavery; white the color of freemen; and the white man, *however poor* . . . feels himself a sovereign. . . ." Thus, despite his despised and wretched condition, the poor white could find psychological comfort in the whiteness of his skin, and he could cherish Calhoun's claim that the "two great divisions of [Southern] society are not the rich and poor, but the black and white." [109] Furthermore, the nonslaveholder, many believed, could become a slaveholder through hard work. Every white man in the South, D. R. Hundley explained, had "just as much right to become an Oligarch as the most ultra fire-eater." A writer for *De Bow's Review* claimed that many wealthy planters had begun their fortunes as nonslaveholders, and that "cheap lands, abundant harvests, high prices gives [sic] the poor man soon a negro." [110] Later, in his story about the young South Carolina Irishman, Wilbur J. Cash would sing about the epic rise of the Old South's one-generation slaveholding aristocracy.

No doubt the African slave-trade radicals recognized that nonslaveholders had interests in slavery. Some advocates even expressed great confidence in the nonslaveholders' allegiance to the peculiar institution. In his essay, "The Non-Slaveholders of the South," James De Bow offered detailed reasons why the interest of the poorest nonslaveholder was "to make common cause with, and die in the last trenches in defence of, the slave property of his more favored neighbor." [111] But many advocates, including De Bow himself, had doubts about nonslaveholders.[112] While De Bow's essay on the nonslaveholders was a declaration of their loyalty, it was also an appeal for their support for

[109] Benjamin F. Stringfellow, *Negro Slavery No Evil* (Boston: 1855), quoted in Naomi F. Goldstein, *The Roots of Prejudice against the Negro* (Boston: Boston University, 1948), p. 72; Calhoun, quoted in Margaret L. Coit, *John C. Calhoun* (Boston: Houghton Mifflin, 1961), p. 292.

[110] See Hundley, p. 30; Alfred Hunger to W. T. Seals, August 8, 1854, in Huger Letterpress Book, Duke University Library; *De Bow's Review*, reprinted in Jackson *Semi-Weekly Mississippian*, December 21, 1860.

[111] De Bow, in *The Interest in Slavery of the Southern Non-Slaveholder* (Charleston: 1860), in McKitrick (ed.), *Slavery Defended*, p. 171.

[112] See De Bow, letter to William Yancey, in *De Bow's Review*, XXVII (1859), p. 234.

slavery. African slave-trade advocates like De Bow and Spratt feared that until white men acquired property in slaves they were not completely committed to the institution, and that high slave prices were making it extremely difficult for nonslaveholders to purchase slaves. If many Southerners could not own or even hope to own slaves, could they be expected to support the peculiar institution? Would they not be antagonistic towards slavery and the slaveholding class? Would they not rally to Hinton Helper's cry for revolution within the South? Worried about the high slave prices, a Louisiana editor offered his readers this gloomy prediction. "Let things go on as they are now tending, and the days of this peculiar institution of the South are necessarily few. The present tendency of supply and demand is to concentrate all the slaves in the hands of the few, and thus excite the envy rather than cultivate the sympathy of the people." [113] Echoing the same anxiety, a Texas editor warned that thousands of citizens were unable to own slaves at the present "exorbitant monopoly prices," and that "the very inability with so many thousands among us to be slaveowners" had a tendency to create an unfriendly feeling towards the institution.[114] If cheap African slaves could be imported, advocates promised, slaves could be more widely distributed, and the tensions between slaveholders and nonslaveholders in the South could be eased.

The South Carolina advocates of the African slave trade were especially suspicious about the loyalty of the nonslaveholder. They believed that the nonslaveholders of South Carolina

[113] Ouachita *Register*, in New Orleans *Daily Delta*, April 3, 1858.
[114] Galveston *Weekly News*, April 5, 1859. For further evidence, see John Mitchel to E. Ruffin, June 12, 1859, Ruffin Papers, University of North Carolina Library; C. W. Miller, *Re-opening the Slave Trade*, p. 8; I. N. Davis, in Jackson *Semi-Weekly Mississippian*, April 26, 1859; Dillon, *Mitchel*, Vol. II, p. 191; Charleston *Mercury*, November 1, 1859; Jackson *Semi-Weekly Mississippian*, June 21, 1859; Edward Delony, "The South Demands More Negro Labor," *De Bow's Review*, XXV (1858), p. 493; Bryan, *Letters to the Southern People*, p. 33; Bryan, *Report on the Message of Gov. Adams*, pp. 43–44; Spratt, "Report, Montgomery," *De Bow's Review*, XXIV (June, 1858), p. 487; J. Adams, in Charleston *Courier*, November 26, 1856.

had failed to support secession during the crisis over the Compromise of 1850. In the 1851 South Carolina election of delegates to a Southern convention at Montgomery, the upcountry, low slave-population counties and Charleston city voted overwhelmingly against secession.[115] Secessionists were able to win only in the high slave-population parishes of the lowcountry. In a letter to the *Southern Reveille* in September 1853, a slaveholder commented on South Carolina's divided response to the Compromise. In the excited political discussions of 1851, he observed, there was a general apprehension over the permanency of slave property. Many reflective Southerners realized the dangerous "absence of a more general diffusion" of an interest in slave property, and they believed a large majority in the state would have been opposed to submission to the Compromise had all white men in South Carolina been slaveholders.[116]

In 1851 South Carolina Unionists made appeals to the nonslaveholders of the state. One Unionist pamphleteer, under the pen name of "Brutus," charged that the secessionists wanted to preserve planter rule in the state. He urged the 200,000 disenfranchised white citizens of South Carolina to appoint delegates to a state constitutional convention rather than to a secession convention. Let that state convention, he continued, draft a new state constitution to provide for the interest of the free laborer and to establish equality of representation in the state legislature. And if the legislature rejected the measure, "Brutus" urged the people to appeal to Congress to secure a truly republican form of state government.[117] It is no wonder that in 1854 the editor of the Charleston *Mercury* feared that with the new rise in slave prices nonslaveholders would not be able to purchase slaves, that they would have little interest in defending slavery, and that "the idea and spirit of that infamous pamphlet 'Brutus'" would spread. "But," continued the editor, "increase

115 Lillian A. Kibler, *Benjamin F. Perry: South Carolina Unionist* (Durham: Duke University Press, 1946), p. 272.

116 *Southern Reveille*, in Boston *Liberator*, September 16, 1853.

117 "Brutus," from Chauncey S. Boucher, "Sectionalism, Representation, and the Electoral Question in Ante-Bellum South Carolina," *Washington University Studies*, IV, Part II (October, 1916), pp. 40–41.

the supply of labor, and thus cheapen the cost of slaves and the South will escape this *internal peril.* The number of slaveowners would multiply, the direct interest in its preservation would be more universally diffused, and that great necessity of the South—union in defense of slavery, more readily accomplished." [118] The wider distribution of slaves to whites in South Carolina could be an antidote to class conflict in the Palmetto State.

Again and again from Virginia to Texas, the advocates of the African slave trade warned the South that slavery was becoming a monopoly. They argued that the number of slaveowners was decreasing daily due to the constantly increasing price of slaves, and that the next census would show a 20 per cent decrease from the number of slaveholders in the 1850 census. They publicized statistics to demonstrate the presence of a slaveholding elite: only a minority of 350,000 out of 6,000,000 whites in the South owned slaves; in Mississippi, less than one third of the voters were slaveholders; and in Louisiana, only about 8 per cent of the white population owned slaves, and 50 per cent of these slaveholders owned about 90 per cent of the slaves.[119] To an important extent, the African slave-trade radicals were correct in their statistical understanding of slave ownership in Southern society on the eve of the Civil War. Actually the number of slaveholders increased 11 per cent between 1850 and 1860. But the white population of the South increased 27 per cent during that decade; thus the percentage increase of the white population was 16 per cent more than the percentage increase of slaveholders. In 1850, 6.2 per cent of the Southern white population owned slaves, while in 1860 this percentage had dropped to 5.5.[120] A comparison between white

[118] Charleston *Mercury,* in Edgefield *Advertiser,* November 16, 1854.

[119] Jackson *Semi-Weekly Mississippian,* April 26, June 21, 1859; New Orleans *Daily Crescent,* January 4, 17, April 13, 1859; Delony, "The South Demands More Negro Labor," *De Bow's Review,* XXV (1858), p. 500.

[120] Bureau of the Census, *Historical Statistics of the United States, Colonial Times to 1957* (Washington: 1960), p. 12; United States Census Office, *Eighth Census, 1860* (Washington: 1864), pp. 247–248.

family units and slaveholders yields a similar pattern. "During the fifties," historian Fabian Linden has pointed out, "the increment in the number of white families in the entire South exceeded the growth in the number of slaveowners by over 25 per cent. Thus we must conclude that the propertied classes of the Old South constituted a relatively shrinking segment of the population."[121] Only about one fourth of all white Southerners were involved in the peculiar institution through direct ownership of family ties. The white Southerner was usually a non-slaveholding small farmer, and the Southern slaveholder was not usually a planter, a slaveholder with at least twenty slaves. While the planters constituted only 12 per cent of the total number of slaveholders in 1860, they owned a majority of all the slaves in the South.[122]

Clearly "only the large capitalists—the very few of our people," the African slave-trade radicals argued, benefited from the system of slave labor. Thus the large number of nonslaveholders was a "smoldering volcano" beneath Southern society, and the permanency of the institution was in danger unless Africans were imported in behalf of the nonslaveholders.[123] The continued decrease in slaveholding social mobility would be fatal to the peculiar institution. "That minute you put it out of the power of common farmers to purchase a negro man or woman to help him in his farm, or his wife in the house, you make him an abolitionist at once."[124] But, if the African slave

[121] Linden, "Economic Democracy in the Slave South: An Appraisal of Some Recent Views," *Journal of Negro History*, Vol. XXXI, No. 2 (April, 1946), p. 178.

[122] Stampp, *The Peculiar Institution*, pp. 30–31.

[123] See Pollard, *A New Southern Policy*, pp. 52–53; *De Bow's Review*, XXVII (1859), p. 234; Bryan, *Report*, pp. 43–44; Spratt, in *De Bow's Review*, XXIV (June, 1858), p. 601; Carolina *Times*, in New York *National Anti-Slavery Standard*, November 8, 1856; Galveston *Weekly News*, June 1, 1858; Mississippi *Cross City*, in Boston *Liberator*, October 14, 1859; Jackson *Semi-Weekly Mississippian*, September 17, 1858, June 10, 1859; New Orleans *Delta*, in Boston *Liberator*, November 14, 1856; *Southern Cultivator*, XVII, No. 3 (March, 1859), p. 84; Richmond *Enquirer*, October 5, 1858; Ouachita *Register*, in New Orleans *Daily Delta*, April 3, 1858.

[124] Sparta *Jeffersonian*, in New Orleans *Crescent*, September 17, 1859, in Roger W. Shugg, *Origins of Class Struggle in Louisiana: A Social History*

trade could be reopened, and if cheap slaves could be made available to all white men, African slave-trade advocates concluded, the South could then prevent the coming of that time when all the slaves would be in the hands of a few wealthy individuals.[125] In 1859 the Augusta *Dispatch* published a letter written by a poor man. "I am a native Georgian," he wrote, "am interested to a limited extent in slave property—and am really a poor man. . . ." But the price of slaves was beyond his reach. "Remove the restrictions upon the Slave Trade, and where is there a poor man in the South who could not soon become a slaveholder—who could not thus become more and more identified with slavery, and more and more ready to defend the institution?"[126] Many slaveholding readers of this letter must have apprehensively wondered what would happen to the poor white man and *to them* if the restrictions were not removed.

While African slave-trade radicals found such expressions of resentment toward the monopolization of slaves disturbing, they also worried about the slave migration from the older Southern states to the new cotton-growing states of the deep South where planters paid handsome prices for slaves. In a report of a South Carolina legislative committee, advocates for the African slave trade offered some ominous statistics on the slave drain. Between 1840 and 1850, Maryland had exported 26,279 slaves, Kentucky, 25,937, and Virginia, 111,259. Even the radical pro-slavery state of South Carolina had lost 40,154 slaves.[127] This movement of slaves had dangerous consequences for slavery in the border and eastern states of the South. It meant that these states, if the slave drain continued, would eventually lose much of their slave population, that free labor

of White Farmers and Laborers during Slavery and After, 1840–1875 (Baton Rouge: Louisiana State University Press, 1939), p. 88.

[125] Goulden, *De Bow's Review*, XXII (1856), p. 222; New Orleans *Delta*, February 14, 1858. In order to encourage every citizen to become a slaveholder, some Southerners proposed that a certain number of slaves be legally exempted from sale for debt. See Memphis *Eagle and Enquirer*, in Charleston *Mercury*, January 16, 1957.

[126] Letter signed "Job," Augusta *Dispatch*, in Savannah *Daily News*, January 27, 1859.

[127] Bryan, *Report*, p. 23.

would replace slave labor, and that these states would there-fore be gradually "abolitionized." We must proclaim the "ap-proaching danger!" the advocates of the African slave trade asserted. "The supply of slave labor for the Southwest must be had elsewhere than the removal of them from the border states, to give place to *free soil voting labor*!" But if the demand for slaves in the deep South could be supplied from Africa, this slave drain could be stopped, and the peculiar institution could be preserved in the border South.[128]

More distressing to the African slave-trade radicals than Northern anti-slavery or the scarcity of slave labor or the peril of social conflict within the South was the presence of Southern doubts about the rightness of slavery. If the South did not have absolute faith in slavery, the radicals questioned, how could their society defend slavery against the Northern assault? If con-fidence in slaveholding social mobility had been an important basis for the nonslaveholding Southerner's commitment to slav-ery, and if the old yeoman-to-planter pattern of social mobility were breaking in the 1850's, how could their society overcome a Southern uncertainty about the morality of the peculiar institu-tion? If slaveholders themselves, moreover, felt guilty about their involvement in slavery, how could Southern society have confidence in the rightness of slavery?

Southern leaders like Yancey, De Bow, and Fitzhugh were only too well aware of the fact that the sentiment of the nine-teenth-century western world was arrayed against the institu-tion of slavery. They found especially disturbing the 1820 federal act that declared the African slave trade piracy. The advocates themselves could not avoid making moral equations. In his mes-

[128] C. W. Miller, *Re-opening the Slave Trade,* p. 7; James Brigham, letter, in *De Bow's Review,* XXVI (1859), p. 482; *American Cotton Plan-ter,* II, No. 10 (October, 1858), p. 325; Fitzhugh, "The Administration and the Slave Trade," *De Bow's Review,* XXVI (February, 1859), p. 146; Galveston *Weekly News,* January 18, 1859; Jackson *Semi-Weekly Mississip-pian,* September 27, 1859; J. Adams, letter to Committee for Bonham Dinner, in Charleston *Mercury,* September 15, 1858; Cartersville (Georgia) *Express,* in Savannah *Daily News,* March 21, 1859.

The Pro-African Slave-Trade Argument

sage to the legislature Governor Adams logically reasoned that "if the trade be piracy, the slave must be plunder." The editor of the Jackson *Semi-Weekly Mississippian* questioned: *"If it is wrong to buy and sell negroes with an intention to enslave them,* IS IT NOT WRONG TO HOLD THEM IN SLAVERY?" Mississippi Governor John J. McRae declared he could see no moral difference between buying a slave in an African market and buying one in a Southern market. In a letter to Pettigrew, Spratt pointed out that if slavery were right, "it must be logically right in its inception." [129]

Ironically, in making the juxtaposition between the African slave trade and slavery, these pro-slavery radicals were in agreement with certain abolitionists. In the late eighteenth century, Anthony Benezet and Samuel Hopkins saw no difference between the trade and slavery.[130] When abolitionists of the 1850's learned about the new proposal to import Africans, some welcomed it for its consistency. James Redpath said he favored the reopening of the African slave trade because it was "neither more immoral in theory or inhuman in practice than the Southern inter-State slave trade." The editor of the New York *Tribune* queried: "And pray what is the vast difference between shipping negroes by sea . . . on a twenty days' voyage from Baltimore into the Gulf of Mexico, and shipping them for the same purposes in the same way on a voyage of forty days from

[129] Adams, "Message, 1856," in Bryan, *Report on Message of Gov. Adams,* p. 48; Jackson *Semi-Weekly Mississippian,* February 26, 1858; John J. McRae, letter to J. Thompson, in Jackson *Semi-Weekly Mississippian,* July 1, 1859; Spratt to J. J. Pettigrew, November 29, 1856, Pettigrew Papers, North Carolina Archives. For further evidence, see Charleston *Mercury,* June 9, 1858; Galveston *Weekly News,* November 23, 1858; Knoxville *Southern Citizen,* in Richmond *Enquirer,* September 8, 1857; New Orleans *Crescent,* in Savannah *Morning News,* May 5, 1859; Nashville *Union,* January 21, 1857; C. W. Miller, *Re-opening of the Slave Trade,* p. 6; Daniel Lee, "Laborers for the South," *Southern Cultivator,* XVI, No. 8 (August, 1858), p. 236; Edgefield *Advertiser,* December 8, 1858.

[130] Mary Locke, *Anti-Slavery in America; from the Introduction of African Slaves to the Prohibition of the Slave Trade, 1619–1808* (Gloucester: Peter Smith, 1965), pp. 28, 55.

the Gaboon River to the lagoons of Florida?" [131] The advocates of the African slave trade were using almost the same language and the same logic to make the opposite point: if slavery were right, then the African slave trade must be right.

The evolution of the Southern awareness of this moral equation can be seen in the thinking of George Fitzhugh—sociologist of the Old South. Initially Fitzhugh condemned the African slave trade as an "infamous traffic," and argued that it would brutalize the institution of slavery. "Slavery with us," he wrote in 1854, "is becoming milder every day; were the slave trade revived, it would resume its pristine cruelty. The slaves we now hold would become less valuable, and we should take less care of them." But then three years later, probably influenced by the incisive and logical arguments of fire-eaters like Spratt, Fitzhugh abandoned his opposition to the African slave trade. "We are now satisfied," he explained, "that the South cannot, consistently, approve the sentence passed by christendom on the slave trade, and yet justify slaveholding." [132] Thus he recognized that the South could not consistently declare the African slave trade immoral and slavery moral.

Like Fitzhugh, many Southerners painfully realized the fundamental contradiction between their acceptance of slavery and their government's prohibition of the African slave trade as piracy. To them the federal laws against the trade represented a stigma, a brand upon slavery, the South, and themselves. "In thus branding it [African slave trade]" the editor of the *Mississippi Baptist* announced, "we condemned ourselves." In a burst of hatred for those laws, Alabama planter William F. Samford expressed the anguish of many Southerners when he cried: "I despise them . . . they are odious to me! They lyingly accuse me and my country of crimes the most infamous and horrible— they hiss the world's stinging scorn into my ears." [133] These

[131] Redpath, in New York *Anti-Slavery Standard*, January 5, 1859; New York *Tribune*, March 7, 1858.

[132] Fitzhugh, *Sociology for the South*, p. 211; Fitzhugh, "The Conservative Principle, or Social Evils and Their Remedies," *De Bow's Review*, XXII (May, 1857), pp. 459, 461.

[133] Charleston *Standard*, in Boston *Liberator*, December 12, 1856;

The Pro-African Slave-Trade Argument

Southerners felt an urgency to deny their guilt, to repudiate the laws condemning them as criminals, as immoral men. Thus they demanded that this federal slur upon them, this "foul imputation" be blotted from the statute book.[134]

The advocates of the African slave trade also bitterly attacked the Webster-Ashburton Treaty. In the Georgia and South Carolina legislatures, they introduced resolutions demanding that the federal government abrogate this treaty, especially the articles providing for the maintenance of an American squadron for the suppression of the slave trade along the African coast. They felt that they were being forced to participate in an act which in effect condemned the South and themselves. They indignantly charged that *slavery itself must be wrong, when the ships and seamen of our country are kept upon the seas to preclude the means to its formation.*" And they pointed out that since Southerners were paying taxes to finance the squadron, they were vindicating the principle that made slaves plunder and slaveholders pirates.[135]

This aggressive Southern attack on the federal laws and the Webster-Ashburton Treaty perplexed ex-president John Tyler of

Mississippi Baptist, in Jackson *Semi-Weekly Mississippian,* July 1, 1859; William F. Samford to Henry W. Hilliard, in Richmond *Enquirer,* October 26, 1858.

[134] Fitzhugh, in *De Bow's Review,* XXVI (1859), p. 148; Spratt to W. P. Miles, February 12, 1859, Miles Papers, University of North Carolina Library; D. H. Hamilton to Miles, April 26, 1860, Miles Papers, University of North Carolina Library; Edgefield *Advertiser,* February 23, 1859; *Mississippi Senate Journal,* 1858, pp. 6–7; Jackson *Semi-Weekly Mississippian,* July 1, 1859; *De Bow's Review,* XVIII (May, 1855), p. 628; Savannah *Daily News,* February 11, 1859; Little Rock *Old Line Democrat,* in Jackson *Semi-Weekly Mississippian,* October 7, 1859; Columbia *Times,* in New York *Anti-Slavery Standard,* December 6, 1856.

[135] Savannah *Morning News,* November 20, 1858; Bryan, *Report,* p. 45; Spratt, *Foreign Slave Trade,* p. 9; Bryan, in Charleston *Mercury,* August 28, 1857. See also Fitzhugh, in *De Bow's Review,* XXII (1857), pp. 450–461; Richmond *Enquirer,* in Charleston *Mercury,* April 1, 1856; Jackson *Semi-Weekly Mississippian,* September 14, 1858, March 1, 1859, April 10, 1860; Bryan, *Letters,* pp. 74–89; Charleston *Mercury,* in Washington *National Intelligencer,* June 24, 1858; William Gilmore Simms to James Hammond, June 11, 1858, in Mary Oliphant, Alfred Odell, and T. Evans, (eds.), *The Letters of William Gilmore Simms,* 4 Vols. (Columbia: University of South Carolina Press, 1955), IV, p. 65.

Virginia. He remembered how the South had voted with "singular unanimity" for the law declaring the African slave trade to be piracy. "How it happens, then," he remarked, "that a provision introduced into a treaty to enforce a law, for which the South had voted, can be rightly regarded as an insult to the South, I must say passes my comprehension." [136] In his bewilderment, Tyler could not understand what these fire-eaters were trying to say: for the sake of moral purity, the federal laws had to be repealed, and the treaty of 1842 had to be annulled.

The Southern criticism of the federal prohibition of the African slave trade had a moral purpose. This was undoubtedly the agitation's most important function. It provided a common ground of agreement among Southerners involved in the agitation. While Southerners like Fitzhugh and Spratt could not agree on the question of secession, they could both assert the African slave trade's morality. Similarly, while Southerners could be divided over whether African slaves should actually be imported, they could be united in the struggle to repudiate the indictment of the African slave trade as immoral. Southerners like Representative William Porcher Miles of South Carolina opposed the actual reopening of the trade. Yet they advocated the repeal of the federal laws. In their view, to repeal the federal laws and to reopen the trade were two different questions. The first was moral and the second economic and political; and thus it was possible to favor the first and oppose the second. On the floor of Congress in 1859, Representative Miles argued: "I, sir, am not prepared to advocate the reopening of the slave trade, but I am prepared to advocate with all my mind and strength, the sweeping away from our statute-book of laws which stamp the people of my section as pirates, and put a stigma upon their institutions." [137] But, for Southerners like C. A. L. Lamar and Leonidas W. Spratt, repeal alone would have been too moderate,

---

[136] Tyler, in Nashville *Union and American*, September 13, 1857.

[137] Miles, in *Congressional Globe*, 35th Congress, 2nd Session, p. 619. For additional evidence, see Richmond *Enquirer*, October 26, 1858; Jackson *Semi-Weekly Mississippian*, June 10, 1859, May 31, 1859; Charleston *Mercury*, in Richmond *Enquirer*, June 18, 1859; New Orleans *Crescent*, in Savannah *Morning News*, July 9, 1859.

too innocuous. They wanted to transport Africans into the South in order to illustrate defiantly the morality of slavery. Nevertheless, while Miles and Lamar differed on the question of actual importations, they were in agreement on the crucial issue: the South had to declare her moral innocence.

The advocates believed that the contest was one of ideas— between the idea of the North and the western world that slavery was morally wrong and the idea of the South that slavery was morally right. The war then, they argued, must be waged on the battlefield of principles. But they knew these contradictory principles were warring within Southern society and within the minds of Southerners themselves. They knew that Southerners in the past, especially before 1832, had admitted to the world that slavery was wrong. During the American Revolution, Southern slaveholders had realized they could not justify slavery, an institution "repugnant to humanity" and "destructive of liberty." [138] Even after the invention of the cotton gin and the expansion of cotton cultivation had given slavery a new profitability, Southerners had continued to apologize for their peculiar institution. During the 1820's, they had called their institution "an evil at best," and "an evil, the curse of which is felt and acknowledged by every enlightened man in the Slave-holding States." A South Carolina Representative had even declared in Congress: "Slavery, in the abstract, I condemn and abhor. . . . However ameliorated by compassion—however corrected by religion—still slavery is a bitter draught, and the chalice which contains the nauseous potion, is, perhaps, more frequently pressed by the lips of the master than of the slave." [139] Three decades later the African slave-trade radicals noticed that many Southerners continued to feel hesitant to defend their institution

---

[138] Patrick Henry, quoted in J. F. Jameson, *The American Revolution Considered as a Social Movement* (Boston: Beacon Press, 1963), p. 23.
[139] Governor Gerald C. Brandon of Mississippi, quoted in Edwin A. Miles, *Jacksonian Democracy in Mississippi* (Chapel Hill: University of North Carolina Press, 1960), p. 123; Edwin Holland of South Carolina, quoted in William W. Freehling, *Prelude to Civil War: The Nullification Controversy in South Carolina, 1816–1832,* p. 80; William Drayton, quoted in Freehling, pp. 76–77.

of slavery on moral grounds. "There was," Spratt observed, "the feeling, that, in some sense, they [slaves] were plunder, which it was enough to get out of the way with." [140] Consequently advocates launched their crusade to reopen the African slave trade in order to convince Southerners themselves—apologetic slaveholders as well as nonslaveholders like our Alabama farmer who said slavery "taant right"—that slavery was right.

For a long time Southerners had been bothered by the fundamental ambivalence of Southern slavery.[141] On the one hand, they regarded the slave as an object of economic value, a thing, a chattel, and a piece of real estate or property. "A slave," the Civil Code of Louisiana declared, "is one who is in the power of a master to whom he belongs. The master may sell him, dispose of his person, his industry, and his labor: he can do nothing, possess nothing, nor acquire anything but what must belong to the master." Slaves were bought, sold, and transferred like horses and cows and other items of property. A Southern newspaper, for example, reported in 1853: "Boys weighing about fifty lbs. can be sold for about five hundred dollars." In his will, a slavemaster bequeathed to his daughter "three negroes . . . also one gray mare and one cow." [142] Slavemasters also viewed the death of a slave as the loss of property, and they recorded such a financial loss in their plantation accounts.

Yet, on the other hand, Southerners also recognized the slave as a person. The slave could be Christianized and also seduced; baptism was an acknowledgment of the slave's soul,

[140] Charleston *Standard,* in New York *Weekly Tribune,* November 18, 1856.

[141] For a discussion on the ambivalence of Southern slavery, see David Brion Davis, *The Problem of Slavery in Western Culture;* Arnold A. Sio, "Interpretations of Slavery: The Slave Status in the Americas," *Comparative Studies in Society and History,* VII (1964–65), pp. 298–303; Wilbert E. Moore, "Slave Law and the Social Structure," *Journal of Negro History,* XXVI (April, 1941), No. 2, pp. 191–201; Kenneth M. Stampp, *The Peculiar Institution: Slavery in the Ante-Bellum South,* pp. 192–236.

[142] Quoted in Wilbert Moore, *op. cit.,* p. 191; Anderson (South Carolina) *Gazette,* and will of John Ensor, quoted in Stampp, *Peculiar Institution,* pp. 201, 204.

and the slavemasters' sexual exploitation of bondswomen was, as David Brion Davis noted, "the clearest recognition of their humanity." [143] Miscegenation in the Old South was, a Kentucky judge admitted, a common practice.[144] The judge's admission could be documented by the half a million mulattoes in the South in 1860. "Under slavery, we live surrounded by prostitutes," a Southern white woman complained. "Like the patriarchs of old, our men live all in one house with their wives and their concubines; and the mulattoes one sees in every family partly resemble the white children. Any lady is ready to tell you who is the father of all the mulatto children in everybody's household but her own. Those, she seems to think, drop from the clouds. My disgust sometimes is boiling over." [145] Slavemasters who had intimacies with slave women could not easily deny the humanity of their mulatto slave children. One such slavemaster "pictured to himself his sons dragged from market to market and passing from the authority of a parent to the rod of a stranger, until these horrid anticipations worked his expiring imagination into frenzy." [146] Many slaveholders found it impossible to relate to slaves simply as property and not as persons, capable of human feelings and friendship. Slaveholders sometimes, perhaps often, developed an affection for certain slaves. A Southern lady described the death of her slave nurse in very human terms: "When I saw that Death had the mastery, I laid my hands over her eyes, and in tears and fervor prayed that God would cause us to meet in happiness in another world. I knew, at that solemn moment, that color made no difference, but that her life would have been as precious, if I could have saved it, as if she had been white as snow."[147] Even the slave's very economic value was based on the fact that he had human qualities. The slave was valuable as a human worker, not as an animal or a machine;

[143] Davis, *The Problem of Slavery,* p. 59.

[144] In Stampp, *op. cit.,* p. 351.

[145] Mary Boykin Chesnut, *A Diary from Dixie* (Cambridge, Massachusetts: Riverside Press, 1961), pp. 21–22.

[146] Alexis de Tocqueville, *Democracy in America,* 2 Vols. (New York: Knopf, 1945), I, p. 396.

[147] Quoted in Stampp, *op. cit.,* p. 324.

his human possessions—his human body, his human skill, and his human intelligence—could be and were used by his master. Southern laws prohibiting the education of the slave implied that the slave, like the white man, was inherently capable of learning how to read and write. Moreover, the slave committed human acts of violence: he rebelled against his bondage and the master class. In this respect, the Nat Turner slave insurrection of 1831 made the slave's humanity frightfully apparent to the South.

Obviously the Southern conception of the slave was a contradiction. Edmund Ruffin's attitude towards his Negro mammy illustrates this paradox. Ruffin, his biographer observes, gave Lucy Lockett "affection in life and a place among his children in death." He buried her in Blandford Cemetery at Petersburg and inscribed a personal tribute on her grave stone: "In rememberance of Lucy Lockett, a slave, yet not the less the friend of her master's family, by whom is offered this testimonial of their esteem for her excellent virtues and true piety, gratitude for her affectionate and faithful services, and grief for her death." Yet, as a slave, Lucy Lockett was undoubtedly also listed as livestock in Ruffin's farm journals. This kind of contradiction was also reflected in the Southern legal system. A Southern court, for example, declared: "Because they are rational *human beings,* they are capable of committing crimes; and in reference to acts which are crimes, are regarded as *persons.* Because they are slaves, they are incapable of performing civil acts; and in reference to all such, they are *things, not persons. . . .*" [148]

For many perplexed Southerners, this ambivalence between the assertion of the slave as property and the admission of the slave's humanity was hard to reconcile. Their tyrannical power over the slave sharpened the anguish of their dilemma. Masters usually employed force to control their slaves—their "troublesome property." Slaves were generally engaged in a "day to day

[148] Craven, *Ruffin,* p. 20; Robert O. Cherry, "Edmund Ruffin: An Analysis of a Southern Fire-Eater," unpublished seminar paper, University of California at Los Angeles, 1969, p. 20; court declaration quoted in Moore, *op. cit.,* p. 198.

resistance" against their oppressive bondage: they shirked labor, feigned illness, destroyed tools and work animals, and ran away. To discipline their slaves, masters often used cruel punishments: they savagely whipped, starved, and even separated slaves from their families. Yet many masters felt guilty about the punishment of slaves, for they recognized that their "troublesome property" was human. When a North Carolina slaveholder willed his estate to his sons, he explained to them this painful predicament of slaveholding. "To manage negroes without the exercise of too much passion, is next to an impossibility. . . . I would therefore put you on your guard, lest their provocations should on some occasions transport you beyond the limits of decency and Christian morality." A South Carolina planter confessed that he whipped his slaves "in a passion & half the time unjustly," and that he suffered "scruples of conscience about slavery." [149]

Even after the Nat Turner insurrection of 1831 had driven Southerners into a fear of race war, even after pro-slavery polemicists like Thomas R. Dew and John C. Calhoun had proclaimed slavery "a positive good," even after the South had supposedly become a closed society, many Southerners were still profoundly uneasy about the morality of their institution. A Virginian exclaimed in 1832: "This, sir, is a Christian community. Southerners read in their Bibles, 'Do unto all men as you would have them do unto you'; and this golden rule and slavery are hard to reconcile." Writing to his wife in 1837, a Southerner expressed a troubled conscience: "I sometimes think my feelings unfit me for a slaveholder." [150] While distressed slavemasters were reluctant and fearful to admit publicly their feelings of guilt over slavery, they sometimes recorded their anguish in diaries. "Oh what trouble," a slavemaster wrote in his diary on December 21,

[149] Quoted in Stampp, *op. cit.*, pp. 91, 177–178; Raymond A. and Alice H. Bauer, "Day to Day Resistance to Slavery," *Journal of Negro History*, XXVII (1942), pp. 388–419; quoted in Freehling, *Prelude to Civil War*, p. 68.

[150] Quoted in Charles G. Sellers, Jr., *The Southerner as American*, p. 48; Gustavus A. Henry to his wife, December 2, 1837, Henry Papers, University of North Carolina Library, quoted in Kenneth M. Stampp, *The Peculiar Institution*, p. 424.

1858, "running sore, constant pressing weight, perpetual wearing, dripping, is this patriarchal institution! What miserable folly for men to cling to it as something heaven-descended. And here we and our children after us must groan under the burden —our hands tied from freeing ourselves." Ten days later he added: "I am more and more perplexed about my negroes. I cannot just take them up and sell them though that would be clearly the best I could do for myself. I cannot free them. I cannot keep them with comfort. . . . What would I not give to be freed from responsibility for these poor creatures. Oh, that I could know just what is right." [151]

Pro-slavery radicals, worried about this Southern moral anxiousness and uncertainty toward slavery, thought they had to declare aggressively that slavery was right in order to help Southerners rid themselves of their inner doubts. During the 1830's a Southern editor asserted that it was not enough for Southerners to believe that slavery had been entailed upon them by their forefathers. "We must satisfy the *consciences,* we must allay the fears of *our own people.* We must satisfy them that slavery is of itself right—that it is not a sin against God. . . ." [152] The pro-slavery argument was to an important extent a response to the psychological need of Southern society to overcome an anxiety based on a feeling of guilt, a feeling that slavery was "a sin against God."

Twenty years later some of the more radical fire-eaters also recognized the need to confront this Southern disquietude towards slavery. Many of these radicals belonged to a post-1830 generation. In their revolt against a history of Southern shame towards the institution, young men of the South like Henry Hughes and C. A. L. Lamar were pressing to its logical extreme the break from the old Southern tendency of apologizing for slavery. They were trying to *create* a new pro-slavery civilization and felt compelled to drive the pro-slavery argument beyond

---

[151] Smith, quoted in Ernest T. Thompson, *Presbyterians in the South, 1607–1861* (Richmond: John Knox Press, 1963), pp. 533–534.

[152] Washington *United States Telegraph*, December 5, 1835, quoted in Sellers, *Southerner,* p. 51. Italics added.

The Pro-African Slave-Trade Argument

the contradictory thinking of Dew and Calhoun. Unlike the older pro-slavery theoreticians, they could not defend the peculiar institution as "a positive good" and continue to describe the African slave trade as "wretched in the extreme."[153] Hence they demanded the repeal of the federal laws against the African slave trade—laws enacted by Southerners like Jefferson and Calhoun—and sought to transform the African slave trade from a symbol of piracy and horror into a symbol of the morality of slavery.

"It is a miserable sophistry," declared a writer to the Charleston *Mercury,* "which views the domestic trade with complacency, but shudders at the buying and selling of the naked Africans. I desire earnestly that we shall not only think consistently, *but feel rightly,* on this subject." [154] The editor of the Galveston *Weekly News* charged that in the past Southern statesmen had acknowledged slavery to be a moral wrong, and that the South could no longer compromise this subject and must assert that slavery was "right in the sight of God." "If you agree to slavery," the editor warned his Texas readers, "you must agree to the trade, for they are one. Those who are not for us must be against us. Those who deny slavery and the slave-trade are enemies of the South."[155] Secessionist William Yancey of Alabama explained that the African slave-trade debate was forcing Southerners to place themselves on the line on the slavery question, and to clarify the slavery issue in their own minds. In his judgment, the agitation had already exposed "much unsoundness in our midst upon the question of slavery, and one of the advantages of discussion will be to correct these erroneous views and to warn our people of those amongst us who are

[153] Dew, *Review of the Debate in the Virginia Legislature, 1831–32,* in *The Pro-Slavery Argument* (Charleston: Walker, Richards & Co., 1852), p. 346; Calhoun, speech in Senate, 1842, in Richmond *Enquirer,* May 28, 1858; Margaret L. Coit, *John C. Calhoun* (Boston: Houghton Mifflin, 1961), p. 285.

[154] Letter signed "P. A. F.," in Charleston *Mercury,* October 20, 1858. Italics added.

[155] Galveston *Weekly News,* November 9, 1858, March 3, 1857.

radically unsound upon the principles which underlie that institution." [156]

Thus, in their ideological attack on the North, these Southern fire-eaters were also aiming at Southerners. They were advancing a radical pro-slavery ideology to discipline the abolitionist Helpers and the distrusted nonslaveholders of the South. While they could not persuade Congress to repeal the federal laws and actually import large numbers of African slaves to restore slaveholding social mobility and thereby reinforce the security of the institution in the South, they sought to wield the pro-African slave-trade argument to intimidate Southern nonslaveholders. They also sought to use their ideological weapon to discipline perplexed and guilt-tortured slaveholders. Advocates of the African slave trade like Spratt and Yancey were defining the norms for Southerners, for themselves.[157] They were trying to give Southerners a new and a consistent pro-slavery identity. They were telling Southerners who they were, or should be—Southerners were *both* slaveholders *and* righteous men. They were leading a Southern crusade to ferret out "unsoundness" on slavery within the South. Support for the African slave trade was a test of Southern loyalty to the peculiar institution.

Their aggressive and insistent affirmation of slavery as the essence of morality could help some of the African slave-trade advocates overcome their private moral qualms about the institution. Public declarations of confidence in slavery sometimes concealed inner misgivings. Even leading pro-slavery theoretician George Fitzhugh confessed privately that he saw "great evils in Slavery, but in a controversial work I ought not to

[156] Yancey, letter, in Montgomery *Advertiser and Gazette*, reprinted in Charleston *Mercury*, July 9, 1859. For further evidence, see Houston *Telegraph*, in Galveston *Weekly News*, March 9, 1858; Galveston *Civilian*, July 19, 1859; *De Bow's Review*, XXIII (September, 1857), p. 317; Bryan, *Letters*, pp. 5–6; Charleston *Standard*, in New York *National Anti-Slavery Standard*, November 8, 1856, December 6, 1856; Charleston *Standard*, in Boston, *Liberator*, December 12, 1856; New Orleans *Delta*, May 18, 1858.

[157] For a suggestive study of norms and deviancy, see Kai T. Erikson, *Wayward Puritans: A Study in the Sociology of Deviance* (New York: John Wiley, 1966).

admit them." Possibly even Edmund Ruffin had not completely conquered his early feelings about slavery as an evil to be abolished someday.[158] In their assault on Southerners who might have been unsound on slavery, some of the advocates were actually trying to convince themselves as well as others that slavery was not a sin.

The African slave-trade agitation's press for a proslavery conformity was related to the thrust for Southern independence. Secession could give the South much more than political independence from the North: it could provide a framework for the reconstruction of values in the South on a sound pro-slavery basis. A Southern Confederacy could reopen the African slave trade, widen the social base of slaveholding, and buttress the commitment to the institution. The presence of numerous blacks in Southern society would compel whites, anxious about their survival, to support slavery, an institution of race control, and condemn the Helper schemes for abolition and colonialization as ridiculous. If the African slave trade could be used to provide labor support for Southern industrialization, then even the industrial society of a Confederacy would be committed to slavery. But even if African slaves were not imported into a Confederate South, the defiance of secession and the violence of war in defense of slavery would surely help to confirm the rightness of slavery in the minds of Southerners. In short, the agitation for the reopening of the African slave trade was designed not only to repel the moral crusade of William Lloyd Garrison but also to help Southerners get right with slavery!

The moral argument for the reopening of the African slave trade was based on a contradiction. Since the slave was property, the advocates argued, Southerners could morally transport slaves from Africa as well as from Virginia. "A man visits a country where negroes are sold as *merchandise*. He buys one, or more . . . just as we would buy a *horse* or any other species of *property;* and there was no more reason for characterizing the

[158] Fitzhugh to Holmes, April 11, 1855, Holmes Letter Book, quoted in Wish, *Fitzhugh*, p. 111; Craven, *Ruffin*, p. 108.

trade in the one as piracy, than in the other." [159] Yet advocates also recognized the slave as person in their emphasis on the missionary function of the African slave trade. They reminded Southerners that Africa was a "benighted land" inhabited by "miserable, naked savages" who worshipped snakes and practiced cannibalism. "Pity the sorrows of a European," they observed, "traveling through the bush and partaking of the hospitality . . . of a native, when as a delicacy reserved for him, there is fished up out of the big pot of soup a black head, with the lips drawn back and the white teeth grinning, and such a painful resemblance of the faces around him that for a moment he wonders which of the younger members of the family has been sacrificed to the exigencies of the occasion. But he is reassured, and discovers that he is not eating man, but monkey." [160] The African slave trade would transport unfortunate, degraded, and barbarous Africans from a depraved continent; and Southern slavery would elevate them to a condition of usefulness, well-being, and morality. In the American South, the African would be transformed from a cannibal to a "submissive," "docile," "patient," and "happy" slave—a Sambo. Slavery would teach the wild African how to work in the cotton fields, "to speak English, to say the Lord's prayer, to trample his fetish, and to loathe raw frogs and redworms, roasted lizards and parched wasps, beetles, bumble-bees and grasshoppers." [161] The African slave trade was a "commerce of mercy," and slavery a missionizing institution. [162] Thus the African slave-trade argu-

[159] Jackson *Semi-Weekly Mississippian*, May 31, 1859. Italics added.

[160] New Orleans *Daily Delta*, October 24, December 21, 1858; November 21, 1858.

[161] Galveston *Civilian*, in Galveston *Weekly News*, June 20, 1857; C. W. Miller, *Reopening*, p. 5; Charleston *Mercury*, June 2, October 20, 1858; J. G. M. Ramsey to L. W. Spratt, April 23, 1858; Ramsey Papers, University of North Carolina Library; New Orleans *Delta*, February 14, 1858.

[162] George S. Sawyer, *Southern Institutes; or an Inquiry into the Origins and Early Prevalence of Slavery and the Slave-trade . . . with Notes and Comments in Defense of the Southern Institutions* (Philadelphia: J. B. Lippincott, 1859), p. 204; Augusta *Dispatch*, in Galveston *Weekly News*, May 3, 1859. For additional evidence, see Charleston *Standard*, in Boston *Liberator*, December 12, 1856; Clayton Banner, in Charles-

ment was actually an extension rather than a resolution of the institution's ambivalent view of the slave as property as well as person.

Yet the message of the African slave-trade argument was clear: since the African slave trade and slavery were moral institutions, Southern moral meekness on the slavery question was unwise. Southerners must launch their own crusade, advance their own principles, and challenge the anti-slavery sentiments of the western world. To accomplish this, the advocates asserted, the South must give to slavery "the moral strength of an aggressive attitude—a position in which there could be no admission of a wrong—no implication of a sense of shame in its condition." [163] Thus in this war of opinion they proposed to plant their standard in the very faces of their adversaries and to declare boldly the renewal of the African slave trade as the leading principle of the South.[164]

Contemporary observers recognized this new aggressiveness. They thought the agitation to reopen the African slave trade represented a spite to the North and a defiance of the opinions of western civilization. William Lloyd Garrison re-

ton *Mercury,* March 3, 1857; Galveston *News,* December 6, 1856; E. Ruffin, Diary, Ruffin Papers, Library of Congress; Richmond *Whig,* September 3, 1859; Edward B. Bryan, *Letters to the Southern People Concerning the Acts of Congress and Treaties with Great Britain, in Relation to the African Slave Trade* (Charleston: Walker, Evans & Co., 1858), p. 17; Presentment of the Grand Jury of Williamsburg, in Consul Bunch to the Earl of Clarendon, December 28, 1854, *British and Foreign State Papers, 1854–1855,* p. 1156; Jackson *Semi-Weekly Mississippian,* September 17, 1858, New Orleans *Crescent,* in Savannah *Morning News,* May 5, 1859; "Southern," in Richmond *Enquirer,* July 28, 1857.

[163] Spratt, in *De Bow's Review,* XXVII (June, 1859), p. 208.

[164] E. Bryan, in Charleston *Mercury,* August 28, 1857; Charleston *Standard,* in New York *Weekly Tribune,* November 8, 1856. For additional evidence, see Fitzhugh, "Southern Thought," *De Bow's Review,* XXIII (October, 1857), p. 339; New Orleans *Delta,* in Charleston *Mercury,* January 16, 1856; J. D. McRae, in *De Bow's Review,* XXVII (1859), pp. 362–363; New Orleans *Crescent,* in Charleston *Mercury,* August 30, 1859; J. G. M. Ramsey to Spratt, April 29, 1858; Ramsey Papers, University of North Carolina Library; Presentments of the Grand Juries of Williamsburg and Richland, in Consul Bunch to the Earl of Clarendon, December 28, 1854, *British and Foreign State Papers, 1854–1855,* p. 1156.

marked that "attempts are now being made to change the views of the Christian world, in regard to slavery; to make it respected." [165] Commenting on the South Carolina proposal to reopen the African slave trade, Frederick Law Olmsted asked: "Why, except for the sake of consistency, or for the purpose of bullying the moral sense of the rest of mankind. . . ?" [166] The editor of the London *Times* shuddered at the new pro-slavery crusade. The revival of the African slave trade, he declared, would mean "a war of principle—a war of religion between the slave-trading states of the North American Union and mankind." [167] But, while these unhappy observers correctly described the African slave-trade agitation as a revolt against the anti-slavery values of western culture, they did not understand that much of the new Southern aggression against the outside western world was actually being directed inward against the uncertain South.

In the supreme expression of Southern pro-slavery defiance, Mississippi State Senator Henry Hughes caustically proposed an identification system for the newly imported Africans.

> The identification of our negroes [from Africa] will not be difficult. Public officers . . . may be ordained and sworned to identify. If necessary bloody letters may by State authority, be branded on the negroes' cheeks or chins. Or if rampant, free-labor philanthropy, fattening on its own abuses but sickening at ours, shall still fall into foaming convulsions at the horrors of our labor system, then, let us in healthy, cool and laughing defiance, identify by other means, the negroes and their children. Let us in hard and staunch protest against what is philanthropy in design but misanthropy indeed; let us in

165 Boston *Liberator*, June 25, 1858.
166 Olmsted, *A Journey in the Seaboard States*, Vol. II, p. 118.
167 London *Times*, in New York *Anti-Slavery Standard*, January 10, 1857; also William Chambers, *Slavery and Colour* (London: W. & R. Chambers, 1857), p. 12; London *Times*, December 16, 1856, in Richmond *Enquirer*, January 9, 1857; Stirling, *Letters from the Slave States*, p. 76; Charles Mackay, *Life and Liberty in America; or Sketches of a Tour in the United States and Canada in 1857–8* (New York: Harper and Brothers, 1859), pp. 249–250.

humorous contempt, in delightful and deliberate detesta-
tion of sanctimonious meddlers; let us if expedient to
identify our new negroes, mark them like hogs and brand
them like beeves; let us slit their nostrils; let us pinch
in their bleeding ears, cross-cuts and underbits, or with
hot and salted irons, fry on their brows and breasts,
lasting letters. . . . Then let freedom shriek till her face
is red, and her voice is cracked as her skull.[168]

Hughes's extreme protest can help us understand an anxiety
at the heart of the internal crisis of the Old South. In his scorn-
ful call for the branding of slaves "like beeves," Hughes was
trying to make it unmistakably clear to Southerners as well as
Northerners what the slave should be: the slave should not be
both person and property, but only property. If the slave were
nothing more than property, nothing more than "hogs" and
"beeves," how could the slaveholder be condemned as sinful and
inhuman? Yet the shrillness of his arrogant and desperate scream
suggests that Senator Hughes himself knew the slave, despite
the bloody letters fried on his brows and breasts, was still
nothing but a man.

[168] Letter signed "St. Henry," in Jackson *Semi-Weekly Mississippian*,
October 4, 1859. "St. Henry" was Henry Hughes's pen name. See Henry
Hughes's scrapbook and diary, Hughes Papers, Mississippi State Archives.

FOUR

PILGRIM'S PROGRESS
OF A SOUTHERN
FIRE-EATER

before he published his *Treatise on Sociology*, before he was elected to the state senate, and before he became Mississippi's leading African slave-trade radical and called for the branding of African slaves "like beeves," young Henry Hughes recorded his most intimate thoughts, ambitions, and anxieties in his diary.[1] His diary, now preserved in the basement of the Mississippi State Archives at Jackson, represents not only a fascinating

[1] Hughes, *Treatise on Sociology* (Philadelphia: Lippincott, 1854); "St. Henry" letters, published in the Jackson *Semi-Weekly Mississippian*, October 4, 1859, February 3, 1860, April 24, 1860; also in Port Gibson *Reveille*, July 30, 1858; Diary of Henry Hughes, in Henry Hughes Papers, Mississippi State Archives, Jackson, Mississippi.

and uninhibited autobiography of a youthful pro-slavery moralist, but also a rare opportunity to study the intersection between the personal crisis of a Southern fire-eater and the crisis of Southern society. In short, the diary of Henry Hughes can serve as an excellent basis for an individual case study to illustrate many of our themes—youthfulness, moral anxiousness over slavery, and pro-slavery aggressiveness.

Since the day of his birth in 1829, Henry Hughes was involved in the peculiar institution. He was born into a slaveholding family of Port Gibson in Claiborne County, and during his childhood he was close to Uncle Aleck, a family slave. "The very first anecdote of myself while I was almost a baby," Hughes later recalled in his diary, "was related to me by a lady; she saw me playing where some little boys were throwing stones, and on asking me whether I was not afraid, I replied seriously, that if my eye was put out, I would get Uncle Aleck who was our teamster, to drive me in his waggon up to heaven; and God there would fix my eye for me." (August 8, 1852) Young Henry saw the slave Uncle Aleck as a friend, as a human being. The fact that Aleck was called "Uncle" had added significance. As Bertram W. Doyle has pointed out, the title "Uncle" was given to a slave who was "considered, more or less, as a part of the family." Hughes's relationship with Uncle Aleck might have been particularly important due to the loss of his father early in his childhood. In his diary, Hughes repeatedly noted the death of his father. Father died "while my life was in its Spring." (January 1, 1848) Hughes's dependence on blacks for friendship continued beyond his childhood days. During the Civil War Hughes took his body servants with him to the battlefront. In a letter to his nephew, he wrote: "Frederic will soon come home to see his wife and child and Mistress. I want him to come. Nobody loves me so much as Frederic and Morgan do. Frederic takes care of me like I belonged to him." [2]

---

[2] Doyle, *Etiquette of Race Relations in the South*, p. 16; Hughes, letter to nephew; quoted in Richard M. Guess, "Henry Hughes, Sociologist, 1829–1862," unpublished M.A. thesis, University of Mississippi, 1930, p. 15.

During the childhood years of Henry Hughes, Mississippi was in an era of great economic expansion. "This country was just setting up," reported the chronicler Joseph G. Baldwin. "Marvellous accounts had gone forth of the fertility of its virgin lands; and the productions of the soil were commanding a price remunerating to slave labor as it had never been remunerated before."[3] In the 1830's Mississippi's cotton production quadrupled and its slave population doubled. By 1840, blacks outnumbered whites. The slave population of Claiborne County increased 222 per cent during this decade, and the county's ratio of slaves to whites rose to 4 to 1 by 1840. These were the "flush times" of Mississippi.[4] This was a crucial decade in Mississippi's history: whites had become dependent on blacks for labor, and on slavery to control the numerous blacks.

No wonder Mississippi white society was fearfully sensitive to the danger of slave insurrections. After the 1831 Nat Turner slave revolt in Virginia, a Mississippian urged the slave patrols of his state to be diligent. "Shall it require the repetition, upon our shores, of the scenes of Southampton to awaken our citizens to a sense of their danger?"[5] Four years later a slave insurrection scare sent Mississippians into a panic. In certain counties, the fear of slave violence was so great that white women and children were gathered into guarded places at night. Lynch mobs savagely whipped slaves to extort information about the alleged plot, and hysterically hanged their victims. "Never was there," a Mississippi lawyer observed, "an instance of more extraordinary or even maddening excitement amid a refined, intelligent and virtue-loving people than that which I had the pain to witness in the counties of central Mississippi in the

[3] Baldwin, *The Flush Times of Alabama and Mississippi* (New York: Hill and Wang, 1957), p. 60.
[4] *Ibid.*, Charles Sydnor, *Slavery in Mississippi* (Baton Rouge: Louisiana State University Press, 1966, pp. 185–186; Edwin A. Miles, *Jacksonian Democracy in Mississippi* (Chapel Hill: University of North Carolina Press, 1960), p. 123; United States Census Office, *Fifth Census, 1830* (Washington: 1832), p. 103; *Sixth Census, 1840* (Washington: 1841), p. 58.
[5] Quoted in Miles, *op. cit.*, p. 124.

summer of 1835." [6] Claiborne County, where young Henry Hughes lived, bordered this circle of fear and paranoia.

Due to the tremendous influx of slaves into Mississippi, the dread of slave rebellions, and the emergence of Northern abolitionism, white Mississippians were driven into an anxious defense of slavery during the 1830's. In 1825 the Governor of Mississippi had admitted that slavery was an evil. But Mississippians began to realize they could no longer make such admissions. A year after the 1835 slave insurrection scare, a state legislative committee declared that the people of Mississippi looked upon slavery "not as a curse, but as a blessing." [7] As Henry Hughes was growing up, Mississippi was becoming a pro-slavery society.

But Henry Hughes was not yet preoccupied with the slavery question. He was too young and too interested in other matters, especially his education. As a child, Hughes was precocious, and at the age of sixteen, he entered the local college. He was a hardworking student and did not "drink, chew, smoke or play cards." [8] Outstanding in mathematics, languages, history, and philosophy, he graduated with honors in 1847. He then studied and practiced law in New Orleans.

As a young lawyer, Hughes devoted much of his time to the reading of legal treatises. But his highly curious mind and his passion for books led him to read Gibbon, Shakespeare, Cicero, Macaulay, Bancroft, Kant, Locke, Carlyle, Fourier, and Mill. Like many Southerners of his day, Hughes was an avid reader of Sir Walter Scott's romantic novels. He also had a keen interest in anatomy and geology, and found time to invent a cotton press, a steam engine, and a screw with a variable thread. He often jotted down his scientific thoughts in his diary. "The force exerted by the magnetism of the Earth," he wrote on March 24, 1850, "varies in different places. (See Almsted's

[6] Henry S. Foote, quoted in Clement Eaton, *The Freedom-of-Thought Struggle in the Old South* (New York: Harper, 1964), p. 97.

[7] Quoted in Miles, *op. cit.*, pp. 123–124; Sydnor, *op. cit.*, pp. 242–244.

[8] Hughes, Diary, January 1, 1848.

Natural Philosophy, Magnetism.) This force, arranges itself about the earth in isodynamic curves. These curves bear towards certain points of the Earth, a certain relation. By this relation those points are made 'magnetic Poles.'" In 1853 Hughes was elected a fellow of the New Orleans Academy of Arts and Sciences. Years later he would employ his scientific knowledge and inventiveness to build fortifications at Bull Run.

Like many young Southern men who became African slave-trade advocates, Henry Hughes had an energetic life style. On June 16, 1850, he recorded his activities for the day.

> During the day: study 1 before breakfast—Gibbon's "Rome"—nearly finished, 2 and then extemporize; 3 after breakfast, study or rather investigate the nature of composition—perfection being the end—4 psychology—the noblest and best—beloved of my investigations—the supporter of all—5 vocalize 6 gesture & principles & practice, 7 composed study Milton's & Getty's oratory; dine; 8 of Civil Engineering, read ten pages, 9 investigate the nature of law with a view to a perfect society; 10 read aloud; study—investigate politics; 12 study Demosthenes translated—a little; 13 study words—synonyms chiefly—writing them; 14 read of law ten pages, walk—sup; 15 read of Civil Engineering ten pages; 16 miscellaneous reflection; 16 before retiring memorize from Yound or Shakespeare alternately, & for principles or classifications, look into law, zoology, ethics; extemporize, jesticulate; 17 retire, pray, thoughts on psychology, miscellaneous thoughts.

Such was a usual day for Henry Hughes.

In his frenzy for knowledge, young Hughes was impatiently hungering for early recognition and success. "When Shall I accomplish Something which will confer visible tangible fame? . . . Am I impatient, Am I too young? . . . Cannot summer produce the fruits of autumn?" (May 21, 1848) Hughes plotted his strategy. "During the Summer of 1847, I joined a Division of the Sons of Temperance, in order to gain the honor of addressing them. I accomplished my aim in two or three months subsequently. The Speech was published in the Port Gibson Herald."

(January 1, 1848) Publication was to be Hughes's vehicle for personal advancement. "Tomorrow, begin writing for publication. This, for power, fame & subsistence." (November 30, 1851)

As an energetic young man possessing a wide diversity of talents and interests, Hughes hated the tedium of his law practice. "My aversion to spending time in the practice of Law, grows." (March 14, 1852) "Why do I abhor the practice yet like the study of the law?" (May 16, 1852) His try at a career in law was a failure; his law business was slow and "quite limited." (December 28, 1851) Clearly Hughes found much boredom and little meaning in his work.

The frustrated young lawyer was also beset with problems of sickness and sex. Hughes was frequently ill and complained about failing eyesight, deafness, and severe chest pains. "My eyes are still very bad. For the last few days I have been attacked with a slight deafness." (July 9, 1848) His relationships with women were often experimental and unfulfilling. "The past week has been fraught with invaluable experience. I have learned the vanity of sensual & forbidden enjoyments, from experiments purposely tried." (January 9, 1848) "I have again reaped a little of the whirlwind of experience; have fully tested the insufficiency of carnal enjoyments." (January 16, 1848) "Have I ever had a pleasure in which woman was not an element. Since my eighteenth year, I have not been unloved. And so again and—still—clasped hands, embracing arms, kissed lips, and pillowing bosoms, Ambition and Love, these are my life." (January 9, 1853)

Disease and women had an important association in Hughes's mind. "Would that the flesh had no weakness. Disease has been preying upon me. . . . Beneath its noiseless influence I feel my nerves relax, strength decrease, energy slacken. . . . But what I most lament is a disposition which is so naturally convival that in the gentle but unguarded excitement of a Society in which are many gay female friends;—I descend from the grave seriousness which should characterize my demeanor, and participate in their levities." (February 27, 1848) These concerns were related to a passionate love for glory. "I love Glory, Power,

Fame. . . . She is my Soul's idol. To her, I, with a lover's hot devotion, kneel. She is my sweet. Romeo never more truly loved. I am her Antony [*sic*]. In her soft arms, on her fair bosom, beneath her warm eyes and balmy breath, I forget all joys & pains." (February 10, 1850) An ambitious man, Hughes worried about illness and women as threats to his quest for knowledge and fame. Both could distract him and dissipate his energy.

A sad loneliness deepened Hughes's anxiousness. The young man had trouble forming genuine human relationships. "I never had many to love me. From my childhood, [I] have been esteemed, honored, flattered, admired, yet there were no spirits with whom I could feel a sympathy." (March 19, 1848) "Nobody ever talks to me. In every conversation, I lead or nothing or little is addressed to me. The little-boy in our office talks to me; that is, if we are by ourselves." (December 28, 1851) A month later, Hughes took polka dance lessons with a class of ladies and gentlemen. Hughes had difficulty relating to people whom he regarded as competitors. "The . . . jealousy even of the name of schoolmates who perhaps may attempt to rival me . . . all force me on" to strive for success. (January 30, 1848) But he could relate comfortably to people who were not in a competitive position: his office boy and especially his slave friends like Uncle Aleck and Frederic. For Hughes, they had clearly defined roles and places.

Young Henry Hughes often thought about suicide. On February 22, 1852, he scribbled in his diary: "Thoughts of suicide. Gloomy, Oh so gloomy." A week later, he cried: "Life grows practical. And such practice. Law—I abhor it. Was I destined to squander precious hours in squeezing from it a scanty & unsatisfactory livelihood?" (February 29, 1852) Yet Hughes's passionate quest for recognition drove him away from self-destruction. "To me annihilation is not terrible. . . . To me, power & fame are almost the only things which invite me from a yearning after annihilation." (October 15, 1848) "Thought on suicide, often have the wish, but something seems to detain me.

. . . If I, in Mississippi, lived; I could, I think, enter Congress, immediately after my twenty-fifth year." (September 15, 1850)

His ambition for political recognition was tied to his need for a lasting and meaningful human relationship, especially his desire for a woman's love and genuine companionship in marriage. Hughes himself made this connection explicit in his diary on May 9, 1852. He wrote that he had attended a citizens' meeting to urge the federal government to establish a navy yard in New Orleans and deepen the mouth of the Mississippi River, and that he would try to secure the appointment as a delegate to Washington. The delegation would be composed of prominent citizens. Hughes wished to be the secretary of the delegation. "The Secretary could perhaps secure from the position, both power & fame." He then continued: "To secure appointments will bring me in contact with some of the Editors & merchants . . . Being thus appointed I shall endeavor to procure appointment as Delegate, from Mississippi, to the Baltimore Convention of the Democratic Party. . . . Thus I shall see & study Congress also; and thus get a distinction slight perhaps, but *useful matrimonially*." [9] But his hopes were quickly dashed. "The Committee on the Navy-Yard resolutions," he wrote in his diary a week later, "was appointed before I applied."

Hughes tried to convince himself that he was destined to become great. "Day after day, I become more firmly convinced that there is a Destiny which shapes my ends. I believe in the Christian Religion. From this day, with the help of my Destiny, I will devote myself, unreservedly, conscientiously with all my heart & with all my strength, to the attainment of that greatness, glory, power, which no mortal man has ever possessed. I will place myself upon a throne from which I can look down on Alexand[er], Caesar, Cicero, Bonaparte, Washington. May my God help me." (January 9, 1848) Hughes's ambition was intertwined with his belief in a personal God. "My Father press to my lips, love me thy Pet, thy Darling." (July 2, 1848) If the weakness of his flesh—his illness and his flirtations—were

[9] Italics added.

sources of anxiety, his image of God offered him assurances about his future. "If I could only believe that there was a God, how happy I should be. I should then be unreservedly confident in my fortunes." (January 16, 1848) But what if God did not exist? Hughes asked this awesome question and felt the horror of nothingness. "My Father, you made me—let me talk so—I was your darling & hero; this was so; but if in what is thus done by me and through you, I am beguiled; if Oh my Soul, there is for me no Father, no caressing God; let then all Earth yawn its chops and gorge with men & blood its gut of fire; let all stars suns and comets shoot short into solid coal and flickers into ashy nothing." (July 4, 1852)

A few days later Hughes left New Orleans, where he was practicing law, and returned to the small town of Port Gibson. He thought about the career options open to him. "I may have here my home. Here I may work out by literature, politics, law, philosophy, science; what God has set me to do. It may be that I shall go to New-orleans to be a money-catcher. That life & prospect, I abhor. If existence is a conflict, death has there the slow victory. There are all hateful things; Sickness is there; there adulteries, seductions, hypocricies [sic], syncopahcies [sic], selfishness; & whatever I have shrunk from, whatever loathed." (July 11, 1852) In Hughes's mind, Port Gibson and New Orleans represented two different worlds. A few years earlier, while on board a steamboat, he had jotted in his diary : "I am on my way to Port Gibson, in Mississippi. It is my native place. I expect to Spend the Summer there. I left New Orleans yesterday evening about five o'clock. It is for the benefit of my eyes & health that I pursue this course. I had hoped to remain longer in the city. Eyes irritated by use & by the dust & glare of Streets & houses; a breast made painful by regular confinement,—have banished me to shadier walks & purer air." (June 11, 1848) Notice the images and associations in these passages : New Orleans was a city—a place of sickness, dust, glare, money, streets, houses, confinement, and seductions ("gay female friends"). New Orleans threatened Hughes's life energies. Port Gibson, on the other hand, was his "native place"—close to nature, open, pure, offering health and the realization of his ambitions.

Unhappy in his law business, Hughes was seeking a career that could bring meaning to his life. "How much I want to grapple with something. I would be a soldier, but not in peace; physician, but not in health; sailor but not in port or calm." (May 16, 1852) While he fretted over his boredom, loneliness, and sickness, he wished for a military career. "I wish that wars were. I detest the practice only of the Law. It is too Mechanical." (June 7, 1852) "Why have I such a passion for war? Why does a soldier's life seem my coming destiny?" (December 12, 1852) Since Southern chivalry had invested much honor and status in the military tradition, Hughes's romantic image of himself as a soldier undoubtedly helped to relieve his sad anguish. A few years later, on the eve of the Civil War, he would offer Southern mothers the following advice on the education of their sons: "Let all such as slapt, slap back, all gallant brats whose crow is like the cock's shrill clarion and whose look is like the lion's, have flags for wrappers, powder boxes for saddles, drums for rattles, and for common playthings, pistols . . . ramrods and scabbards, let them play most with the rod that they may long for the rifle, and most with the scabbard that they may prize the sword. Soon swords only can save us. . . ." [10] Here was the extreme expression of the Southern cavalier's cult of the military.

In his search for some kind of meaning, Hughes even considered the possibility of becoming an abolitionist! "It has this morning, occurred to me that the chief aim of my life shall be to unite the great powers of the earth in one Republic, to abolish slavery, and to reform the system of human laws and human society." (November 16, 1848) Occasionally in his diary he expressed moral doubts about slavery. "The relation of landlord & tenant is as sinful as that [of] master & slave. Both relations shall be abolished; but not to the hurt of the South." (April 13, 1851) But how could slavery be abolished? Hughes, like

[10] "St. Henry," in Jackson *Semi-Weekly Mississippian*, October 4, 1859. For a discussion of the Southern cult of the military, see Osterweis, *Romanticism and Nationalism in the Old South*, pp. 90–94.

Thomas Jefferson and Hinton Helper, considered colonization—the mass transportation of blacks to Africa. (March 9, 1851)

But Hughes's views on slavery were profoundly ambivalent. During this very time of personal crisis, he was also becoming involved in pro-slavery ideology and politics. On August 31, 1851—five months after he had condemned the master-slave relationship as "sinful"—he recorded two important thoughts in his diary. "Examined the morality of slavery. Thoughts of becoming a candidate for the legislature." The juxtaposition of his interest in the morality of slavery and his political ambitions could hardly have been coincidental. His hopes for a political career were identified with the defense of slavery. For Hughes, political recognition could be "useful matrimonially." But his study of "the morality of slavery" had much more than political and matrimonial meaning. Hughes could not support abolition and colonization for he was too dependent on blacks for human relationship. He did not want to be separated from his slaves like Uncle Aleck or Frederic. Yet he still felt morally uncomfortable about slavery. If he could work out a theory for a moral and humane master-slave relationship, then possibly he could come to terms with his own qualms about slavery. Soon he was investigating the question of the right of secession and reading pro-slavery novels and treatises. He avidly read Calhoun's writings on nullification and slavery. "Began Calhoun's Disquisition on Government; able work—pleased. Looked through 'Uncle Tom's Cabin,' by Mrs. Beecher Stowe. That book is womanish & I am afraid absurdly unprincipled; written by a woman clearly. I feel like I am the man for times coming." (August 15, 1852) On October 24, 1852, he called himself "the devotee" of "Slavery Perfect Society." By then he had already begun writing his own wordy analytical justification of Southern slavery.

In 1854, at the age of twenty-five, Henry Hughes published his *Treatise on Sociology*. His book immediately received favorable recognition in the South. The famous Southern writer, William Gilmore Simms, described it as a profound and conclusive defense of slavery. Another reviewer praised the book as a worthy effort to overcome the Southern "habit" of admitting that slavery was "an evil in the abstract." Sociologist George Fitzhugh thought Hughes's book had helped to revolutionize Southern public opinion on slavery.[11] Like Leonidas W. Spratt's essay on "The Destiny of the Slave States," Hughes's *Treatise* represented a departure from the old Southern inclination to apologize for slavery. Literary recognition had political implications for the youthful author. Reprinting Simms's review of the *Treatise,* the editor of the Port Gibson *Reveille* declared that Hughes was "well qualified by natural talents and astute learning for any position that the people of his native State might assign him. We know of no man who would represent the views of the Southern people in Congress with more ability and fidelity than Mr. Hughes." [12] Two years later the editor would be able to announce the election of Henry Hughes to the Mississippi State Senate.

In formulating the concepts for his *Treatise,* Hughes was influenced by the socialistic writings of John Stuart Mill and Charles Fourier, and by the sociological theories of Auguste Comte. In his diary, he reported that he had read Mill's *Principles of Political Economy;* and then he added: "Thoughts of a method of gradual Socialism." (March 16, 1851) Fourier, the theoretician of utopian socialism who advocated the reorganization of society into communities called phalanxes, also had an impact on Hughes's thinking. "Finished the first volume of Fourier's 'Passions of the Human Soul.' That book's influence on me!" (May 2, 1852) "Continued Fourier on the Passions. I do not think that this book will mislead, nor make me visionary. It will generate conceptions; it will supply elements." (May 23, 1852) The following year Hughes studied in Paris where he probably met Comte. The French philosopher's influence on Hughes was apparent in Hughes's use of Comte's terms such as "sociology" and Comte's assumption that social phenomenon

[11] Simms, in Port Gibson *Reveille,* December 30, 1854, in Hughes scrapbook, Hughes Papers, Mississippi State Archives; Review, unidentified newspaper clipping, Hughes scrapbook; Fitzhugh to G. F. Holmes, March 27, 1855, Holmes Letterbook, Duke University Library, quoted in Genovese, *World the Slaveholders Made,* p. 130.

[12] Port Gibson *Review,* December 30, 1854, in Hughes scrapbook.

could be reduced to science and laws. But Hughes was interested in these European thinkers only because he wanted to use their ideas and methods to refute the charges that slavery was "morally evil, and civilly inexpedient." [13]

In his sociological defense of slavery, Hughes asserted that there were two forms of "societary organization"—the "free sovereign" society and the "ordered sovereign" society.[14] He explained that the labor system of the "free sovereign" society involved a private relationship between the capitalist and the free laborer. Their interests were antagonistic. The laborer was a victim of injustice, want, and pauperism. The "rich and poor, conflict. . . . Strikes and riots are not eliminated." [15] Thus class conflict and social anarchy threatened "free sovereign" societies, such as the society of the North. The South, on the other hand, had an "ordered sovereign" society. Its labor system, which Hughes called "warranteeism" rather than slavery, involved an institutional relationship between the white master and the black servant, between the "warrantor" and the "warrantee." "Property in man," he explained, "is absurd. Men cannot be owned. In warranteeism, what is owned is the labor-obligation, not the obligee. The obligee is a man." [16] Both the "warrantor" and the "warrantee" shared common interests. As a valuable "material product," the black laborer was appreciated and given sufficient food and necessities. Hence poverty and strikes were absent in the "ordered sovereign" society of the South. "Warranteeism" in the South also guaranteed the control of black laborers and the preservation of political and social order. Like Leonidas W. Spratt who claimed that slavery was "intensely conservative of peace and order," Hughes argued that black workers in the South were "manageable." They had no military organizations and no power to meet in "riotous assemblies" without fear of punishment. White Southerners had military might and organi-

13 Hughes, *Treatise*, p. v.
14 *Ibid.*, p. 286.
15 *Ibid.*, pp. 289–290.
16 *Ibid.*, pp. 167–168.

zation, and thus "a white regiment can keep the peace of a black nation." [17]

Southern "warranteeism," moreover, maintained the caste subordination of Negroes and racial purity in Southern society. White Southerners, Hughes declared, had a "moral duty" to continue the preservation and progress of their race. "Degeneration is evil. . . . Impurity of races is against the law of nature. Mulattoes are monsters." [18] Society had to be divided between white and black. There must be economic divisions along racial lines; whites must "mentalize" and blacks must "manualize." Otherwise "economic amalgamation" would lead to "sexual amalgamation." [19] Blacks must also be kept out of the political structure, for "political amalgamation is sexual amalgamation; one is cause of the other. . . . For power to rule, is power to marry, and the power to repeal or annul discriminating laws." [20] In the caste system of the South, "the purity of the females of one race" was systematically preserved. [21] Like the illiterate Alabama farmer who told Olmsted he did not want to "hev a nigger steppin' up to" his "darter," the educated Hughes was concerned about the protection of white women. But his statement about "the females of one race" could have been ambiguous; it could have been a reference to black women. In an earlier discussion in his book, Hughes had explained that interracial marriage would take place if it were lawful. Black women would choose white men from "natural preference" or ambition, and avaricious or ignorant white men would choose black women. "These motives are certain; and certainty of motive, is certainty of movement. . . . The law must therefore forbid amalgamation," declared Hughes, a man aware of his own sexual passions. [22] While Hughes undoubtedly knew about the sexual relations between white men and black women already taking

[17] *Ibid.*, pp. 220–221, 280, 286–287.
[18] *Ibid.*, pp. 239–240.
[19] *Ibid.*, pp. 264–265. For some recent thoughts on these divisions, see Eldridge Cleaver, *Soul on Ice* (New York: McGraw-Hill, 1968).
[20] Hughes, *Treatise*, p. 241.
[21] *Ibid.*, p. 288.
[22] *Ibid.*, pp. 241–243.

place under slavery, he feared that the repeal of legal pro-
hibitions against interracial marriage would mean the dangerous
loss of controls over white men and black women and the un-
restrained rise of a population of mulatto "monsters."

"Warranteeism" provided order—economic, political, and
especially social order in the biracial society of the South. In
a great burst of poetic flurry, Hughes ended his *Treatise* with
a description of the harmony and happiness of his "warrantee"
society of Southern plantation phalanxes.

> Then, in the plump flush of full-feeding health, the
> happy warrantees shall banquet in PLANTATION-RE-
> FECTORIES; worship in PLANTATION-CHAPELS;
> learn in PLANTATION-SCHOOLS; or in PLANTATION-
> SALOONS, at the cool of evening, or the green and
> bloomy gloom of cold catalpas and magnolias, chant old
> songs, tell tales; or to the metred rattle of chattering
> castanets, or flutes, or rumbling tamborines, dance down
> the moon and evening star, and after slumbers in PLAN-
> TATION-DORMITORIES, over whose gates Health and
> Rest sit smiling at the feet of Wealth and Labor, rise
> at the music-crowing of the morning-conchs, to begin
> again welcome days of jocund toil, in reeling fields. . . .
> When these and more than these, shall be the fulfilment
> of Warranteeism; then shall this Federation and the
> World, praise the power, wisdom, and goodness of a
> system, which may well be deemed divine; then shall
> Experience aid Philosophy, and VINDICATE THE WAYS
> OF GOD, TO MAN.[23]

Like Spratt, Hughes sought to "vindicate" the slaveholding
society of the South against the censure of the western world.
He, too, saw the important relationship between the vindication
of slavery and the reopening of the African slave trade. Hughes
had begun to think about this relationship even before the
publication of Spratt's essay on "The Destiny of the Slave
States." On November 14, 1852, he had written in his diary: "Is
Savage freedom better than civilized Slavery? Is the American
slave's condition better than that of the native African?" Such

[23] *Ibid.*, p. 292.

questions helped to guide Hughes to a radically pro-slavery conclusion: the South must demand the reopening of the African slave trade in order to affirm the rightness of slavery. Like Spratt, Hughes also advocated the revival of the African slave trade as a means to check the monopolization of slaves and the increasing class tensions within the South, to shore the South against Northern "freesoilism" and Northern "freeloveism," and to preserve the institutional basis of social order and controls in the biracial Southern society. During the late 1850's, Hughes almost equalled Spratt in his active involvement in the African slave-trade agitation. He wrote pamphlets and newspaper articles, supported bills and resolutions in the state legislature for the importation of Africans, and gave speeches at public meetings and Southern Commercial Conventions.[24] His was the life of a busy fire-eater.

The making of Henry Hughes into a Southern fire-eater was a very personal experience. Possibly the young Hughes had undergone what Erik Erikson has called an *"identity crisis."* This crisis, Erikson has explained, "occurs in that period of the life cycle when each youth must forge for himself some central perspective and direction, some working unity, out of the effective remnants of his childhood and the hopes of his anticipated adulthood. . . ." This crisis can be critical for some individuals, and they can "resolve it through participation in ideological movements passionately concerned with religion or politics, nature or art." [25] Hughes was a young man, anxious about his future and frantic in his search for a meaningful career which would satisfy his ambitions and his need for social relationships. He was frustrated in the practice of the law and in his relation-

[24] Hughes, *State Liberties; or the Right to African Contract Labor* (Port Gibson: 1858); Jackson *Semi-Weekly Mississippian,* January 12, 1858; August 18, 1859; October 4, 1859; February 3, 1860; April 24, 1860; New Orleans *Crescent,* April 15, 1856; *Journal of the House of Representatives of the State of Mississippi, 1858* (Jackson: 1858), p. 95; Jackson *Eagle,* August 31, 1858; October 16, 1858, in Hughes scrapbook; Port Gibson *Reveille,* July 30, 1858; October 19, 1858, in Hughes scrapbook.

[25] Erikson, *Young Man Luther: A Study in Psychoanalysis and History* (New York: W. W. Norton, 1859), p. 14.

ships with women. Like many young Southern men of his day, Hughes became actively involved in the defense of slavery and found himself in a circle of literary recognition and political rewards. But Hughes's crisis involved more than identity: he was also trying to resolve his own moral doubts about slavery. In his diary, he had *privately* condemned slavery as "sinful" and had considered abolition and colonization. As a pro-slavery theoretician and African slave-trade advocate, Hughes was seeking to vindicate slavery to himself as well as to the world. A "warranteed" society would permit him to care for blacks, to make them "happy," to keep his black friends like Uncle Aleck near him, and to reconcile his inner scruples about the "sinful" institution.[26] The importation of thousands of African slaves, if accomplished, could help Hughes suppress his abolitionist thoughts and rule out the possibility of colonization.

Yet, Hughes did not find peace of mind. Like many Southerners, he could not overcome the troublesome contradiction of his slaveholding society: he remained imprisoned in the institution's ambivalent view of the slave as person and property. In his loneliness, Hughes found much comfort in the friendship of certain blacks. He knew that the slave was a person and that his childhood friend—Uncle Aleck—was no "thing." In his *Treatise on Sociology*, he recognized the "warrantee" as a "man." But, in his aggressive cry for the reopening of the African slave trade, Hughes felt compelled to degrade blacks into property and call for the branding of slaves "like beeves." [27] To fry hot letters on the brows and breasts of slaves like Uncle Aleck or Frederic would have been an excessively painful contradiction for Henry Hughes.

---

[26] Hughes, *Treatise*, p. 292; Hughes, Diary, November 16, 1848, April 13, 1851.

[27] Hughes, *Treatise*, pp. 167–68; Hughes, Diary, August 8, 1852; Jackson *Semi-Weekly Mississippian*, October 4, 1859.

FIVE

THE
LOYAL
OPPOSITION

the pro-slavery crusade to reopen the African slave trade provoked fierce and articulate Southern opposition. Like the African slave-trade advocates, the Southern critics of the trade proposal were concerned about the nature and future of Southern slaveholding society. They, too, had to confront the distressing problems of Northern abolitionism, diminishing slaveholding social mobility, white social conflict within the South, and Southern moral disquietude towards the peculiar institution. In their arguments against the revival of the trade, the Southern critics were actually echoing many of the anxieties troubling the advocates of the African slave trade.

True to slavery, the Southern critics of the African slave-trade proposal were worried about the new Southern political powerlessness due to the sectional imbalance in Congress and the formation of the Republican Party. But the Southern critics, representing secessionists as well as Unionists, viewed the agitation to reopen the African slave trade as a foolish and suicidal political strategy for the defense of slavery. Consequently they condemned the pro-slavery crusade for the revival of the trade as a misguided effort and a threat to the peculiar institution and Southern society.

Some of the Southern critics desired secession and Southern independence as ardently as African slave-trade advocates. Critics like John Cunningham and Lawrence Keitt were committed to the destruction of the Union. But they saw that secession required a united South and that the African slave-trade question was dividing the South. Thus, while many of them would have supported the demand for the importation of Africans, they sought instead to suppress the clamor of fire-eaters like Spratt and Hughes. In a letter to a South Carolina newspaper, a secessionist explained why he opposed the trade proposal. The Southern states, "St. James Santee" wrote, could never be united or the Union dissolved, upon the issue of reopening the African slave trade.[1] This fear of the trade proposal as a source of schism in the South may be seen by tracing the positions of the disunionist Charleston *Mercury* on the African slave trade. In 1854 the *Mercury* enthusiastically raised Spratt's banner. But in April 1857 it expressed doubts about the possibility of reopening the trade and suggested instead the importation of coolies. Coolie laborers were cheap and could work "like the negro on Southern plantations." In June the *Mercury* argued that the South could not be united on the African slave-trade question, and that consequently silence on the issue was a better policy. Two years later the *Mercury* denounced the agitation to reopen the African slave trade, especially the agitation's determination to expose Southern

[1] Charleston *Mercury,* October 10, 1859.

unsoundness on slavery. Support for the African slave trade, the editor declared, was "no test of soundness to southern insti-tions." He warned that the attempt to impose certain narrow standards of loyalty upon Southerners tended to alienate and kindle "distrust amongst our own people." [2] In the judgment of secessionists like "St. James Santee" and the *Mercury* editor, the agitation to reopen the African slave trade was helping to pro-long the existence of the Union.

Many Southern critics of the trade proposal, however, feared the agitation for a completely different reason: they saw the agitation as a danger to the Union. Unlike advocates of the African slave trade as well as secessionist critics of the trade agitation, Southerners like James Hammond, Benjamin F. Perry, and Henry Foote thought slavery could best be protected through Unionism. They wanted to continue doing what the South had so long done—"rule the Union in the Union." For them, the protection of slavery by the Constitution and the federal government was "the true Southern doctrine." They were convinced there would always be a Northern minority honest and wise enough to sustain the Constitutional rights of the South.[3] Indeed, the South, explained Senator Hammond of South Carolina in 1858, could "always divide the North & govern it essentially." [4]

Many Southern critics of the African slave-trade agitation were well known Unionists. Benjamin F. Perry, J. L. Petigru,

<hr/>

[2] Charleston *Mercury*, in Edgefield *Advertiser*, November 16, 1854; Charleston *Mercury*, in Boston *Liberator*, April 17, 1857; Charleston *Mer-cury*, June 25, 1857; Charleston *Mercury*, in Milledgeville *Federal Union*, July 5, 1859.

[3] Quoted in Merritt, *James Henry Hammond*, p. 130. See also Ham-mond to Edmund Ruffin, August 17, 1858, in Craven, *Edmund Ruffin*, pp. 167–168; Hammond to William G. Simms, March 23, 1858; Ham-mond Papers, Library of Congress; Hammond, "Barnwell Speech," in James Hammond, *Selections from the Letters and Speeches of the Hon. James H. Hammond, of South Carolina* (New York: J. F. Trow & Co., 1866), p. 333; Foote, in *De Bow's Review*, XXVII (August, 1859), p. 218; Perry to Hammond, April 18, 1858, Hammond Papers, Library of Congress.

[4] Hammond to Simms, March 26, 1858, Hammond Papers, Library of Congress.

Richard Yeadon, and Alfred Huger had been leaders of the South Carolina Union Party in 1832. During the nullification crisis, Perry had castigated Calhoun and voted against the Ordinance of Nullification, and Petigru had written a protest against the action of the convention. African slave-trade critics like James L. Orr, Walker Brooke, John Minor Botts, Samuel Houston, Henry W. Hilliard, and Henry Foote had strongly favored Southern acceptance of the Compromise of 1850.

Of course Southern Unionists of the 1850's realized that the South had to deal with the problem of decreasing Southern *vis à vis* Northern representation in both houses of Congress. Unlike African slave-trade advocates, however, they had little enthusiasm for the expansion of slavery into the territories. Aware of Northern political opposition to slavery in the territories, they had lost hope for the extension of the peculiar institution and the addition of more slave states.[5] Some of them had even admitted a belief that slavery had practically reached its natural limits. Senator Hammond, for example, thought that "the borders of our [slave] States had reached the great desert which separates the Atlantic from the Pacific States of this confederacy. No where is African slavery likely to flourish in the little oases of that Saharah of America." [6] Since slavery could not be extended into the territories, Southerners like Hammond asked, why should the South import slaves from Africa?

But if the African slave trade could not be used to expand slavery into the territories, could it bring an influx of population into the slave states to help restore the political equilibrium between the North and the South? The editor of the Charleston *News* thought such an effort would be ridiculous. He calculated

[5] Lumpkin, J. Garrett, in Jackson *Semi-Weekly Mississippian*, September 13, 1859; Benjamin Fitzpatrick to Clement Claiborne Clay, August 30, 1859, C. C. Clay Papers, Duke University Library; Garnett Andrews, Letter, *Southern Cultivator*, XVII, No. 3 (March, 1859), p. 69. See also letter signed "R. G. H.," in Richmond *Enquirer*, January 4, 1858.

[6] Hammond, "Barnwell Speech," in Hammond, *Letters and Speeches*, pp. 335–336. See also Hammond, in Edgefield *Advertiser*, March 23, 1859; Hammond to Simms, January 20, 1858; Hammond Papers, Library of Congress; Simms to Hammond, January 28, 1858, in Oliphant, *et al.* (eds.), *Simms*, Vol. IV, p. 24.

that the 1860 census would indicate a Northern population of 18,000,000 and a Southern population of 12,000,000. Thus the North would have a majority of 6,000,000 and based on the three-fifths ratio, a federal majority of 7,600,000. By 1870 Northern population would have increased by 8,000,000 (births over deaths: 5,000,000; immigration: 3,000,000), and thus the 1870 majority would be 15,600,000. The Southern population increase by 1870, on the other hand, would be 3,600,000 (births over deaths: 2,866,000; immigration: 734,000). If Southerners wished to challenge Northern political power, they would have to import 20,000,000 Africans in the next ten years. Since a third of the Africans would die during the middle passage, 30,000,000 would have to be obtained in Africa. The editor then concluded: "Is not the proposition absurd?"[7]

Since they believed the South could not expect to restore its political power by means of slave expansion into the territories and mass migrations of Africans, many Southern critics of the trade proposal pursued a coalition strategy: the South should cooperate with friends in the North and depend on the National Democratic Party to countervail the growing power of the Republican Party. Benjamin F. Perry and Congressmen James L. Orr tried to convince South Carolinians that the National Democracy was able to maintain Southern rights within the Union.[8] In his letter of acceptance for the nomination of governor in 1855, Hershel V. Johnson urged Georgians to cooperate with the Northern Democrats.[9] Senator Hammond, certain the slave states would forever constitute a numerical minority, believed the South could accomplish nothing in the Union without the aid of faithful allies in the free states.[10]

[7] Charleston *News,* in Washington *National Intelligencer,* January 13, 1859. See also George R. Hunter of Georgia, in Richmond *Enquirer,* June 11, 1858.

[8] Perry, *Biographical Sketches,* p. 147; Schultz, *Nationalism and Sectionalism,* pp. 89, 122. Orr, in Richmond *Enquirer,* August 27, 1858; see also Orr, in Edgefield *Advertiser,* June 4, 1856.

[9] H. V. Johnson, Letter of Acceptance, June 8, 1855, Johnson Papers, Duke University Library.

[10] Hammond, "Barnwell Speech," in Hammond, *Letters and Speeches,* p. 353. For additional evidence see Perry to Hammond, January 8, 1858,

These Southern politicians were the forerunners of post-Civil War Southerners who sought national power through coalitions with conservative Northerners.

For Senator Hammond, cooperation with the National Democratic Party meant the forging of a South-West alliance. He was attracted to the idea of an "interior Party," which would form an axis between the Mississippi Valley and the South, dominate the East, and erase sectional strife.[11] He asserted that the South should fight the battle in the Union, and that the West would be the key to Southern safety. "For this census will place the power of the union in the hands of those whose produce goes down the Ohio, Miss. and Missouri rivers and is mainly sold to the Slave holders who own the mouths of those rivers and the outlet to the world. These people, Yankees and Foreigners chiefly, may not now be so friendly to us as we desire, but Yankee & Foreigner will soon wear out, while those rivers, that produce, the Southern Market and the Southern Port will remain forever."[12] Senator Hammond hoped to use the Western dependence on the Southern market to cement a South-West alliance within the National Democratic Party.

But the African slave-trade agitation could divide the National Democracy along sectional lines. Apprehensive about the trade agitation, Southerners like Roger Pryor of Virginia and Governor Hershel V. Johnson of Georgia warned that the South needed Northern allies as a shield against abolitionist aggression, and that Southern support for the African slave trade would mean the sacrifice of the National Democracy. "Many men, North," they explained, "have manfully stood by

and April 18, 1858, Hammond Papers, Library of Congress; Milledgeville *Federal Union*, December 5, 1854, April 7, 1857, and October 13, 1857; *South Carolinian*, in Edgefield *Advertiser*, August 6, 1856; Edward Noble to F. W. Pickens, August 10, 1859, Pickens Papers, Duke University Library, Edgefield *Advertiser*, June 4, 1856; Peter Gray, *Address to the Citizens of Houston* (1859), p. 27.

[11] W. M. Corry to Hammond, January 14, 1858, and November 11, 1858, Hammond Papers, Library of Congress.

[12] Hammond to I. W. Hayne, September 19, 1869, Hammond Papers, Library of Congress.

our rights. . . . But we cannot expect, if they have the African slave trade to shoulder, but that the camel's back will be broken." Unless the agitation could be suppressed, Southern National Democrats concluded, it would alienate their friends in the North and guarantee a Republican victory in the 1860 Presidential election.[13]

This Southern advocacy of Unionism was based more on policy than principle. No doubt Southern Unionists like Charleston *Courier* editor Richard Yeadon, Governor Samuel Houston, and South Carolina State Representative M. P. O'Connor might have felt a true love for the Union. But for many Southern critics of the African slave-trade proposal, Unionism was tactical.[14] Should the time come when Unionism endangered their institution, these Southerners would not have hesitated to break the nation. Congressman W. W. Boyce of South Carolina viewed the National Democracy on a *quid pro quo* basis: he was willing to abandon it when it ceased to serve the South. If the Republican Party captured control of the national government, South Carolina Representative James L. Orr was prepared to join hands with Yancey and Rhett.[15] In a private letter to Benjamin Perry, the leading South Carolina Unionist, Senator Hammond wrote: "From what I know of you personally & otherwise, I do not doubt, that *if ever the time arrives* that you think the South & Southern Institutions—(i.e., slavery) are endangered by Northern & anti-slavery aggression, actually & practically, you will show yourself a thorough Southern man

[13] Pryor, in *De Bow's Review*, XXIV (1858), p. 582; Pryor to Hammond, October 13, 1858, Hammond Papers, Library of Congress; Johnson, in *Republican Banner and Nashville Whig*, January 27, 1857; Garnett Andrews in *Southern Cultivator*, XVII, No. 3 (March, 1859), p. 70. For additional evidence, see H. J. Harris to Jefferson Davis, June 7, 1859, in Rowland, *Davis*, Vol. IV, pp. 55–56; Richmond *Enquirer*, April 14, 1857, and December 29, 1857.

[14] Richard Yeadon to Hammond, August 30, 1858, Hammond Papers, Library of Congress; Anna Irene Sandbo, "Beginnings of the Secession Movement in Texas," *The Southwestern Historical Quarterly*, XVIII, No. 1 (July, 1914), p. 50; Mary D. O'Connor, *The Life and Letters of M. P. O'Connor* (New York: Dempsey & Carroll, 1893), pp. 18–19.

[15] Boyce, in Richmond *Enquirer*, August 27, 1858; Schultz, *Nationalism and Sectionalism*, p. 94.

'born to the manor.' I therefore venture to write to you—(not to your paper nor for print) very frankly in the hope of eliciting equal confidence from you." Hammond's judgment of Perry was accurate. "It may be," wrote Perry on the eve of Lincoln's election, "that I am mistaken in supposing slavery to be out of reach of the assault of its foes, and if so I will be as ready as anyone to defend it at the sacrifice of the Union itself, as much as I value the Union." [16]

To African slave-trade critics like Hammond and Perry, Northern aggression did not yet "actually & practically" endanger slavery. Consequently they resisted efforts to reopen the African slave trade, for they saw the agitation as a conspiracy to destroy the Union. "Many, very many who advocate it," warned H. W. Walter, Whig candidate for governor of Mississippi in 1859, "use it, not for the ulterior purpose of cheapening and increasing slaves, but with the covert desire of producing disunion." [17] Even as early as 1854, Perry charged that the advocates of the African slave trade were seeking to agitate, excite and unite the South on this question, and then point to a dissolution of the Union as the only means of accomplishing their purpose. Charles Colcock Jones of Georgia, after witnessing the furor over the African slave trade at the Savannah Southern Commercial Convention, wrote to his wife: "It [the African slave trade] is thought to owe its paternity to South Carolina—& to be a measure looking towards disunion." [18]

Obviously the proposal to reopen the African slave trade was shocking to Northerners. Hence many Southerners feared

[16] Quoted in Kibler, *Perry,* p. 288. Italics added. Perry, *Biographical Sketches,* p. 177.

[17] H. W. Walter, in Jackson *Semi-Weekly Mississippian,* September 16, 1859.

[18] Perry, Greenville *Southern Patriot,* October 12, 1854, quoted in Kibler, *Perry,* p. 282; Charles C. Jones to Mary Jones, December 13, 1856, C. C. Jones Papers, Tulane University Library. For further evidence, see Wade Hampton, in Washington *National Intelligencer,* December 29, 1859; Roger Pryor, in *De Bow's Review,* XXIV (1858), p. 582; John M. Botts, *The Great Rebellion, Its Secret History, Rise, Progress, and Disastrous Failure* (New York: Harper & Bros., 1866), pp. 104–105; Richmond *Enquirer,* July 13, 1858; Charleston *Courier,* in Boston *Liberator,* September 17, 1858.

that the agitation for the African slave trade would force Northerners into the Republican camp and place a Seward or a Lincoln in the Presidency. Former Congressman H. W. Hilliard of Alabama regarded the African slave-trade proposition as an invitation to every anti-slavery "fanatic" to demand the overthrow of Southern institutions. "Is it the policy of the South," asked the editor of the Richmond *Enquirer*, "to still further embarrass its position, still more scornfully to defy the opinion of the world— to enflame the zeal, and multiply the number of its enemies? . . . If not, then let us stop this talk about reviving the African slave trade."[19] Convinced the African slave-trade agitation was calculated to strengthen support for Northern anti-slavery senti- ment and political power, Senator Hammond condemned the trade proposal as "abolitionism in disguise" and "treasonable to the South."[20] Ironically, the African slave-trade advocates, totally committed to slavery, were branded as abolitionists and traitors to the South.

But how could the South meet the increasing demand for cotton and overcome the problem of soil exhaustion without reopening the African slave trade? African slave-trade critics contended that the best way to meet the demand for more cotton would be to improve the methods of cultivation and the management of land. They also argued that a new supply of African labor would encourage slaveholders to wear out their lands and move on to new fields, and consequently, the blight of soil exhaustion would continue to plague the South.[21] The opponents of the African slave trade, furthermore, denied the

[19] Hilliard, in *De Bow's Review*, XXIV (June, 1858), pp. 590–592; Emerson Etheridge, in *Republican Banner and Nashville Whig*, March 6, 1857; Boyce, in Charleston *Mercury*, September 3, 1859; Hammond, in Edgefield *Advertiser*, September 14, 1858; Hammond to Simms, July 30, 1859; Hammond Papers, Library of Congress; Richmond *Enquirer*, November 28, 1856; New Orleans *Picayune*, October 17, 1859; Richmond *Dispatch*, in Richmond *Enquirer*, December 9, 1856.

[20] Hammond to Marcus Hammond, July 23, 1859; August 10, 1858, Hammond Papers, Library of Congress.

[21] New Orleans *Picayune*, January 6, 1857; Thomas P. Miller, Letter, *Southern Cultivator*, XVI, No. 12 (December, 1858), p. 363; Richmond *Enquirer*, December 31, 1858.

danger of foreign cotton competition. In a rebuttal to Governor Adams's message on the slave trade, the editor of the Richmond *Enquirer* argued that the governor's fears of British and French efforts to cultivate cotton in India and Algeria were unwarranted. Had not England and France, asked the editor, been "taxing their ingenuity and the resources of their philosophy for years, in the vain search after some substitutes for American cotton? It is demonstrated beyond dispute that India and Algeria in combination cannot produce cotton in sufficient quantity to supercede the demand for American cotton."[22]

If the African slave trade remained closed, however, would the peculiar institution be economically viable? Would not the high slave prices jeopardize the profitability of the slave labor system? In their arguments against the reopening of the African slave trade, Southern critics contended that the high prices were due to the high productiveness of slave labor rather than to a scarcity of labor. Of course they knew that the high slave prices also reflected an increasing demand for slave labor, and that a supply of new laborers from Africa could help to reduce those prices. But they had misgivings about some of the consequences of lower slave prices. One critic of the trade proposal charged that the importation of African slaves would hurt rather than help South Carolina because "it would depreciate so much the value of the Slaves she now holds without a corresponding gain on account of the inferiority [of our] cultivated lands to those of the newer states." [23] A writer to the Richmond *Enquirer* argued that "the slave himself is a part of the proprietor's 'vested interest.' He see-saws on the same plank with his master; and when he goes down, his master goes with him and the vested interests go too."[24] In other words, if the African slave trade

22 Richmond *Enquirer*, November 28, 1856. See also J. J. Pettigrew, in *De Bow's Review*, XXV (August, 1858), p. 179; Roger Pryor, in *De Bow's Review*, XXIV (June, 1858), pp. 579–582; Letter signed "Edgefield," in Charleston *Mercury*, October 23, 1858.

23 W. D. Porter to James Hammond, November 3, 1858, Hammond Papers, Library of Congress. See also Fitzhugh, *Sociology*, p. 210.

24 Letter signed "R. G. H.," in the Richmond *Enquirer*, December 31, 1858; Thomas P. Miller, letter, in *Southern Cultivator*, XIV, No. 12 (December, 1858), p. 363; Macon *Telegraph*, in Savannah *News*, June

were reopened, the slaveholder could expect a financial loss in the value of his slave property. This concern about the economic impact of the African slave trade on slaveholding assets was related to a much greater anxiety. "If the price of slaves comes down," former governor Henry Foote of Mississippi reasoned, "then the permanency of the institution comes down. Why? Because every man values his property in proportion to its actual intrinsic worth." [25] To these Southern critics of the trade proposal, the African slave trade represented a way to destroy rather than defend slavery.

Like African slave-trade radicals, many Southern critics of the trade proposal had a great enthusiasm for Southern industrialization. They wanted machine shops and factories in the South; they wanted to make Southern industry as important as Southern agriculture. But where could the South find laborers for the workshops? White laborers, the critics answered, could be used to develop industrialism in the South. In his essay on Southern industrialism, James L. Orr encouraged the employment of whites as mechanics and factory workers. "We want enterprising, intelligent, inventive mechanics," he wrote. "We want them to increase until their labor will furnish us every machine and fabric for man's use that can be as cheaply manufactured here as elsewhere." Southern industrialist William Gregg called the idea that the South needed Africans "preposterous" and pointed to "the hundreds of families moving from place to place in wretched poverty, seeking employment as factory operatives." If the Southern white population could not satisfy the demand for labor, European workers would move into the South. "Who would not prefer them to wild Africans?" In his answer to the charge that the foreigner would be subversive to slavery, Gregg replied: "Foreigners who settle among us are generally true to the country and its institutions." [26]

17, 1858; State Senator Dawson of Georgia, in Washington *National Intelligencer*, November 27, 1858.
[25] Foote, in *De Bow's Review*, XXVII (September, 1859), p. 219; Walker Brooke, in *De Bow's Review*, XXVII (September, 1859), p. 361.
[26] William Gregg, "Southern Patronage to Southern Imports and

Time and again the African slave-trade advocates had claimed that the importation of Africans was designed to benefit the nonslaveholders of the South by broadening the distribution of slaves. Southern critics of the trade proposal agreed that a new supply of Africans would lower the prices of slaves. But they argued that it would also reduce the value of labor and thus depress wages for white workers. The reopening of the African slave trade would lead to a perilous conflict between slaveholding capitalists and white workers: the importation of cheap laborers from Africa would allow "a few bloated capitalists" to "absorb the products of labor" and degrade the white masses.[27] If the African slave trade were reopened, Jacksonian Sam Houston argued, nonslaveholding whites in the South would be forced into poverty and wretchedness. "Not a poor man," he argued, "would be able to stay in the country, because labor would be so cheap that he would not be able to get bread for himself and family."[28] Thus the depressed wages for whites resulting from the influx of African slaves, critics warned, would polarize the white classes in the South and plunge them into greater conflict.

Critics of the African slave trade pointed out that the

Domestic Industry," *De Bow's Review*, XXIX (November, 1860), pp. 623–624; James Orr, "Development of Southern Industry," *De Bow's Review*, XIX (July, 1855), pp. 4, 11, 13; James Hammond, "Progress of Southern Industry," *De Bow's Review*, VIII (June, 1850), p. 510; Roger Pryor, in *De Bow's Review*, XXIV (June, 1858), pp. 579–582; Pryor, in Herbert Wender, *Southern Commercial Conventions, 1837–1859* (Baltimore: Johns Hopkins, 1930), p. 215.

[27] Athens *Southern Banner*, March 3, 1859, in Phillips, *Plantation and Frontier Documents*, Vol. II, pp. 358–359; Letter signed "R. G. H.," in Richmond *Enquirer*, January 4, 1858. For further evidence, see Joseph Koger letter in Jackson *Semi-Weekly Mississippian*, October 14, 1859; Roger Pryor, in *De Bow's Review*, XXIV (June, 1858), p. 581; State Senator Gibson of Georgia, in Washington *National Intelligencer*, November 27, 1858; letter signed "Madison," in Milledgeville *Federal Union*, July 5, 1859; A. G. Brown, in Jackson *Semi-Weekly Mississippian*, June 14, 1859, and May 16, 1859; Natchez *Free Trader*, October 13, 1859.

[28] Houston, in Galveston *Weekly News*, July 21, 1859. See also Houston, speech at Montgomery, in Amelia W. Williams and Eugene C. Barker (eds.), *The Writings of Sam Houston, 1813–1863*, 8 Vols. (Austin: University of Texas Press, 1941–1943), Vol. VII, p. 375; Eastern *Clarion*, in Natchez *Free Trader*, October 13, 1859.

reduction of wages would render it impossible for the white laborers whose source of wealth was their labor to accumulate enough money to purchase slaves. "Their labor," Benjamin Perry logically contended, "is their capital, and as their labor is depreciated their capital is diminished in value. It is non-sense to talk about a poor man's being able to purchase slaves if they are cheaper, when his labor is cheapened, too, by the same operation. . . ." [29] In homespun language, Senator Albert Gallatin Brown offered his nonslaveholding Mississippi followers some sober advice in 1859:

> Let not the nonslaveholder indulge the hope that (except in rare instances) he was to be benefited by this policy [of the African slave trade]. If he could not pay family expenses and buy a negro for fifteen hundred dollars and pay for him in cotton at twelve cents, he might take it for granted he could never pay expenses and buy at five hundred dollars in cotton at seven cts. . . . And when he came to buy a cheap negro he would be much in the condition of the Irishman who boasted that he could buy as much in Ireland for a quarter of a dollar as he could in this country for a dollar. An intense American asked why he did not stay in Ireland. "Bejabers," said Pat, "I could niver get the quarter of a dollar." [30]

Clearly in the judgment of these critics of the trade agitation, the importation of Africans would not bring flush times to the nonslaveholders of the South.

A deeper fear was expressed in a letter from a poor white man published in the Savannah *Republican* in 1859. His fear was not that the influx of African workers would reduce his

[29] Perry, in Greenville *Southern Patriot,* October 12, 1854, in Kibler, *Perry,* p. 282.

[30] Brown, speech, in Jackson *Semi-Weekly Mississippian,* June 14, 1859. For additional evidence, see Pettigrew, in *De Bow's Review,* XXV (1858), pp. 184–185; Foote, in *De Bow's Review,* XXVII (August, 1859), p. 219; letter signed "Madison," in Milledgeville *Federal Union,* July 5, 1859; John Hope to Hammond, February 26, 1859, Hammond Papers, Library of Congress; Houston, in Williams and Barker (eds.) *Sam Houston,* Vol. VII, p. 375; Gray, *Address of Judge Peter W. Gray,* p. 26.

wages but that the newly imported Africans would replace his labor. "My opposition to it [the African slave trade]," he wrote, "springs from interest. . . . If we are to have negro labor in abundance, where will my support come from? for I say it with all bitterness and regret, I am poor—very poor. If my labor is to be supplanted by that of negroes, how can I live? . . . In short, with an abundance of negroes, a poor white man will stand no chance at all to make a support . . . and the poor would grow poorer while the rich grew richer." [31]

This class resentment towards slaveholders was associated with a racist hatred towards Negroes. The most extreme expression of the fusion of these two feelings was Hinton Helper's *The Impending Crisis.* Helper, as we observed earlier, wanted to eliminate the slaveholding class and to exclude Negroes from the South. Southern critics of the trade proposal did not advocate such a drastic program. But, in their arguments against the revival of the African slave trade, they sometimes made or noted a connection between racist exclusionist sentiment and hostility towards the slaveholding class. Senator Albert Gallatin Brown, the spokesman of Mississippi nonslaveholders, declared that he wanted to keep out "an influx of untold millions of wild Africans." Clearly his statement had a racial meaning. Then he added: "Thousands on thousands of white laborers would be crowded out, to make room for the negro operators." A Georgia state senator asked: "Does the laboring man of Georgia demand that the savage barbarians of Africa shall be imported and planted side by side with him in the field and factory?" A Missouri critic of the trade proposal thought it would be a grave mistake to import Africans and increase the numbers of "the *inferior* race" in the South. "The white laborers of the South might be aroused, by such a policy, into a distrust more injurious to the planters than any Northern fanaticism: for it is too plain for argument that an introduction of cheap slave labour will reduce prices of all labour, including that of the

[31] Letter signed "Nothing Laid Up," in Savannah *Republican,* in Savannah *Daily News,* January 5, 1859.

whites. In such a contest it is but natural that men should stand by their interests and their 'class'." [32]

Southern society was in trouble. Faith in slaveholding social mobility was, as Wilbur Cash has shown, an essential basis of the civilization of the Old South. Yet this old optimistic assumption was cracking in the 1850's. Both the advocates and the critics of the African slave trade agreed that slave prices were high, and that the class lines between slaveholders and non-slaveholders were becoming distressingly rigid. Both of them noticed that white farmers and mechanics had begun to define their interests *vis-à-vis* the interests of the slaveholders. While the advocates hoped the importation of African slaves would help to ease class tensions within the South, the critics feared it would only intensify them. But both sides no longer felt much confidence in the belief that a young white Southerner could rise from yeoman to planter.

The African slave-trade agitation encountered sectional as well as class opposition. Spratt and other advocates repeatedly noted the danger of the slave drain from the border and Atlantic states to the Gulf states, and insisted that the African slave trade would check this movement and keep the older Southern states true to slavery. But Southern critics of the African slave trade saw that the movement of slaves was not caused simply by the high slave prices of the Southwest but also by the soil exhaustion of the Southeast. "The property of slavery," wrote William Simms to Senator Hammond in 1858, "is to seek new lands as the old become unprofitable; for negro slavery rarely improves exhausted lands," and thus slaves would continue to be moved out of Virginia, North Carolina, and Kentucky.[33] In reference to the emigration of South Carolina slaves to Mississippi and Louisiana, South Carolina State Representative J. J. Pettigrew pointed out that this emigration was mainly from the

[32] Brown, in Jackson *Semi-Weekly Mississippian*, June 14, 1859; Gibson, in Washington *National Intelligencer*, November 27, 1858; Thomas C. Reynolds to J. J. Pettigrew, October 9, 1858, in Pettigrew Papers, North Carolina Archives.

[33] Simms to Hammond, January 28, 1858, in Oliphant, *et al.* (eds.), *William Gilmore Simms*, Vol. IV, pp. 24–25.

upcountry, that the chief reason for it was soil exhaustion, and that a new supply of Africans would not solve the problem.[34] Pettigrew's argument was probably valid. James De Bow in *Encyclopaedia of the Trade and Commerce of the United States* and Lewis C. Gray in his classic study of agriculture in the South confirm the existence of soil exhaustion in upper South Carolina.[35] Furthermore, a comparison of the 1840 and 1850 census reports reveals a tremendous loss of slaves in the upcountry districts, while the slave population in the lowcountry districts remained stable or even increased. Upcountry Greenville and Spartanburg lost over 62 per cent of their slave population, while lowcountry Beaufort lost only 10 per cent and Colleton increased its slaves by 24 per cent.[36]

For many slaveholders in the border and South Atlantic states, the profitability of slavery depended in large part upon the sale of surplus slaves to the cotton-growing states of the Southwest.[37] "The slaves in Virginia," wrote Thomas R. Dew of Virginia, "multiply more rapidly than in most of the Southern states;—the Virginians can raise cheaper than they can buy, in fact, it is one of their greatest sources of profit."[38] Another Virginian, Edmund Ruffin, noted that the slaveholders of his state derived a portion of their income from the breeding and

[34] Pettigrew, in *De Bow's Review*, XXV (August, 1858), p. 182; see also Perry, in Greenville *Southern Patriot*, October 12, 1854, in Kibler, *Perry*, p. 282.

[35] James De Bow, *Encyclopædia of the Trade anad Commerce of the United States*, 3 Vols. (London, 1854), Vol. III, p. 137; Gray, *History of Agriculture*, Vol. I, p. 446, Vol. II, p. 910.

[36] United States Census Office, *Sixth Census, 1840* (Washington: 1841), p. 46; and United States Census Office, *Seventh Census, 1850* (Washington, 1853), pp. 338–339. Greenville's slave population dropped from 17,839 to 6,691; Spartanburg's from 23,669 to 8,039; Beaufort's from 35,794 to 32,279; and Colleton's increased from 25,548 to 31,771.

[37] See Alfred H. Conrad and John R. Meyer, "The Economics of Slavery in the Ante-Bellum South," *Journal of Political Economy*, LXVI, No. 1 (April, 1958), pp. 95–130, Gray, *History of Agriculture*, Vol. II, pp. 661–662; Bancroft, *Slave-Trading in the Old South*, pp. 291, 393; E. Ruffin, "The Effects of High Prices of Slaves," *De Bow's Review*, XXVI (June, 1859), pp. 647–657.

[38] Dew, quoted in Gray, *History of Agriculture*, Vol. II, p. 661.

selling of slaves.[39] In 1854 a traveler in the South compared the average decennial ratio of slave increase in all the states with the difference in the number of the actual slave population of the slave-breeding states, and calculated that more than 20,000 slaves a year were exported to the cotton-growing states.[40] The exportation of slaves from Virginia was noticeable during the 1850's. In his impressive *Slave-Trading in the Old South,* Frederic Bancroft estimated that between 1850 and 1860 Virginia exported slightly more than 17 per cent of its slave population.[41] Virginia newspaper reports of slave movements support Bancroft's calculation. These newspapers noted the daily heavy shipments of slaves for the far South, and the "almost endless outgoing of slaves from Virginia to the South." The Norfolk *Argus,* commenting on the high slave prices in 1857, observed that as many as ten thousand Virginia slaves had been transplanted to the cotton-growing states during the past year.[42]

Unlike the cotton-producing states, the older Southern states, especially Virginia, had a vested interest in the domestic slave trade, and consequently they strongly opposed the proposal to reopen the African slave trade. "What is there in such a policy," asked the editor of the Lexington (Virginia) *Valley Star,* "for slave-holders of Rockbridge? For several years the State Revenue of the country has been paid by the sale of her slaves. Open the Slave Trade and what will our Negroes be worth?"[43] The editor of the Lynchburg *Virginian* declared that a considerable portion of the slave population of Virginia was annually transferred to the cotton states, and that Virginia

[39] Ruffin, quoted in *ibid.,* pp. 661–662.

[40] Olmsted, *Seaboard,* I, pp. 60–61.

[41] Bancroft, *Slave-Trading in the Old South,* p. 393.

[42] Petersburg *Express,* quoted in Bancroft, *Slave-Trading,* p. 291; Portsmouth (Virginia) *Transcript,* in Jackson *Semi-Weekly Mississippian,* January 28, 1859; Norfolk *Argus,* in Richmond *Whig,* May 1, 1857.

[43] Lexington *Valley Star,* September 13, 1860, in Ollinger Crenshaw, *The Slave States in the Presidential Election of 1860* (Baltimore: Johns Hopkins, 1945), p. 138.

therefore had a paramount interest in maintaining the law against the African slave trade.[44]

Even critics of the trade proposal from the deep South agreed that the South should protect the domestic slave trade of the border states. They feared that the reopening of the African slave trade, though designed to check abolitionism in the border states due to the slave drain, would actually hasten the abolition of slavery in those states. S. B. Newman warned Mississippians that the legalization of the foreign slave trade would force Virginia slaveholders to sell their slaves as fast as possible, and thus only serve to increase the slave drain. *"Why is it apprehended,"* questioned Henry Foote of Mississippi, *"that Virginia and the other middle States are very much inclined to emancipation? Because slave labor is unprofitable. It is an admitted fact now, that if you stop the exportation of slaves from Maryland, Delaware, and Virginia, these States would be compelled . . . to emancipate their slaves. . . . Therefore, the permanence of the system depends on keeping the prices high."* [45] The fears of Newman and Foote, however, were largely unwarranted. If the African slave trade had been reopened, and if slavery had become unprofitable in the border states, it is highly doubtful that the border states would have abolished slavery. Slavery was a multifunctional institution: it was not only a system of labor but also a system of race control.[46] Nevertheless, these critics of the African slave trade

[44] Lynchburg *Virginian*, in Washington *National Intelligencer*, November 1, 1860. For further evidence, see New Orleans *Delta*, in Boston *Liberator*, January 23, 1857; Richmond *Enquirer*, May 25, 1858; W. G. Simms to W. P. Miles, February 22, 1861, Miles Papers, University of North Carolina Library; E. Ruffin to A. H. Stephens, August 3, 1859, Stephens Papers, Library of Congress.

[45] S. B. Newman, in Jackson *Daily Mississippian*, November 26, 1856; Foote, in *De Bow's Review*, XXVII (August, 1859), p. 219. For further evidence, see Brandon (Mississippi) *Republican;* in Olmsted, *A Journey in the Back Country*, pp. 285–286; Peter Gray, *Address of Judge Peter Gray*, p. 26; Charleston *Courier*, September 4, 1858; Report of the South Carolina Legislative Committee on Coloured Population, in Consul Bunch to the Earl of Clarendon, December 28, 1854, *British and Foreign State Papers, 1854–1855*, p. 1157.

[46] For a discussion of the race control function of slavery, see U.

correctly understood that the importation of Africans would threaten the economic security of slavery in the border states. They could also understand why many slaveholders in the border South, economically dependent on the domestic slave trade, could not advocate the reopening of the African slave trade as a means to assert the morality of slavery.

While the Southern critics of the new pro-slavery crusade regarded the African slave-trade agitation as a danger to the Union as well as to Southern class and Southern regional unity, they probably worried most about the agitation as a threat to the South's moral position. Some Southern opponents of the trade proposal tried to ignore the western world's condemnation of the South. In a letter to the Charleston *Mercury,* a South Carolina planter expressed his indifference to world opinion. After pointing out that the South had a monopoly on cotton production, he asked: "Do we want the whole world to grow cotton too? If we don't, let the whole world outside the South abuse and hate slavery. We want no 'moral victories' on slavery outside the South. The more fools persist in refusing to use Africans as slaves, the better for us. If we could convert all other nations to the truth, concerning African slavery, we of the South would be ruined, stock, lock and barrel." Such a conversion, he concluded, would mean the revival of slavery in the West Indies and the end of the Southern cotton monopoly.[47]

But could white Southerners turn away from a confrontation on the issue of the morality of slavery and still develop and maintain their own moral confidence in the peculiar institution? Could Southerners, in other words, refuse to challenge the outside world and still win "moral victories" for slavery within the South? This was a crucial and anxious question most Southern critics of the trade proposal could not ignore.

B. Phillips, "The Central Theme of Southern History," in E. M. Coulter (ed.) *The Course of the South to Secession* (New York: Hill and Wang, 1964).

[47] Letter signed "Edgefield," in Charleston *Mercury*, October 23, 1858.

Like the African slave-trade advocates, they felt the lash of the western world's judgment on slavery. They, too, sought to prove their innocence to outsiders as well as to themselves. Hence, though they knew that slavery was an economic system designed to enable the capitalist master to accumulate the wealth derived from the labor of his slave, though they knew that the institution's control over the slave was based essentially on the principle of fear, and though they knew about the discontent of many slaves and the rebelliousness of Denmark Vesey and Nat Turner, these Southern critics of the African slave trade made proud claims about the loyalty of slaves and the kindness of masters. They fondly explained that the master-slave relationship was bound together by ties of affection. From birth to death, both the master and the slave were engaged in the interchange of protection and service. "At present we have in South Carolina," Benjamin F. Perry boasted, "two hundred and fifty thousand civilized and peaceable slaves, happy and contented in their slavery. . . ." J. J. Pettigrew noted the "pleasant intercourse between master and slave," and Roger Pryor reminded the Southern Commercial Convention at Montgomery that "ours is a patriarchal institution now, founded in pity and protection on the one side, and dependence and gratitude on the other."[48] Under the direction of paternalistic masters, they insisted, slavery had transformed the savage African into a Sambo—a loyal, dependent, and happy slave.

Whether or not the reality of slave behavior and motivation outside of the Southern white mind was indeed Sambo-like is, of course, a vital question. Sambo might have been an imagined person, created by Southerners for propagandistic and psychological purposes: the image of the happy slave could have been used to help convince the world that slavery was right and also calm the stormy and guilt-ridden consciences of slaveholders. If Negroes were "happy and contented in their slavery,"

[48] Perry, in Greenville *Southern Patriot,* October 12, 1854, in Kibler, *Perry,* p. 282; Pettigrew, in *De Bow's Review,* XXV (September, 1858), p. 293; Pryor, in *De Bow's Review,* XXIV (June, 1858), p. 582; Milledgeville *Federal Union,* December 16, 1856; Richmond *Enquirer,* March 12, 1858.

how could the peculiar institution and slavemasters be condemned? Few slaveholders, a European traveler observed, could "openly and honestly look the thing [slavery] in the face. They wind and turn about in all sorts of ways, and make use of every argument . . . to convince me that the slaves are the happiest people in the world. . . ." Or Sambo might have been real. But the question of reality in this case is highly complicated, for slaves who behaved like Sambos might have been playing a role in order to survive, or they might have actually internalized their role.[49] Slavemasters themselves recognized how difficult it was to determine a slave's true personality. "So deceitful is the Negro," a slavemaster explained, "that as far as my own experience extends I could never in a single instance decipher his character. . . . We planters could never get at the truth."[50] Nevertheless, slavemasters were quick to accept expressions of slave contentment, and Southern critics of the African slave trade were equally quick to defend the integrity of the South and their peculiar institution on the basis of their conception of the slave as a Sambo.[51]

The African slave trade, Southern critics argued, would threaten the master-Sambo relationship, for it would change slavery from a kind and paternalistic institution into a cruel and insensitive system of labor. Since slave prices were high, a Georgian reasoned, it was economical to take good care of them. But if the value of slaves dropped, would not many slaveholders

[49] Quoted in Sellers, *op. cit.,* p. 61; "It is a blessed thing," ex-slave Frederick Douglass explained, "that the tyrant may not always know the thoughts and purposes of his victim." *Life and Times of Frederick Douglass* (New York: Collier, 1962), p. 192.

[50] Quoted in Stampp, *Peculiar Institution,* p. 88.

[51] For a discussion of the Sambo personality, see Stanley M. Elkins, *Slavery: A Problem in American Institutional & Intellectual Life* (New York: Grosset & Dunlap, 1963). While Elkins assumes that slaves in the South did in fact behave according to the way Southerners like Edward Pollard (a pro-slavery writer) thought they behaved, I am here only saying that Southerners like Benjamin Perry *thought* or wanted to think slaves were Sambos. It is not my intention to suggest that slaves were Sambos, or that they were not Sambos.

"work one to death to buy two more?" [52] Judge Peter Gray of Texas predicted that if Africans were imported, the slaves "would become mere brutes—animals of labor. Instead of the patriarchal institution we now boast, it would become a mere matter of work and profit. . . . One of our strongest grounds against abolition fanaticism would fall." [53] The need to justify slavery as a paternalistic and hence moral institution compelled these Southerners to condemn the reopening of the African slave trade. If they could invoke images of Sambos and kind slavemasters and proclaim the "affection" between master and slave, then they could challenge the western world's moral criticism of Southern slavery.

While critics of the African slave trade imaged the domestic slave as a Sambo, they viewed the African as a wild savage.[54] If the African slave trade were reopened, they argued, a "black inundation" of African barbarians would destroy the identity of Southerners as white and civilized men. White men and their families would be subjected to the barbarities of the Africans and Southern society would be "Africanized." "Was our noble land," the editor of the Charleston *News* asked, "most designed for the white race or the negro?"[55] The introduction of heathen Africans, the critics added, would undermine Southern efforts to civilize and Christianize the slaves already in the South. The Southern slaves would be "contaminated and demoralized by immediate contact and association with a race of savages." The Christian influence surrounding slaves in the South would be overwhelmed by "the heathen immoralities attending the influx of a horde of African barbarians." If Christianized slaves were placed in contact with untamed Africans, they would

[52] Garnett Andrews, letter, *Southern Cultivator,* XVII, No. 3 (March, 1859), p. 70.

[53] Gray, *Address of Judge Peter Gray,* p. 26.

[54] A Georgian had an altogether different view. He said that Africans were already civilized. In their native land, they were "a thrifty, industrious people, sharp in trade and fond of money, possessing a knowledge of many useful arts and trades" such as carpentry, shoemaking, and weaving. See letter signed "J. M. W." *The American Cotton Planter,* III (January, 1859), p. 12.

[55] Charleston *News,* in Galveston *Weekly News,* February 1, 1859.

quickly degenerated into their basic and original savagery. Thus, their missionary commitment to Southern slaves, the critics felt, required the prohibition of the African slave trade.[56]

The critics' emphasis on paternalism and the Christian mission to the slave was rooted in the recognition that the slave, despite his definition as property, was nevertheless a person, capable of "affection" and conversion. But their interest in the moral welfare of the slave was also based in large part upon their fear of slave insurrections. In the past Southerners had associated the African slave trade with servile rebellions. As early as 1714, South Carolina imposed high duties on imported slaves because the increasing number of slaves seemed to endanger the white population of the colony; in 1740 and 1764 South Carolina, fearful of slave insurrections, enacted £100 duties on imported slaves to prohibit the African slave trade.

During the 1850's, however, the chief concern of the African slave-trade opponents was not the increase in slave population but the political contamination of the slaves already in the South. While the opponents of the African slave trade contended that the Southern slave was a Sambo, they also feared that under the influence of newly imported "savages" and "heathens" from Africa, Sambo could be transformed into a violent rebel.[57] The editor of the Charleston *Courier* opposed the African slave trade because he thought it would "introduce the insurrectionary element among our now orderly and contented slaves. . . ."[58] In a report against the repeal of the federal laws prohibiting the African slave trade, a committee of the Louisiana legislature argued that the introduction of Africans among "our present civilized and happy negro population" would "render them unhappy, discontented and insubordinate, the spirit of insurrection and revenge would take the place of

[56] Richmond *Enquirer*, March 12, 1858; see also Milledgeville *Federal Union*, December 16, 1856; Pettigrew, in *De Bow's Review*, XXV (September, 1858), p. 293.

[57] New Orleans *Bulletin*, in New Orleans *Daily Delta*, March 9, 1858.

[58] Charleston *Courier*, September 4, 1858. See also New Orleans *Bee* (French edition), January 30, 1858.

the respect and affection they have for their owners now." [59]
During the slave insurrection scare of 1856, the editor of the
Richmond *Enquirer* declared the slave unrest illustrated the
"utter folly" of the African slave-trade proposition. Slave revolts,
he explained, originated in the "blind passions of the ignorant
and brutal mass—a mass to which it is the interest of the South
to make no addition from the savage wilds of Africa." [60] And
a Florida farmer saw the African slave trade as an abolitionist
plot to "crowd the Southern State with rude Africans, who . . .
would be taught to render the slaves we have dissatisfied, and
to aid them in a general insurrection and massacre. The white
people would be butchered, as they were in St. Domingo." [61]
While these Southerners allowed happy and docile Sambos to
live among them, they insisted that "rude" and "insubordinate"
savages be kept separate from Southern society.

This argument was part of a Southern view on the question
of the physical proximity between whites and blacks. So long
as slaves in the South knew their place and so long as they
did not threaten the racial order, they were permitted to have
a hierarchic *integrated* relationship with their masters. [62] The
Southern mammy and other servants spent much of their time
in their master's house and in close proximity to the white
family. Slaves "live with us," a Southerner explained, "eating
from the same storehouses, drinking from the same fountains,

[59] Quoted in Joe G. Taylor, *Negro Slavery in Louisiana* (Baton Rouge:
Louisiana Historical Association, 1963), p. 58.

[60] Richmond *Enquirer*, December 16, 1856.

[61] Letter by "A Florida Farmer," in *De Bow's Review*, XXVII (July,
1859), p. 38. For additional evidence, see James B. Ranck, *Albert Gallatin
Brown: Radical Southern Nationalist* (New York: A. Appleton-Century,
1937), p. 173; Hundley, *Social Relations*, p. 295; Samuel Houston to
Ferdinand Flake, July 2, 1859, in Williams and Barker (eds.), *Sam Houston*, Vol. VII, p. 341; Alfred Huger to Wade Hampton, December 17,
1856, Huger Letter Press Book, Duke University Library; Pettigrew, in
De Bow's Review, XXV (September, 1858), p. 305.

[62] For a brilliant discussion on this point for post-Civil War race
relations in the South, see Lawrence Friedman, *The White Savage: Racial
Fantasies in the Post-Bellum South*, to be published by Prentice-Hall.

dwelling in the same enclosures. . . ." [63] But if slaves behaved impudently, they were often *segregated* from whites.[64] Thus Southerners had a dual attitude towards slaves: they drew submissive slaves close to them, and they shunned insolent slaves. A South Carolina planter expressed this sort of attitude shortly after the Civil War when he complained about the rudeness of Negro waiters in a Charleston hotel. "A part of the satisfaction," he declared, "is that I am perfectly independent of having negroes about me; if I cannot have them as they used to be [servile and docile], I have no desire to see them except in the field [at a distance]." [65] During the 1850's, Southern critics of the African slave trade wanted to keep defiant and dangerous African savages away from Southern whites.

But was not the trembling about slave unrest, the African slave-trade radicals asked their worried Southern critics, an unwarranted exaggeration of irrational fears? Could not slaveholders simply tighten up their slave-control machinery to break the spirit of the imported African slaves? And did not Southern society have the power to squash slave rebellions? If slaves revolted, would not the "entire extermination" of black insurrectionists "be but a day's bloody toil"?[66] Yet, for many Southerners, this awesome power to discipline and destroy black human beings involved a terrible agony.

In order to control the dangerous slaves imported from Africa, the slave-trade critics argued, whites would be forced to adopt cruel and harsh laws and penalties, and thus the slaveholders themselves were in danger of being demoralized and

[63] John B. Adger, quoted in Thompson, *Presbyterians in the South*, pp. 441–442.

[64] See Richard C. Wade, *Slavery in the Cities: The South, 1820–1860* (New York: Oxford University Press, 1964), pp. 266–278.

[65] Quoted in Joel Williamson, *After Slavery: The Negro in South Carolina During Reconstruction, 1861–1877* (Chapel Hill: University of North Carolina Press, 1965), p. 277.

[66] Newspaper clipping, "Quartette of Objections to African Labor Immigration," in Henry Hughes Scrapbook, Hughes Papers, Mississippi State Archives; see also New Orleans *Delta,* March 9, 1858.

brutalized.[67] This Southern anxiety about the moral welfare of the slaveholder was not new. During the late eighteenth century, Thomas Jefferson had worried about the evil impact of slavery upon the slaveholder and his children. "The whole commerce between master and slave," the slaveholding statesman observed, "is a perpetual despotism on the one part, and degrading submissions on the other. Our children see this, and learn to imitate it. . . . If a parent could find no motive either in his philanthropy or his self-love, for restraining the intemperance of passion towards his slave, it should always be a sufficient one that his child is present. But generally it is not sufficient. The parent storms, the child looks on, catches the lineaments of wrath, puts on the same airs in the circle of smaller slaves, gives loose to the worst of passions, and thus nursed, educated, and daily exercised in tyranny cannot but be stamped by it with odious peculiarities." [68] Several decades later, during the 1850's, the opponents of the African slave trade echoed Jefferson's fears. Ex-senator Walker Brooke of Mississippi, for example, warned his fellow Southerners that if Africans were imported, "every semblance of humanity would have to be blotted out from the statute-books, and the slaveholder would become—instead of the patriarchal friend and master of his slave—a bloody, brutal, and trembling tyrant." [69] The slaveholder's inhumanity to the slave would make the slaveholder himself less than human.

The opponents believed the reopening of the African slave trade would not only corrupt themselves as slaveholders, their loyal slaves, and their humane peculiar institution, but would also invite everyone to view the ideal slave society of the South in association with the odious traffic. Conscious of the western world's abhorrence of the African slave trade, they argued that they wanted to defend slavery as a paternalistic and civilizing institution. If Southerners reopened the African

67 Foote, quoted in Rainwater, *Mississippi*, p. 79.

68 Jefferson, *Notes on Virginia*, quoted in Dumas Malone, *Jefferson in Virginia* (Boston: Little, Brown, 1948), p. 265.

69 Brooke, in *De Bow's Review*, XXVII (September, 1859), p. 361. See also Pryor, in *De Bow's Review*, XXIV (June, 1858), p. 582; Richmond *Enquirer*, March 12, 1858.

slave trade, they would offer a "vulnerable spot for the lance of the enemy." [70] Thus the critics of the African slave trade advised Southerners to ponder long on the trade question: did they wish to bring down upon themselves the wrath of the civilized world? Former Senator Reverdy Johnson of Maryland insisted that the reopening would shock civilized society, and B. H. Richardson of Maryland, a slaveholder, admitted he was not prepared to go before the Christian world as an advocate of the African slave trade.[71] The implication of their protest was clear: Southerners could not reopen the African slave trade and still be regarded as civilized and Christian. These critics saw what was obvious to Spratt. The real issue, they recognized, was not the African slave trade but slavery itself. Thus, like Spratt, they had to face the disturbing and basic question: could the South be a slaveholding as well as a civilized and Christian society?

In the judgment of these critics, the reopening of the African slave trade would make it impossible for the slaveholding South to be regarded as a moral society. For a few opponents of the trade proposal, however, this reluctance to irritate the moral sensibilities of western civilization was largely tactical. Their resistance to the reopening was chiefly designed to accommodate, not to accept, world opinion against the African slave trade. Congressman William R. Smith of Alabama, for example, opposed the reopening of the African slave trade because he did not want to antagonize certain European nations. In his opinion, the African slave trade was not immoral: it took the African from the jungle and placed him in a civilized land.[72] Thus some Southern critics of the African slave trade believed

[70] Albert Pike, in *De Bow's Review*, XXII (January, 1858), p. 219.
[71] Andrew Hunter, in *ibid.*, p. 223; Johnson, letter, in Richmond *Enquirer*, January 30, 1857; Richardson, in *De Bow's Review*, XXII (January, 1857), p. 223. For further evidence, see R. Pryor, in *De Bow's Review*, XXIV (June, 1858), p. 582; Washington *National Intelligencer*, August 27, 1859; Montgomery *Advertiser*, in Washington *National Intelligencer*, January 5, 1859.
[72] Smith, in Smith, *Alabama Convention*, p. 204; Smith, quoted in Easby-Smith, *William Russell Smith of Alabama, His Life and Works* (Philadelphia: 1931), p. 113.

that Spratt was correct morally. But many other Southern critics shared the western world's deep moral repugnance for the traffic. Joseph Day, speaker of the Georgia House of Representatives, regarded the African slave trade as a "system of the most unnatural cruelty, savage barbarity, and unnecessary and unjustifiable suffering, that ever was practiced in any age or country, professing to be civilized." These opponents of the African slave trade were trying to make one point singularly clear to their Southern society: *as civilized men,* Southerners could not support such an inhuman and "gigantic wickedness." [73]

These Southern critics drew a clear moral distinction between the domestic and the foreign slave trades. The editor of the *Republican Banner and Nashville Whig* rejected the advocates' assertion that the domestic slave trade equalled the African slave trade, and argued that the first involved the buying and selling of slaves while the second involved the enslavement of free Africans.[74] The African slave trade was not, Judge Peter Gray explained to his Texas listeners, "the same as the internal trade among the states. There negroes are already slaves, in an improved condition. In Africa it is not so. There they make slaves by war. Captives are taken by force, with all the horrors of barbarian war, for the purpose of being made slaves." [75] While African slave-trade advocates like Spratt and Adams could perceive no moral difference between slavery and the African slave trade, many opponents saw a vast moral hiatus between the two. They regarded slavery as a moral institution, for the condition of the slave in "this civilized

[73] Day to Hunter, in Milledgeville *Federal Union,* September 13, 1859; B. H. Richardson, in *De Bow's Review,* XXII (January, 1857), p. 223; Charleston *Courier,* September 4, 1858; New Orleans *Picayune,* May 22, 1857; Henry A. Wise, in Richmond *Enquirer,* August 2, 1859; Richmond *Enquirer,* in New York *Anti-Slavery Standard,* December 13, 1856; J. L. Orr to J. J. Pettigrew, April 20, 1857, Pettigrew Papers, North Carolina Archives, Raleigh, North Carolina; Etheridge, in *Republican Banner and Nashville Whig,* March 6, 1857; John C. Underwood, in Jackson *Semi-Weekly Mississippian,* July 29, 1859.
[74] *Republican Banner and Nashville Whig,* February 3, 1857.
[75] Gray, *Address of Judge Gray,* p. 25.

and Christian country" was "infinitely better than that in his native land." But the "odious" traffic was "a different thing altogether" for it forced Africans into bondage. "How monstrous, then," the editor of the *Republican Banner and Nashville Whig* complained, "to place slavery, as it exists here, on a footing, in point of morality, with the African slave trade." [76] While Governor Henry A. Wise of Virginia felt he could easily justify Southern slavery, he found the African slave trade offensive to his moral sense. In his rebuttal to Governor Adams's message, J. J. Pettigrew attacked Adams's syllogism of the African slave trade as piracy and the slave as plunder. He argued that it was "not worth while to stick in the bark of this objection, and show that piracy and plunder are not necessarily correlative terms." [77] In the minds of these Southern critics of the African slave trade, the distinction between the African slave trade and slavery served not only to condemn the trade but also to underscore the rightness of slavery. Indeed, in their very repudiation of the African slave trade, they reaffirmed their peculiar institution.

Important religious leaders of the South also distinguished between the immorality of the African slave trade and the morality of slavery. Bishop William Meade, the long-time ruler of the Episcopal Church in Virginia, argued that the Biblical passages forbidding "manstealing" required the church to condemn the African slave trade as a "sin" attended by great cruelty.[78] Reverend James Henley Thornwell of South Carolina, whose dominating influence in the Presbyterian Church of the South earned him the appellation, the "Calhoun of the Church," was certain that the great mass of Southern people viewed the African slave trade as an abhorrent system of kidnapping and

[76] *Republican Banner and Nashville Whig,* February 3, 1857; Robert G. Harper, in Jenkins, *Pro-Slavery Thought,* p. 97; Charleston *Courier,* September 4, 1858.

[77] Wise, in Richmond *Enquirer,* August · 2, 1859; Pettigrew, in *De Bow's Review,* XXV (September, 1858), p. 293.

[78] Bishop William Meade to Bishop Leonidas Polk, December 10, 1856, Meade Papers, Library of Congress.

manstealing.[79] In his criticism of Governor Adams's African slave-trade message, Reverend John B. Adger, editor of the distinguished *Southern Presbyterian Review,* charged that the African slave trade was responsible for horrible evils such as African wars and the "involuntary separation of the negro from his relatives." [80] But while these custodians of Southern Christianity condemned the African slave trade in moral terms, they at the same time confirmed the religious legitimacy of the institution of slavery.[81] Yet their very assertion that the Scriptures sanctioned slavery and that slavery was a blessing to the slaves in the South led to contradictions. If slavery were a divinely established institution, had it not been made possible by the African slave trade? If slaves living in the American South were in a blessed state of Christianity, should not the church encourage the importation of more Africans? The contradictions posed by these questions may be seen in the distinction between slavery and the African slave trade set forth in two resolutions adopted by a meeting of the Rocky Creek Baptist Church of South Carolina in 1859:

> *Resolved,* That we do not oppose the existence of Slavery as we have it among us, but are willing to defend it with all the means that God has given us.
> *Resolved,* That to bring untrained negroes from Africa and land them upon any portion of the soil of South Carolina, for the purpose of making slaves of them, meets our unqualified disapprobation, and we will oppose it with all the legal means within our power.[82]

[79] J. H. Thornwell, in R. L. Stanton, *The Church and the Rebellion* (New York: Derby & Miller, 1864), p. 64.

[80] John B. Adger, "A Review of the Reports to the Legislature of South Carolina on the Revival of the Slave Trade," *Southern Presbyterian Review* (October, 1858), pp. 113–115.

[81] See John B. Adger, *A Review of Reports to the Legislature of South Carolina on the Revival of the Slave Trade* (Columbia: R. W. Gibbs, 1858), p. 15; H. Shelton Smith, "The Church and the Social Order in the Old South as Interpreted by James H. Thornwell," *Church History,* VII, No. 2 (June, 1938), p. 119; Meade to Polk, December 10, 1856, Meade Papers, Library of Congress.

[82] Reprinted in Boston *Liberator,* January 28, 1859. For additional evidence, see Charleston *Courier,* September 4, 1858; Charleston *Evening*

On the above resolution, William Lloyd Garrison caustically commented: "Who ever can reconcile the logic and morality of these resolutions will be competent to reconcile any absurdities and contradictions, however monstrous." [83] Such a statement, ironically, could easily have been made by Leonidas W. Spratt!

Southern society was in moral crisis. As defenders of slavery, both the advocates and opponents of the African slave trade could not ignore the biting criticism of Northern abolitionists as well as the troubled consciences of many Southern slaveholders. While the African slave-trade radicals proclaimed the rightness of slavery by scornfully screaming for the importation of African slaves, their Southern critics did this by emphasizing the humaneness of the master–Sambo relationship. But both of them felt the anguished need not only to affirm their commitment to the peculiar institution but also to assert the morality of their commitment. Slavery, they recognized only too painfully, was a moral problem in western culture.

News, in Edgefield *Advertiser,* March 2, 1859; Governor Henry Wise, in Richmond *Enquirer,* August 2, 1859; *The Southern Episcopalian,* reprinted in Charleston *Mercury,* April 9, 1859.

[83] Garrison, in Boston *Liberator,* January 28, 1859.

SIX

GETTING RIGHT
WITH SLAVERY:
THE METHODIST
EPISCOPAL CHURCH,
SOUTH

Since slavery was a moral problem in western culture, Christians North and South could not avoid the burning issue. Their efforts to grapple with the problem led to sectional schisms in the Baptist, Presbyterian, and Methodist Churches. But, as our study of the Southern Methodist Episcopal Church will show, after they had withdrawn from their anti-slavery Northern brethren, Southern white Christians discovered they still had to face their own consciences. The pro-slavery crusade to reopen the African slave trade, moreover, demanded they do so immediately.

Inevitably the issue of the African slave trade became a controversy in the Methodist Episcopal Church, South, for one of the General Rules of this church prohibited the African slave trade. At their General Conference held at Nashville in May 1858, the Southern Methodists confronted this troublesome rule. Though the delegates at this conference strongly believed in the separation of church and state, and though they certainly wished to shun any involvement in the sound and fury over the African slave-trade revival, their need to reckon with the contradiction between slavery and a church rule was driving them into an ironic relationship between the church and the political agitation to import African slaves. But the representatives of this major Southern church could not avoid this predicament; they were being compelled by resolutions from the annual district conferences to expunge from the General Rules of the church the rule forbidding "the buying and selling of men, women and children, with the intention to enslave them." [1] In their effort to expunge this rule, these churchmen were revealing an anxious need to overcome their doubts about their Christian integrity and to confirm the rightness of slavery.

The Methodists at the Nashville General Conference had to face many questions charged with significant implications. Were not slavery and the African slave trade civil matters? Hence did not the rule on buying and selling of human beings involve the church in a civil matter? Did not Southern Methodist ministers and editors firmly assert the Biblical sanction of slavery? Did not the Methodist Episcopal Church, South, then have an obligation to defend the peculiar institution? Should not the church expunge the rule on the slave trade? But what would be the relationship between the expunction of the rule and the efforts to reopen the African slave trade? Had not the influential Nashville *Christian Advocate* approved the charge that the African slave trade was the "supreme unrighteousness"?

[1] Nashville *Christian Advocate,* in Milledgeville *Federal Union,* May 25, 1858; *The Quarterly Review of the Methodist Episcopal Church, South, 1858,* XII, No. 3 (Richmond: 1858), p. 384; Washington *National Intelligencer,* September 11, 1857; Charlotte (North Carolina) *Whig,* in Charleston *Mercury,* December 5, 1857; Charleston *Mercury,* October 4, 1858; Nashville *Union,* October 22, 1858; Jackson *Semi-Weekly Mississippian,* January 19, 1858.

Would expunction mean the church's endorsement of the revival of the African salve trade? And was the church ready for that? [2]

On May 19, 1858, the General Conference of the Methodist Episcopal Church, South, expunged the slave-trade rule by a vote of 143 to 8. The conference agreed:

> *Whereas,* The rule in the General Rules of the Methodist Episcopal Church, South, forbidding "the buying and selling of men, women, and children, with an intention to enslave them," is ambiguous in its phraseology, and liable to be construed as antagonistic to the institution of slavery, in regard to which the Church has no right to meddle, except in enforcing the duties of masters and servants, as set forth in the Holy Scriptures; and whereas, a strong desire for the expunction of said rule has been expressed in nearly all parts of our ecclesiastical Connection: therefore,
> *Resolved,* 1. . . . that the rule forbidding "the buying and selling of men . . ." be expunged from the General Rules of the Methodist Episcopal Church, South.
> *Resolved,* 2. That in adopting the foregoing resolution this Conference expresses no opinion in regard to the African slave-trade, to which the rule in question has been "understood" to refer.[3]

The Southern Methodists at the Nashville General Conference tried to show that the expunction of the rule did not signify support for the reopening of the African slave trade. They carefully announced that they were simply expunging the rule and expressing "no opinion" on the African slave trade. Furthermore, the bishops emphatically denied that the expunction favored the agitation to import African slaves. Bishop

[2] Lewis M. Purifoy, "The Southern Methodist Church and the Proslavery Argument," *Journal of Southern History,* XXXII (1966), pp. 324–325, 332, 341; Charles B. Swaney, *Episcopal Methodism and Slavery* (Boston: Richard G. Badger, 1926), p. 279; *Quarterly Review of the Methodist . . . South, 1858,* pp. 422–423; Charles Elliott, *South-Western Methodism—A History of the Methodist Episcopal Church in the South-West from 1844 to 1864* (Cincinnati: Poe & Hitchcock, 1868), p. 37.

[3] *Quarterly Review of the Methodist . . . South,* p. 384; *Richmond Enquirer,* June 1, 1858; New Orleans *Picayune,* May 28, 1858; Washington *National Intelligencer,* May 28, 1858.

George F. Pierce explained that it was not within the province of the church to decide a question related to slavery, "a purely civil institution." By expunging the rule, the church was only withdrawing herself from a civil matter. Bishop Pierce begged the brethren to be "easy," for there was nothing here to warrant any construction looking towards a repeal of the federal laws against the African slave trade.[4] In their pastoral address of 1858, Bishops Joshua Soule, James O. Andrew, Robert Paine, George F. Pierce, John Early, and Hubbard H. Kavanaugh argued that slavery was a subject belonging to Caesar, and ecclesiastical legislation upon it was contrary to the teachings of Christ and the examples of the apostles. Hence the church had to strike out the rule on the slave trade. But the bishops also declared the church's opposition to the African slave trade. "And if, contrary to expectation, the African slave trade should ever be revived in the face of the law which declares it to be piracy, we have rule and authority enough by which to hold our membership to a rigid responsibility. Nor would we fail in this, sustained as we would be by our own convictions of duty, the law of the land, and what we know to be the moral sentiment of the people among whom we dwell."[5] Such assurance, however, represented an ironic contradiction to their belief that the church should render unto Caesar the things that were his, for the bishops were claiming jurisdiction over their constituents' activity in the African slave trade, a civil matter. Furthermore, in the case of the expunction of the slave-trade rule, the separation of the church and state actually involved the church in the defense of a civil institution. The church had eliminated a rule "liable to be construed as antagonistic to the institution of slavery."[6]

Despite the "no opinion" qualification included in the resolutions for expunction, and despite the clarifying explanations of the bishops, for many white Southerners the expunction of

[4] Bishop George Pierce, in Richmond *Enquirer*, June, 1858.
[5] "Pastoral Address of the South General Conference of the Methodist Episcopal Church, South," in *Quarterly Review of the Methodist . . . South*, pp. 421–426.
[6] *Quarterly Review of the Methodist . . . South*, p. 384.

the rule signified support for the African slave trade. The editor of the Richmond *Whig*, for example, remarked: "When a whole Christian denomination sees nothing wrong, or immoral, or improper in the 'buying and selling of men, women and children, *with an intention to enslave them*,' why should mere politicians presume to pronounce as wicked and atrocious the re-opening of the African slave trade?"[7] Some Methodist supporters of expunction, moreover, were advocates of the African slave trade. According to Reverend D. Stevenson, who wanted to maintain the rule on the slave trade as a barrier against pro-slavery extremism, some delegates at the Nashville General Conference did express pro-African slave-trade sentiment, and this "sentiment seemed to be spreading in the church."[8] A few months before the General Conference, Methodists in Texas had boldly announced their approval of the African slave trade.[9] For these Texas Methodists, the expunction of the rule on the slave trade was designed not simply to separate the church from the state but also to encourage the effort to reopen the African slave trade. Clearly expunction meant different things to different Methodists.

But the expunction of the rule forbidding the buying and selling of men, women, and children involved a broader question than the reopening of the African slave trade. It was part of the movement to transform the Methodist Church into a pro-slavery institution.

Only 14 years before the expunction of the slave-trade rule, the Southern Methodists had protested against the Northern Methodists' criticism of slaveholding ministers. The Methodists of the South were deeply implicated in the institution of slavery: hundreds of ministers and thousands of laymen were slaveholders. Consequently Southern Methodists found the abolitionist spirit of their Northern brethren intolerable, and in 1845 they withdrew from the Methodist Episcopal Church and

[7] Richmond *Whig*, June 4, 1858.

[8] D. Stevenson, in Swaney, *Episcopal Methodism*, p. 249.

[9] Houston *Telegraph*, April 14, 1859, in Earl Wesley Fornell, *The Galveston Era: The Texas Crescent on the Eve of Secession* (Austin: University of Texas Press, 1926), p. 220.

founded an independent Southern church.[10] The 1846 General Conference of the Methodist Episcopal Church, South, was reluctant to eliminate the rule condemning slavery from the church *Discipline;* but the conference agreed that the church should not interfere with the civil institution of slavery.[11] The General Conference of 1854 successfully struck from the *Discipline* the section pronouncing slavery an evil and requiring ministers to be nonslaveholders. The conference also tried to expunge the rule on the slave trade but failed to secure a constitutional majority of two-thirds. Nevertheless, the conference did in effect sanction the domestic slave trade in a compromise resolution, declaring that "the General Rule on the subject of the 'buying and selling of men, women, and children, with the intention to enslave them,' is understood as referring exclusively to the slave trade, as prohibited by the Constitution and laws of the United States." [12] And four years later, the General Conference at Nashville decided that this rule, despite the narrow interpretation imposed upon it in 1854, had to be expunged, for it was still "ambiguous in its phraseology, and liable to be construed as antagonistic to the institution of slavery."[13] Clearly the expunction was the logical conclusion of the drive to transform the Methodist Church below the Mason-Dixon line into a Southern pro-slavery church.

The expunction of the rules condemning slavery and the slave trade from the *Discipline* represented a Methodist demand for consistency between their theology and their church. For many years, Southern Methodists had been proclaiming a theo-

---

[10] Donald G. Mathews, *Slavery and Methodism: A Chapter in American Morality, 1780–1845* (Princeton: Princeton University Press, 1965), pp. 246–282; Purifoy, "Southern Methodist Church," *Journal of Southern History,* p. 325; Eugene P. Southall, "The Attitude of the Methodist Episcopal Church, South, toward the Negro from 1844 to 1870," *Journal of Negro History,* XVI, No. 4 (October, 1931), p. 360.

[11] Southall, "Methodist Episcopal Church, South," *Journal of Negro History,* p. 367; Arthur E. Jones, Jr., "The Years of Disagreement, 1844–61," in Emory Stevens Bucke (ed.), *The History of American Methodism,* 3 Vols. (New York: 1964), Vol. II, p. 157.

[12] Jones, *op. cit.,* p. 191; Swaney, *op. cit.,* pp. 246–247.

[13] *Quarterly Review of the Methodist . . . South,* p. 384.

logical defense of slavery. "We believe," the South Carolina Methodist Conference of 1836 declared, "that the Holy Scriptures, so far from giving any countenance to [the] delusion [of abolitionism], do unequivocally authorize the relation of master and slave." [14] During the intense sectional conflict of the 1850's, the bothersome contradiction between this belief in the Biblical approval of slavery and the anti-slavery church rules compelled Southern Methodists to press for the expunction of the rule against slavery in order to act in "truth and plain-dealing with the world," and to take a position "on the immutable principles of Scriptural testimony." [15]

The expunction of the rule on the slave trade culminated this struggle for Southern self-purity in the Methodist Church. This act of purgation gave a great sense of relief to the bishops. "We rejoice ourselves," exclaimed the bishops in their pastoral letter of 1858, "and confidently expect your sympathy and approbation, that Southern Methodism at last stands disentangled from this vexed and vexing question [of slavery], erect upon a scriptural basis—at liberty to circulate everywhere in our bounds her book of laws, without note or comment; and that *a rule of doubtful interpretation no longer exists to embarrass our ministers and friends,* or to justify the suspicion and assaults of our enemies." [16] Thus, while African slave-trade advocates like Leonidas Spratt and William Yancey were demanding the expunction of certain federal laws in order to harmonize the federal government with slavery, the Methodist Episcopal Church, South, had expunged a church rule in order to harmonize a religious institution with the peculiar institution.

This pro-slavery quest for Southern self-purity involved an aggressive attack upon Southern Methodist dissenters opposed to the expunction of the rule on the slave trade. After the Texas Methodist Conference at Waco had urged the 1858 General Conference to expunge the rule on the slave trade, Texas

---

[14] Mathews, *op. cit.*, pp. 73–74.

[15] Charleston *Christian Advocate*, February 28, 1851, in Purifoy, "Methodist Episcopal Church, South," p. 204.

[16] *Quarterly Review of the Methodist . . . South,* p. 423. Italics added.

Methodists opposed to the African slave trade attempted to organize a "M. E. Church North." But in a mass meeting, Methodists of Houston and Galveston declared their support for the efforts to import African slaves, and "gave all persons connected with said M. E. Church North, as itinerant preachers or Bishops or propagators of their views, 60 days to leave the state." [17] Meanwhile in Mississippi, the Methodist ministers meeting at Brandon adopted resolutions for the expunction of the rule by a vote of 70 to 7. Mississippi newspaper editors immediately excoriated the seven dissenting ministers.[18] *"We want to know the names of the seven abolition preachers,"* thundered the editor of the Oxford *Mercury*. "It is due to the high standing and character of the Methodist Church, *that the seven negro worshippers should be exposed, and held up to the scorn and condemnation of every honest man.* We have no use for abolitionists in our state; there is no room for them, and their presence should and will not be tolerated. If we can get the names of the immortal seven, we will promise to give them an advertisement free of cost, which will make them known all over the country. We have fully determined to show no favor to any abolitionists . . . and we should always denounce in unmeasured terms such characters as vile reptiles, who ought to be driven from the land." [19] While Northern condemnation of slavery was abominable, Southern dissent against a pro-slavery movement was intolerable in Southern society. In the eyes of Mississippians like the editor of the Oxford *Mercury*, such dissent represented internal doubts about the morality of slavery and internal infidelity to the peculiar institution. Hence the Southern dissenters were quickly labeled "abolitionists" and "vile reptiles," worthy of Mississippi scorn and even Mississippi violence. Clearly such violence against individuals regarded as social deviants would help to expose what Yancey called "un-

[17] Houston *Telegraph*, April 14, 1859, in Fornell, p. 220.

[18] Jackson *Semi-Weekly Mississippian*, January 19, 1858; Panola (Mississippi) *Star*, in New York *Anti-Slavery Standard*, January 30, 1858.

[19] Oxford *Mercury*, in Jackson *Semi-Weekly Mississippian*, January 19, 1858. See also Jackson *Semi-Weekly Mississippian*, February 26, March 2, March 23, 1858.

soundness in our midst on the question of slavery," and to instruct white Southerners who they should be and should *not* be. Such violence would define sharply and underscore strongly the norms and the values of Southern slave society.[20]

But what concerned the Southern Methodists at the Nashville General Conference of 1858 was not the need to suppress Southern dissent but the need to identify themselves as *both* pro-slavery *and* Christian. Their expunction of the rule on the slave trade was part of an old and continuing effort to reconcile a Methodist ambivalance towards the institution of slavery. On the one hand, the Methodists in the South had inherited the tradition of John Wesley's commitment against slavery. The founder of the Methodist Church abhorred slavery. In 1743 he had written the rule against the buying and selling of human beings into the General Rules. To Wesley, the African slave trade was "that execrable sum of all villanies", infinitely exceeding "in every instance of barbarity, whatever Christian slaves suffer in Mahometan countries." In a letter to William Wilberforce, the famous English crusader against the African slave trade and slavery, Wesley declared: "Go in the name of God, and in the power of his might, till even American slavery (the vilest that ever saw the sun) shall vanish away before it."[21] The anti-slavery impulse within American Methodism found expression in the leadership of Bishops Thomas Coke and Francis Asbury and in the Methodist conferences of the late eighteenth century.[22] On the other hand, the Southern Methodists had also accepted the tradition of George Whitefield's commitment to the Christianization of slaves. Unlike Wesley, the fiery circuit-rider of the Great Awakening believed in the legitimacy of slavery. "As for the lawfulness of keeping slaves,"

[20] Yancey, in Charleston *Mercury*, July 9, 1859.

[21] John Wesley, in Mathews, *Slavery and Methodism*, pp. 5–6; W. B. Posey, "Influence of Slavery upon the Methodist Church in the Early South and Southwest," *Mississippi Valley Historical Review*, XVII (1931), pp. 530–531.

[22] Mathews, *op. cit.*, p. 10; Posey, *op. cit.*, p. 531; Lewis M. Purifoy, "The Methodist Episcopal Church, South, and Slavery, 1844–1865," unpublished Ph.D. thesis, University of North Carolina, pp. 2, 3, 4.

Whitefield explained, "I have no doubt, since I hear of some that were bought with Abraham's money, and some were born in his house." [23] In his justification of slavery, Whitefield emphasized the church's obligation to convert slaves. Lecturing to slaveholders in 1740, Whitefield queried: "Think you" that your children "are any better by Nature than the poor Negroes? No, in no wise. Blacks are just as much, and no more conceived and born in Sin, if White Men are. Both, if born and bred up here, I am persuaded, are naturally capable of the same [religious] improvement." In 1751 Whitefield told Wesley that the presence of Negroes in Georgia was an opportunity "for breeding up their posterity in the nurture and admonition of the Lord." [24]

Clearly Methodist ministers in the South faced a dilemma. If they condemned slavery, they could be banned from preaching to the slaves on the plantations. If they approved the institution, they could be banished from Wesley's church. During the late eighteenth century, the Methodist Church bravely attacked the institution of slavery. The General Conference of 1784 declared slavery "contrary to the laws of God, man, and nature, and harmful to society; contrary to the dictates of conscience and true religion." [25] Four years later the church threatened to suspend slaveholding preachers and to discipline slaveholding church members. But Methodist opposition to slavery provoked slaveholding resistance to the church's efforts to bring the Word of God to the slave. The reaction of the slaveholders jeopardized the church's contact with the slaveholder as well as the slave and hindered the growth of Methodism in the South.[26] Thus in the early nineteenth century, the Methodists began to withdraw from the Wesley antislavery commitment in order to promote the Whitefield ministry to the slaves. They explained that unless the church modified its anti-

[23] Whitefield, in Jenkins, *Pro-Slavery Thought,* p. 42.
[24] Whitefield, in Winthrop D. Jordan, *White Over Black, American Attitudes Toward the Negro, 1550–1812,* pp. 213–214.
[25] James W. Patton, "The Progress of Emancipation in Tennessee, *Journal of Negro History,* XVII, No. 1 (January, 1932), p. 84.
[26] *Ibid.;* Mathews, *op. cit.,* p. 22.

slavery position, it would alienate slaveholders and consequently destroy the mission to the slaves. They argued that the salvation of the slave's soul was more important than his personal liberty. Such a Methodist concern to prove that the church was safe on slavery in order to gather black souls into the Methodist fold helped to persuade the General Conference of 1804 to suspend the *Discipline's* Section on Slavery in the states south of Virginia.[27]

Fifty years later, during the crisis of the 1850's, the Southern Methodists completely eliminated the Section on Slavery. Significantly, while the General Conferences of the 1850's were revising the General Rules, they were also zealously declaring their commitment to the salvation of slaves. "The gospel is God's gift to the black man as well as to the white," the Nashville General Conference of 1858 announced, "and Christian masters should see to it that all their dependents are regularly supplied with the preaching of the word of God." [28] Obviously a pro-slavery Methodist Church, blessed with the confidence and support of the master class, would be a more powerful missionary to the slaves.

This Southern Methodist zeal to save black souls had a profound psychological significance. The mission to the slaves was a symptom of a Southern Methodist need to justify their connection with slavery before the Christian world, and perhaps also *to convince themselves that they were not guilty of sin.* As Southern Methodists became more and more proslavery and as they expunged the church rule against the slave trade, they increasingly felt a distressing sense of isolation from their brethren in the world, and an anxious need to escalate their efforts to Christianize slaves in order to witness their own righteousness. In their dedication to the "salvation of the colored race," the Nashville General Conference of 1858 added: "Let us earnestly seek to meet our responsibilities and then whatever 'evil thing' ignorance and prejudice shall say of us, we shall

[27] Mathews, *op. cit.*, pp. 13, 26; Purifoy, "Methodist Episcopal Church, South," pp. 8, 9, 13, 203, 208.
[28] Purifoy, "Methodist Episcopal Church, South," p. 118.

have the testimony of a *good conscience,* and the blessing of Him who is Judge of all." [29] In their 1858 call for greater missionary activity in the South, the bishops explained to their Southern brethren: "The position we, of the Methodist Church, South, have taken for the African, has to a great extent cut us off from the sympathy of the Christian Church throughout the world; and it behooves us to make good this position in the sight of God, of angels, of men, of churches, and to *our own consciences.*" [30]

Cast into the hell of irony, Southern Methodists were desperately seeking for a way to be granted the slaveholders' permission to preach to slaves and labor fervently in the missionary tradition of Whitefield, and *at the same time* to win the recognition of the Wesleyan Christian world and to confirm their Christianity in their own minds. The doctrine of the separation of church and state enabled them to expunge the rules against slavery and the African slave trade from the *Discipline,* reinforce the slaveholders' confidence in the Methodist Church of the South, and advance their crusade for black souls and for their own moral legitimacy to be a Christian church.

[29] *Ibid.* Italics added.

[30] Jones, *op. cit.,* p. 203. Italics added. Perhaps no wonder the Southern Methodist Church spent more than a million dollars between 1844 and 1864 for mission work among Negroes. See Southall, *op. cit.,* p. 364.

SEVEN

SANCTUARIES
FOR PRO-SLAVERY MEN:
THE SOUTHERN
COMMERCIAL
CONVENTIONS

While the Southern Methodists were building a pro-slavery church during the 1850's, African slave-trade advocates like Leonidas W. Spratt, James De Bow, and William Yancey were radicalizing the Southern Commercial Conventions. Both the Methodists and the African slave-trade advocates were seeking to bring institutions below the Mason-Dixon line into the defense of slavery. Both groups, moreover, were attending yearly conventions and proclaiming what they as Southerners anxiously wanted to hear. They were addressing themselves to the Southern need to affirm the rightness of slavery, and aggressively declaring that their society was *both* slaveholding *and* moral.

146

The radicalization of the Southern Commercial Conventions of the late 1850's represented a sharp departure from the interests and purposes of earlier conventions. Concerned chiefly with commercial questions, the conventions at Memphis, Baltimore, and New Orleans in the 1840's and early 1850's discussed the construction of the Pacific railroad, the exportation of cotton, federal aid to build levees along the Mississippi River, direct trade and steamship communication between the South and Europe, the employment of slaves as factory operatives, and the encouragement of manufacturing in the South.[1] The commercial interest in these early conventions was linked to the defense of slavery. John C. Calhoun, the philosopher of nullification, supported these conventions as a means to promote Southern economic independence from the North. At the 1837 Augusta Convention, George McDuffie of South Carolina called for direct trade with Europe and pointed out that the South had to develop her foreign commerce in order to be prepared for the contingency of disunion. The Charleston Convention of 1839 recommended support for the *Southern Review,* a magazine devoted to Southern interests. The conventions at Baltimore in 1852 and Memphis in 1853 urged Southerners to educate their youth in Southern schools with Southern teachers and Southern textbooks.[2]

While these early conventions had a Southern orientation, they sought to defend the interests of the South within the Union. Southerners attending expressed Unionist sentiments. At the 1838 Augusta Convention, they drank toasts: "To our country—The whole must prosper when every part takes care of itself," and "The Northern States—Let us show that in honor-

---

[1] J. H. Easterby, "The Charleston Commercial Convention of 1854," *The South Atlantic Quarterly,* XXV, No. 2 (April, 1926), p. 184; John G. Van Deusen, *The Ante-Bellum Southern Commercial Conventions* (Durham: Duke University Press, 1926), pp. 21–27, 62; Russel, *Economic Aspects of Southern Sectionalism,* pp. 127, 131, 142–43; *De Bow's Review,* I (January, 1846), pp. 10–13.

[2] Wender, *Southern Commercial Conventions,* pp. 11, 15, 21; Van Deusen, *Southern Commercial Conventions,* pp. 10, 19; Russel, *Economic Aspects of Southern Sectionalism,* p. 131.

able enterprise brothers may compete and be brothers still." [3]
The 1845 Memphis Convention, which had elected Calhoun as
its president, resolved that "this convention, far from desiring
to engender sectional prejudices, or encourage attempts to
alienate any portion of our country from the rest, regard the
North and the South, the East and the West, as ONE PEOPLE,
in sympathy and interest, as in government and country, and
hold their countrymen of every State to the duties and responsibilities of a closely connected and indissoluble Union." [4] Seeking
to forge a South-West alliance, Calhoun announced at this convention his support for federal aid to improve the "inland sea"
—the Mississippi River.[5] In his presidential address to the Memphis Southern Commercial Convention of 1853, Senator William
C. Dawson of Georgia explained that the zeal for Southern
commercial development did not signify an antagonism to the
North.[6] A year later Albert Pike of Arkansas, an enthusiastic
advocate of the Pacific railroad, told the Charleston Southern
Commercial Convention that Southern economic progress and
equality with the North were the only assurances of Southern
safety within the Union.[7]

During the late 1850's the Southern Commercial Conventions underwent a radicalizing process. The conventions at
Savannah (1856), Knoxville (1857), Montgomery (1858), and
Vicksburg (1859) became noticeably less commercial and Unionist and more political and disunionist. They were increasingly
transformed from innocuous affairs resembling gatherings of the
chamber of commerce to intense political meetings. At these
conventions, Southerners made pronouncements about their
commitment to secession rather than their love for the Union;
they were more interested in the expansion of slavery into
Kansas and the Walker filibuster into Nicaragua than in the

---

[3] Charleston *Courier*, April 6, 1838, in Wender, *Southern Commercial Conventions*, p. 21.

[4] *De Bow's Review*, I (January, 1846), p. 9.

[5] Calhoun, in Wender, *Southern Commercial Conventions*, p. 57.

[6] Dawson, in Easterby, "The Charleston Commercial Convention," *The South Atlantic Quarterly*, pp. 184–185.

[7] Pike, in Wender, *Southern Commercial Conventions*, p. 127.

improvement of the Mississippi River. "It is not to be disguised," a writer to the Nashville *Union and Republican* correctly observed, "that these Conventions at first originated for the *sole* purpose of developing the commercial and industrial resources of the slave States are verging on to political questions. . . ." [8] The editor of the New Orleans *Picayune* complained that the Southern Commercial Conventions had neglected their proper mission and had degenerated into sectionalist and political assemblies.[9] Aware of the conventions' political purpose, the editor of the Milledgeville *Federal Union* remarked: "When the South gets ready to dissolve the Union, all she has to do is, to reassemble the Southern Commercial Convention which met at Montgomery." [10] The election of James De Bow as president of the Knoxville Southern Commercial Convention symbolized the radicalization of the conventions. In his presidential address to the convention, De Bow declared that the Southern Commercial Conventions should have a political purpose. They should show Southerners that they had "rights more to be valued and defended than any theories or sentiments about Union," and that the South had resources sufficient "to exist without the Union and to maintain the rank of a first class power whenever it shall be deemed necessary to establish a separate confederation." [11]

As the Southern Commercial Conventions became increasingly radicalized, they gave greater attention and support to the proposal for the reopening of the African slave trade. The Knoxville Convention demanded the annulment of the Webster-Ashburton Treaty's eighth article—a provision requiring the presence of an American squadron off the African coast to

[8] Nashville *Union and Republican*, September 9, 1857; Knoxville *Register*, in *Republican Banner and Nashville Whig*, December 28, 1856; C. C. Jones to Mary Jones, December 13, 1856, C. C. Jones Papers, Tulane University Library; Richmond *Examiner*, in Washington *National Intelligencer*, August 3, 1857.

[9] New Orleans *Picayune*, May 20, 1858; August 22, 1857; Charleston *Mercury*, September 14, 1857.

[10] Milledgeville *Federal Union*, May 18, 1858; Richmond *Enquirer*, May 25, 1858.

[11] De Bow, in Wender, *op. cit.*, p. 187.

suppress the slave trade. The convention also formed an African slave-trade committee headed by Leonidas W. Spratt. The Southern Commercial Convention at Vicksburg was virtually an African slave-trade convention. The convention devoted four out of five days to a discussion of the subject, and adopted a resolution demanding the repeal of all state and federal laws against the African slave trade.[12]

The radicalization of the Southern Commercial Conventions was related to the changing composition of the delegates. The early commercial-oriented conventions were attended by politicians, editors, and businessmen—merchants, bankers, manufacturers, and railroad and steamship promoters. The delegates were appointed by governors, city councils, mayors, chambers of commerce, citizens' meetings, and agricultural associations. Anyone able to pay his way could secure an appointment.[13] Clearly it would be easy to pack the Southern Commercial Conventions with African slave-trade advocates like De Bow, Spratt, and Hughes. A study of the membership of the conventions reveals a definite change in composition. Unlike the earlier conventions, the Savannah Southern Commercial Convention, assembled a month after the tense Presidential election of 1856, was composed largely of politicians rather than businessmen. The members of the Savannah Convention, a delegate from Tennessee reported, were politicians rather than men immediately and mainly interested in the promotion of Southern commercial development.[14] The Southern Commercial Conventions at Knoxville, Montgomery, and Vicksburg followed the same pattern: very few businessmen and very many politicians were present. Commenting on the composition of the Mont-

[12] *De Bow's Review*, XXIII (May, 1855), p. 628; XXIII (September, 1857), pp. 303, 310–317, 440; XXIV (June, 1858), p. 491, 582; XXVI (June, 1859), p. 713.

[13] Easterby, "The Charleston Commercial Convention of 1854," *South Atlantic Quarterly*, p. 184; Van Deusen, *Southern Commercial Conventions*, pp. 108–109; Russel, *Economic Aspects of Southern Sectionalism*, pp. 144–145; Richmond *Enquirer*, November 7, 1856.

[14] Knoxville *Register*, in *Republican Banner and Nashville Whig*, December 28, 1856; Russel, *Economic Aspects of Southern Sectionalism*, p. 158; Van Deusen, *Southern Commercial Conventions*, p. 54.

gomery Southern Commercial Convention, the editor of the Montgomery *Daily Confederation* observed: "Every form and shape of political malcontent was there present, ready to assent in any project having for its end a dissolution of the Union, immediate, unconditional, final." [15] A month before the Southern Commercial Convention met at Vicksburg, the editor of the New Orleans *Picayune* complained that extremist politicians had taken over the conventions.[16] The Southern Commercial Conventions of the late 1850's had become meetings for pro-slavery politicians.

This change in the composition of the conventions was no coincidence. Fire-eaters were urging their colleagues to attend the conventions and to radicalize the meetings. William Yancey of Alabama invited Robert Barnwell Rhett of South Carolina to attend the Montgomery Southern Commercial Convention.[17] In a letter to Senator James Hammond of South Carolina, Virginia secessionist Edmund Ruffin wrote: "I wish you to go to the Knoxville Commercial Convention in August. I want to have a true *southern* convention, in which southern men of the highest ability . . . shall lead & direct the proceedings for the real benefit (Commercial & general) of the southern states. Here-to-fore, these 'commercial conventions,' have been mostly composed of delegates (self-nominated too) from the towns only, & most of these were agents of northern merchants, or otherwise intimately connected with northern trade, & the keeping the south tributary to the north." [18] This kind of letter writing campaign helped to ensure the presence of a large number of fire-eaters at the convention. Furthermore, African slave-trade advocates like De Bow took control of the program committee and announced *in advance* the extremist pro-slavery topics to be

[15] Montgomery *Daily Confederation*, in Russel, p. 143; Ruffin, Diary, April 30, 1858, Ruffin Papers, Library of Congress.
[16] New Orleans *Picayune*, March 31, 1859; Wender, *Southern Commercial Conventions*, p. 228; Van Deusen, *Southern Commercial Conventions*, p. 67.
[17] Du Bose, *Yancey*, I, 358–359.
[18] Ruffin to Hammond, July 4, 1857, Hammond Papers, Library of Congress.

discussed at the next convention. The published call for the meeting at Vicksburg used the title "Southern Convention" rather than Southern Commercial Convention.[19] Such tactics turned many Southerners, especially businessmen, away from the Southern Commercial Convention. The editor of the Milledgeville *Federal Union*, for example, called the Southern Commercial Convention a farce, and suggested that Georgia refuse to send delegates to the Vicksburg meeting.[20] This sort of reaction facilitated the fire-eaters' effort to control the Southern Commercial Conventions.

A crucial step in the radicalization of the Southern Commercial Conventions was the alienation of the border states. Concerned about the protection of the domestic slave trade, the delegates from the border states played an important role in the suppression of the African slave-trade agitation in the conventions. They effectively defeated African slave-trade proposals at the Savannah Southern Commercial Convention. They also forced the Southern Commercial Convention at Montgomery to table Spratt's resolutions for the reopening of the African slave trade.[21] But the delegates from border states like Virginia, Kentucky, and Maryland did not attend the meeting at Vicksburg in 1859. "I fear [the Vicksburg Convention] indicated less than former interest in these meetings," Ruffin commented. "Members from but 8 states were present—& not one from Virginia." [22] Virginians were unwilling to participate in a convention seeking to reopen the African slave trade. Consequently Spratt and company were able to dominate the Vicksburg Convention and pass their resolutions favoring the reopening of the African slave trade. A significant change in the composition of the conventions

[19] *De Bow's Review*, XXIV (May, 1858), pp. 466–467; Natchez *Free Trader*, May 10, 1858; New Orleans *Picayune*, March 31, 1859.

[20] Milledgeville *Federal Union*, in Washington *National Intelligencer*, April 8, 1859.

[21] *De Bow's Review*, XXII (1857), p. 89; New Orleans *Picayune*, December 18, 1856; *De Bow's Review*, XXIII (September, 1857), pp. 303, 310; Ruffin, Diary, May 13, 1858, Ruffin Papers, Library of Congress; New Orleans *Delta*, May 18, 1858.

[22] Ruffin, Diary, May 28, 1859, Ruffin Papers, Library of Congress.

had taken place in 1859. The African slave-trade advocates did not have to worry about the 33 votes of Maryland, North Carolina, and Virginia—states which had voted against the African slave trade in previous conventions. Compare, for example, the votes of the 1856 Savannah Convention on the resolution to appoint a committee to investigate the propriety of reopening the African slave trade with the votes of the Vicksburg Convention on the resolution to repeal the laws against the trade.[23]

	1856 Savannah		1859 Vicksburg	
	Yes	**No**	**Yes**	**No**
Alabama	9		9	
Arkansas			4	
Florida		3		3
Georgia		10	10	
Kentucky				
Louisiana	3	3	6	
Maryland		8		
Mississippi			7	
North Carolina		10		
South Carolina	8		4	4
Tennessee		12		12
Texas	4		4	
Virginia		15		
	—	—	—	——
	24	61	44	19

Had the delegates from Maryland, North Carolina, and Virginia been present at the Vicksburg Convention, the African slave-trade resolution would have been defeated by a vote of 52 to 44. The evolution of the Southern Commercial Convention into an African slave-trade convention was a simple process: most of the delegates from the border states had withdrawn, and African slave-trade advocates had crowded into and taken over the meeting.

[23] *De Bow's Review*, XXII (January, 1857), p. 92; XXVI (June, 1859), p. 713.

But why did the advocates of the African slave trade want to carry their agitation into the Southern Commercial Conventions? A review of the African slave-trade resolutions introduced in these conventions shows that the advocates were trying to educate Southern society in pro-slavery thought. They were seeking to point out the moral contradictions on the question of slavery held by Southerners themselves. At the New Orleans Southern Commercial Convention of 1855, Dr. J. W. P. McGimsey of Louisiana presented a resolution favoring the African slave trade.

> In view of the fact that African slavery is an institution clearly sanctioned by the volume of inspiration—that it is the only conservative power of the south end of the Union—and that it constitutes the best state of society, where the African and Caucasian races are compelled to dwell together in the same community, therefore—
>
> *Resolved,* That this convention recommend our Senators and Representatives in Congress, from the slaveholding States, to introduce a bill to repeal all laws suppressing the slave trade, and that they exert all their influence to have such a law passed.[24]

McGimsey's preamble gave his resolution a special meaning. McGimsey could hardly have expected the repeal of the federal laws. In the context of his preamble, his resolution was an aggressive assertion that slavery was divinely sanctioned and constituted the "best state" of a biracial society. Thus McGimsey was simply requesting a convention of Southerners to make this declaration in an endorsement of the African slave trade, and to articulate what they as slaveholders should believe. Similarly the actions of the Knoxville Southern Commercial Convention were designed in part to enlighten white Southerners on the question of slavery. In their protest against the Webster-Ashburton Treaty, the African slave-trade advocates at the Knoxville Convention argued that the American commitment to police the African coast was a contradiction to the Southern

[24] *De Bow's Review,* XVIII (May, 1855), p. 628.

belief in the integrity of slavery. Unless slaveholders were prepared to admit their slaves were plunder, the advocates reasoned, they must deny the African slave trade was piracy and repudiate the insulting provision in the treaty. The Knoxville Convention also appointed a committee to collect information on the reopening of the African slave trade and to make a report at the next convention. Refusal to discuss the African slave-trade issue in the convention, the advocates argued, would imply that the delegates considered "the matter wrong, and that they regarded slavery as objectionable." [25]

In the Southern Commercial Conventions, African slave-trade advocates were aiming their resolutions and arguments at their fellow delegates and Southern society. This was one of Spratt's purposes at the Montgomery Southern Commercial Convention. After reading an elaborate report on the African slave trade to hundreds of politicians assembled at this convention, Spratt recommended three resolutions:

> 1. *Resolved,* That slavery is right, and that being right there can be no wrong in the natural means to its formation.
> 2. *Resolved,* That it is expedient and proper the foreign slave trade should be re-opened, and that this Convention will lend its influence to any legitimate measure to that end.
> 3. *Resolved,* That a committee, consisting of one from each slave State, be appointed to consider of the means, consistent with the duty and obligations of these States, for re-opening the foreign slave-trade, and that they report their plan to the next meeting of this Convention. [26]

Like McGimsey and the Southern critics of the Webster-Ashburton Treaty, Spratt was asking Southerners to proclaim boldly the rightness of slavery. He was calling upon Southerners to declare that slavery was right and hence there could be "no

[25] *De Bow's Review,* XXIII (September, 1857), pp. 303–317, 440; New Orleans *Picayune,* August 23, 1857.
[26] *De Bow's Review,* XXIV (June, 1858), p. 491.

wrong in the natural means to its formation." Thus the advocates of the African slave trade were using the Southern Commercial Conventions to establish the values essential for a Southern slaveholding society.

The advocates of the African slave trade used the Southern Commercial Conventions to create an image of Southern support for their measure in order to influence the sentiments of the South towards the African slave trade. Actually the Southern Commercial Conventions' interest in the African slave trade did not indicate growing Southern support for the proposal: it only meant that the African slave-trade radicals had captured the conventions. Nevertheless, the advocates pointed to the actions of the Southern Commercial Conventions as indications of Southern public opinion. "Such Conventions," a New Orleans editor observed, "profess to represent the Southern people; and though the Southern people have about as much voice in them as they would have in an assemblage of Seminoles, and care as little about them, yet their action would go forth to the country as the voice of the South. . . ." [27]

Thus the Southern Commercial Conventions had an important function in the agitation to reopen the African slave trade. In these conventions, fire-eaters like De Bow and Spratt adopted extremist resolutions on the African slave trade; and then in their magazines and newspapers, they reported these resolutions as expressions of the enthusiastic and increasing Southern demand for the reopening of the African slave trade. The editor of the Galveston *Weekly News* praised the Montgomery Southern Commercial Convention for its interest in the revival of the African slave trade. "It was only a year or two ago," he remarked, "that we heard the first suggestion of the necessity of reopening the slave trade as the only means to supply the South with labor, and then the very idea of such a thing was denounced by our very conservative and Union-saving journals, as a most dangerous heresy. But what a change has taken place in this short time!" [28] A few months after the

[27] New Orleans *Bulletin*, August 12, 1857.
[28] Galveston *Weekly News*, May 22, 1858.

Montgomery Southern Commercial Convention, *De Bow's Review,* a propaganda magazine for the African slave trade, reported that the subject was attracting growing interest throughout the entire South, and that in "most of these States a very large party; in some, it would be safe to say, almost a controlling portion of the population look to a limited revival of the African slave-trade. . . ."[29] The editor of the Jackson *Semi-Weekly Mississippian* applauded the Vicksburg Convention for its endorsement of the African slave trade, and observed that the action of the meeting represented a rising tide of support for the reopening of the African slave trade. "We regard this as undeniable evidence that the movement is still advancing, and that the hope of effecting the repeal of all anti-slave trade laws is gaining strength and boldness in the South."[30] In their reports on the meetings, African slave-trade advocates were raving about the "advancing" movement to reopen the African slave trade and the wonderful "change" in Southern sentiment on the trade question. They were presenting "undeniable evidence" to the South and to the world that Southern public opinion was moving in their radical pro-slavery direction.

The Southern Commercial Conventions, moreover, were sanctuaries for pro-slavery men. At these conventions, fire-eaters could get together to discuss their common interests and anxieties. They could create a miniature pro-slavery society within the convention hall. Under radical pro-slavery control, the Southern Commercial Convention became what Ruffin called a "true *southern* convention," and served certain social and psychological needs of many fire-eaters.[31] A few days before the meeting of the Montgomery Southern Commercial Convention, Ruffin wrote in his diary: "Though these Conventions have been of no *direct* use, they may be of indirect benefit. I shall go to meet & exchange views with men of the south, & for the possible chance of forwarding the union & welfare of the

[29] *De Bow's Review,* XXV (August, 1858), p. 116.
[30] Jackson *Semi-Weekly Mississippian,* June 10, 1859.
[31] Ruffin to Hammond, July 4, 1857, Hammond Papers, Library of Congress.

southern states, & in my *private capacity* instigating secession from the northern states." When Ruffin arrived at the convention, he met and talked with Southerners *like himself*. He was happy to find among them "a strong feeling of disunion." [32] The Southern Commercial Convention provided a place where Southerners like Ruffin could gather to express to each other a commitment to secession and to satisfy their desire for a radical pro-slavery fellowship.

In the Southern Commercial Conventions, fire-eaters like Spratt, Yancey, and Hughes had a platform, a stage to declare annually the rightness of the African slave trade to their Southern society as well as to themselves. The conventions offered these men opportunities for them to imagine a sense of powerfulness. Obviously they had no power in Congress to repeal the federal laws against the African slave trade. But they attended their Congress-like Southern Commercial Conventions and acted almost like congressmen. In their conventions, they delivered eloquent speeches and elaborate reports, and voted on resolutions instructing Congress to repeal certain federal laws. The editor of the Richmond *Examiner* depicted the Southern Commercial Conventions as

> the best places in the world for clever visionaries and distinguished riders of hobby horses. Neglected genius, nursing in obscurity magnificent schemes for benefiting mankind, gentlemen who are so tremendously ahead of the fastest of young Americans as not to be comprehended, inventors so magnificent in their plans as to fail to get them into the patent office at Washington, receive a respectful and attentive consideration in a Southern Convention. The utmost charity and the kindest considerations are manifested by the delegates to a Southern Convention for the widest vagaries of their fellow members. The enthusiast from Mississippi, when he has let off a notable plan for converting cotton seed into cheese, listens complacently to the gentlemen from Kentucky who propose manufacturing silk from the refuse of the hemp stalk. The Western speculator who makes a

[32] Ruffin, Diary, April 30, 1858; May 9, 1858, Ruffin Papers, Library of Congress.

speech in favor of employing the Crows, Blackfeet, and Sacs to construct a railroad out of old tomahawks, and to issue wampum as a substitute for the ordinary railroad stock, is not the man to object to the gentleman from Virginia, who proposes running a daily line of flat-boats to the Arctic Ocean to supply Massachusetts with ice and Polar bear meat.[33]

In his sarcastic commentary, the editor had caught a part of the significance of the Southern Commercial Conventions of the late 1850's.

The advocates of the African slave trade were gathering yearly at the Southern Commercial Conventions. They were withdrawing into a fellowship of fire-eaters to articulate and applaud their radical pro-slavery proposals. In these pro-slavery sanctuaries, Southerners like McGimsey and Spratt were professing what they as Southerners believed, or should believe, and avowing their faith in the rightness of the peculiar institution.

[33] Richmond *Examiner*, in Washington *National Intelligencer*, August 3, 1857. The Milledgeville *Federal Union* made a similar observation. See *Federal Union*, May 18, 1858.

EIGHT

TURMOIL
IN THE
SOUTHERN STATES

t he controversy over the reopening of the African slave trade was largely a *Southern* tempest—a political and social storm raging below the Mason-Dixon Line. The slave-trade issue was entangled in a mesh of Southern tensions between the border and cotton states, upcountry and lowcountry, nonslaveholders and slaveholders, Democrats and Whigs, and even Democrats and Democrats. Different and often antagonistic moral, regional, class, and political concerns within the South produced a variety of Southern responses to the African slave-trade question. The complexity of the Southern responses cannot be fully understood unless the African slave-trade agitation is analyzed within the context of individual states. Indeed greater attention to state histories is essential for a proper understanding of sectional and national behavior. As Professor Charles G. Sellers has pointed out, "scholarly indifference to local and particular ends that are often the springs of political behavior has shrouded much of our political history in a pervasive unreality." [1] Much of our analysis so far has focused on the African slave-trade agitation in relationship to Southern pro-slavery politics and ideology, and Southern institutions like the Methodist Church and the Southern Commercial Conventions. But we need to study what happened in the states. Thus, in order to deepen our understanding of the agitation to reopen the African slave trade, we now turn to an analysis of the turmoil in the Southern states.

The turmoil over the issue in Virginia exposed the conflict of economic interests between the border states and the cotton states. Unlike Mississippi and Texas, Virginia was a slave-selling state. Consequently the proposal to reopen the African slave trade provoked great opposition in Virginia. In their arguments against the revival of the trade, Virginians expressed different attitudes about the morality of the African slave trade. The editor of the Richmond *Enquirer,* for example, was "glad" to see the agitation of the African slave-trade issue. "The odium cast upon slavery by existing Federal laws," he argued, "should never have been submitted to by the Southern people, and the sooner it is removed the better." [2] The editor of the Charlottesville *Review,* on the other hand, condemned the African slave trade as "contrary to the civilization of the age." But while they had conflicting opinions about the morality of the traffic in African slaves, both editors agreed that Virginia's vested interest in the domestic slave trade required the prohibition of the African slave trade, and sternly warned that Virginia would not tolerate competition in the slave market. Virginians had a "vested right" in the selling of slaves to the cotton states, they

[1] Charles G. Sellers, Jr., "Jackson Men with Feet of Clay," *American Historical Review* (April, 1957), p. 551.
[2] Richmond *Enquirer,* May 25, 1858, October 19, 1858.

declared, and the reopening of the African slave trade would "destroy that right." [3]

Virginia's opposition to the African slave trade was a depressing experience for Edmund Ruffin. The singleminded fire-eater could see that Virginians were prostituting themselves to Mammon in their resistance to the importation of African slaves. Virginia critics like the editors of the Richmond *Enquirer* and the Charlottesville *Review* were behaving like Yankees: they were hypocritical and acquisitive. They were hardly Southern gentlemen conscious about honor and oblivious to money-making. They were invoking rhetorical expressions of moral approval or abhorrence towards the African slave trade, and selfishly protecting their economic monopoly over the supply of slave labor. They had sold their cavalier birthright for the right to sell slaves. They represented Virginia's apathetic defense of slavery. Dismayed by the opposition to the African slave trade in the Old Dominion, Ruffin soon found intolerable his fellow Virginians' chary attitude towards pro-slavery radicalism. He painfully felt he was a prophet without honor in his own state. During the final crisis of 1860–61, Ruffin was so disgusted with Virginia's cowardly reluctance to secede, so alienated by Virginia's calculating view towards joining the Southern Confederacy that he rushed to South Carolina. "If Virginia remains in the Union, under the domination of this infamous, low, vulgar tyranny of Black Republicanism and there is no other state in the Union that has bravely thrown off the yoke," Ruffin bitterly declared in Charleston, "I will seek my domicile in that state and abandon Virginia forever. If Virginia will not act as South Carolina, I have no longer a home, and I am a banished man." [4] As a pro-slavery cavalier, Ruffin felt more comfortable among South Carolinians committed to the principle of slavery rather than among Virginians concerned

[3] Charlottesville *Review*, December 14, 1860, in Washington *National Intelligencer*, December 15, 1860.

[4] Ruffin, quoted by Craven, *Ruffin*, p. 198. For a study of Ruffin in the context of the tension between Cavalier and Yankee, see Taylor, *Cavalier & Yankee*, pp. 312–318.

about the profitability of the domestic slave trade. Ruffin had hoped the pro-slavery crusade to reopen the African slave trade would "stir the sluggish blood of the South" and *redeem* Virginia from her abominable lethargy. But Edmund Ruffin did not despair: he knew the "letting of blood" and a certain "64 pound Columbiad" cannon aimed at Fort Sumter would bring him and Virginia together again.[5]

Not all border states were as concerned as Virginia about the domestic slave trade. Tennessee had only a limited interest in the sale of slaves to the Gulf states: during the 1850's Tennessee's slave exportations amounted to less than a third of the slaves sold out of Virginia.[6] The need to protect the domestic slave trade was not an important motivation for Tennessee's opposition to the African slave trade. The hostility to the African slave-trade proposal in Tennessee was based largely on a moral repugnance for the trade as well as a commitment to Unionism as a means to preserve an institution of race control.

This may be seen in Representative Emerson Etheridge, Tennessee's leading critic of the African slave trade. Author of the 1856 Congressional resolution condemning the extremist effort to reopen the trade, Etheridge was morally opposed to the African slave trade. "If the trade were legalized tomorrow," he declared to his fellow Congressmen, "I would first have to consider myself an outlaw from the society of good men everywhere, before I would, for any reason, engage in it, and I think it would be no cause for national sorrow if every ship thus manned and thus destined were to go down to the bottom of the sea."[7] But like most Southern opponents of the African slave trade, Etheridge had no anti-slavery intentions: to the contrary, he was against the African slave trade because he was for slavery. A slaveholder himself, Etheridge sought to

[5] Ruffin, quoted in Craven, pp. 171, 212; Ruffin, Diary, May 15, 1857, Ruffin Papers, Library of Congress.

[6] Bancroft, *Slave-Trading in the Old South,* pp. 386, 403.

[7] Etheridge, in *The Congressional Globe,* 34 Congress, 3rd Session, Appendix, p. 336. See also Etheridge, in *Republican Banner and Nashville Whig,* March 6, 1857.

frustrate the African slave-trade advocates' secessionist efforts, for he feared the chaos of disunion would destroy slavery and the "liberty of the white race." [8] Etheridge was determined to keep the black man in his place. Even after legal emancipation and the Civil War, Etheridge continued to defend white control over blacks. "The negroes are no more free than they were forty years ago," he declared in 1867, "and if one goes about the country telling them they are free, shoot him. . . ." [9] Clearly, Etheridge, like Ruffin, was committed to white supremacy and the peculiar institution.

The editor of the Trenton [Tennessee] *Independent Journal* did not understand that Etheridge was actually a pro-slavery critic of the African slave-trade agitation, and denounced Etheridge as "the Black Republican Representative of the 9th Congressional District of Tennessee." [10] In a more perceptive evaluation of Etheridge's opposition to the African slave trade, the editor of the Nashville *Union and American* sharply criticized Etheridge's repugnance of the trade as an obvious moral inconsistency. "The abstract morality of the slave trade," he argued, "is identical with the morality of slavery. There would be no more immorality, if the laws permitted it, in the act of buying a slave from his despotic master in Africa, than from his humane master in Tennessee." [11] Like Spratt and Fitzhugh, the Nashville editor saw a logical moral correlation between slavery and the African slave trade.

Pitted against Etheridge in Tennessee was the Irish patriot and African slave-trade agitator, John Mitchel. In 1857 Mitchel began the publication of the Knoxville *Southern Citizen*, a newspaper dedicated to the agitation for the reopening of the traffic in African slaves. In the prospectus of the newspaper,

[8] United States Bureau of the Census, 1860 Census Population Schedules, Tennessee Slave Schedule, Weakly County, p. 50, MSS microfilm copy in the University of North Carolina Library; Etheridge, *The Congressional Globe*, p. 366.

[9] Etheridge, quoted in Knoxville *Whig*, April 24, 1867.

[10] Trenton *Independent Journal*, in Nashville *Union and American*, January 14, 1857.

[11] Nashville *Union and American*, January 21, 1857.

Mitchel announced that slavery was a "sound, just, wholesome institution," and that the newspaper would address itself to the African slave trade and the economic needs of the South.[12] Mitchel's interest in the African slave trade was stimulated by Leonidas W. Spratt. "The precise line of politics (American politics) which I have followed," wrote Mitchel to Spratt in 1859, "was promoted and governed by you, more than any other merely personal influence." [13] Unlike Spratt, however, Mitchel did not have an actual concern for the South and slavery. In his diary, Mitchel confessed that while he was defending the South and demanding African slaves, he was thinking of Ireland and contending for the South as the "Ireland of this continent." [14] Since he viewed the Southern struggle for independence from the North in terms of the conflict between Ireland and England, his involvement in the pro-slavery crusade was psychologically satisfying to him as an Irish patriot. As an African slave-trade advocate, Mitchel was also defiantly twisting the lion's tail. In a letter to Father John Kenyon, Mitchel explained that the institutions and aspirations of the South represented a special hostility to the British system. While the South was trying "one form of civilization," England had tried "the other" and was "going shortly to ruin." And he added: "I want to promote the success of the one and the ruin of the other." [15] For the fire-eating Mitchel, the advocacy of the African slave trade served a unique personal need: his quest for Irish independence and his hatred of England.

Despite his zealous activity, Mitchel could not persuade Tennessee to support or even condone the importation of African slaves. Like Etheridge, most Tennesseans felt morally uncomfortable about the African slave trade. In a "private" letter

[12] Knoxville *Southern Citizen,* in *De Bow's Review,* XXIII (October, 1857), p. 447; Mitchel, in Dillon, *Mitchel,* II, p. 100; Charleston *Standard,* in Nashville *Union and American,* September 18, 1857; Knoxville *Southern Citizen,* in Jackson *Semi-Weekly Mississippian,* December 14, 1858.

[13] Mitchel to Spratt, July 30, 1859, in Charleston *Mercury,* August 4, 1859.

[14] Mitchel, in Dillon, *Mitchel,* II, p. 101.

[15] Mitchel to Kenyon, in *ibid.,* II, pp. 105–106.

to Spratt in 1858, Dr. James G. M. Ramsey, a Tennessee advocate of the African slave trade, admitted the people of his state would not "sanction" the African slave trade at that time. It "may be necessary to delay for a few years the renewal of the slave traffic without shocking too suddenly the prejudices or the judgment of the border States." [16]

But the border states' antagonism to the African slave trade should not be overemphasized. Opposition to the African slave trade was also present in the cotton-growing states. Clearly, as our analysis of the African slave-trade controversy in Georgia, Louisiana, Mississippi, Texas, and South Carolina will show, the proposal to reopen the trade involved much more than an effort to increase the Southern slave labor supply.

Dr. Ramsey's evaluation of public opinion towards the African slave trade in Tennessee could have been applied to Georgia. "Prejudices" against the African slave trade also existed in the cotton-growing state of Georgia. Georgia leaders like Governor Hershel Johnson, Senator Robert Toombs, and United States Secretary of the Treasury Howell Cobb announced their moral disapproval of the African slave trade. Much of their opposition was also politically motivated. As Unionists and as political allies and patronage friends of President James Buchanan, they were moored to the National Democratic Party. Governor Johnson expressed this fusion of moral and political concerns in his 1857 message to the state legislature. The proposal to reopen the African slave trade, he declared, was adverse to the sentiments of the civilized world and divisive for the National Democracy.[17]

[16] Ramsey to Spratt, April 29, 1858, Ramsey Papers, University of North Carolina Library; *Republican Banner & Nashville Whig,* January 15, 1857; Memphis *Eagle and Enquirer,* in *Republican Banner and Nashville Whig,* January 29, 1857; John Wright, in *Congressional Globe,* 34 Congress, 3rd Session, p. 125.

[17] Johnson, message, in *Republican Banner and Nashville Whig,* January 27, 1857. For information on the African slave-trade controversy in Georgia, see Milledgeville *Federal Union,* December 16, 1856; Savannah *Republican,* December 13, 1858; Savannah *News,* May 25, 1858, June 17, 1858, December 18, 1858; Brunswick *Herald,* September 21, 1858.

But the moderate political lid of Cobb and Toombs was almost blown off in 1859. In a speech at Augusta, one of their close political associates—Congressman Alexander Stephens—declared that the South could not expect "to see many of the territories come into the Union as slave states, unless we have an increase of African stock. The law of population will prevent us. We have not the people. . . . It takes people to make States; and it requires people of the African race to make slave states." [18] Stephens's speech fell like a bomb on the Georgia political scene. Friends of Stephens were surprised and bewildered. In a letter to Stephens, M. J. Crawford described his reaction to the reports on the Augusta speech: "The Chronicle charged that you 'advocated' the reopening of the slave trade. I heard that on the Streets and I offered to bet 85 negroes upon it all I had, and then stated what I believed that you had said—but soon the Constitutionalist gave us the positions taken and put a stop to the false account given by that . . . most unprincipled of all newspapers." [19] The advocates of the African slave trade, on the other hand, welcomed Stephens into their camp. Spratt sent Stephens a pamphlet on the African slave trade by John Cowden of Mississippi, and in an accompanying letter, he wrote: "In common with many others in the South he seems to have come to the conclusion that you are an advocate for the foreign slave trade. . . ." [20] But the African slave-trade advocates had misunderstood the Georgia leader. Stephens himself explained to his brother: "I did not advocate the reopening of the Slave Trade. I simply told the people that we should have but few if any more Slave States . . . unless there was an increase of African stock. . . . If we lost the new

[18] Stephens, in Henry Cleveland, *Alexander H. Stephens in Public and Private with Letters and Speeches before, during, and since the War* (Chicago: National Publishing Company, 1866), p. 646.

[19] Crawford, to Stephens, July 7, 1859, Stephens Papers, Library of Congress. See also J. H. Smith to A. Stephens, July 24, 1859, *ibid.*; P. Thweatt to A. Stephens, July 8, 1859, *ibid.*; Linton Stephens to A. Stephens, July 3, 1859, Stephens Papers, Manhattanville College of the Sacred Heart, microfilm copy in the Library of Congress.

[20] Spratt to Stephens, August 23, 1859, Stephens Papers, Library of Congress.

States it would not be because of abolition or the injustice of the South but for the want of the people to make Slave States. I told them I considered our institutions safe in the union or out of it." [21]

Actually Stephens wanted to secure Southern rights and interests within the Union. Like Cobb and Toombs, he had supported the Compromise of 1850 as a means to save both the South and the Union. As a Congressman, he had been instrumental in the enactment of the Kansas-Nebraska Act, an invitation for Southern expansion into the territories and a hope for Southern power within the Union. "I agree with you thoroughly," Stephens wrote to a friend in January 1857, "that the very best thing that could happen for the Country would be for Kansas to come in as a Slave State." [22] The defeat of the Lecompton Constitution in 1858, however, drove Stephens into deep pessimism about the future of the South. Like Spratt, he now realized that the South could not expand into the territories without African slaves and that the South was doomed to powerlessness within the Union. "This great truth," Stephens explained in a private letter to J. Henly Smith in July 1859, "seems to take the people by surprise. Some shrink from it as they would from death. Still it is true as death." [23] His choice of the word "death" was deliberate: it expressed the intenseness of his despair. Yet Stephens, undoubtedly aware the reopening of the trade would mean the destruction of the Union, shrank from Spratt's conclusion—the South should reopen the African slave trade.

While Congressman Stephens was viewing the African slave-trade issue in the context of power realities, many of his fellow Georgians were involved in a debate over the African slave trade as a moral question. Their debate focused on the

[21] A. Stephens to L. Stephens, July 5, 1859, Stephens Papers, Manhattanville College of the Sacred Heart, microfilm copy in Library of Congress.

[22] Stephens to Thomas W. Thomas, January 16, 1857, Stephens Papers, Duke University Library.

[23] Stephens to Smith, July 29, 1859, in Phillips (ed.), *Correspondence of Toombs, Stephens, Cobb*, p. 446.

Georgia constitutional prohibition of the African slave trade. For many Georgia legislators, this state prohibition was more repugnant than the federal laws against the traffic. On November 5, 1858, State Representative Luffman and State Senator Alexander Atkinson introduced bills to strike out of the Georgia Constitution the section prohibiting the importation of African slaves.[24] Senator Atkinson explained that this section had to be removed because "the Southern people ought to pluck the beam out of their own eyes before they attempt to cast the mote out of the eyes of our Northern brethren. If we first purge our Constitution and our laws of these abolition heresies, we can then consistently ask the North to believe with us; but while we acknowledge the evil of slavery by prohibiting it from our shores, can we expect to call it anything but a sin?" [25] Atkinson's point was clear: Georgians had to resolve the moral contradiction between their state constitution and their peculiar institution. Like Spratt, Yancey, and other African slave-trade radicals, Senator Atkinson was demanding that Southerners "purge" themselves of "abolition heresy" and clarify their own confusion about the morality of slavery.

After a bitter debate, the senate defeated Atkinson's bill by a close vote of 46 yeas to 47 nays, and the house tabled Luffman's bill by a vote of 72 yeas to 61 nays.[26] Many Georgians voted against the revision of the state constitution because they feared the African slave trade as a divisive issue in the South. But the opposition involved more than a strategic concern for Southern unity. Like Congressman Etheridge of Tennessee,

[24] *Journal of the House of Representatives of the State of Georgia, 1858* (Columbus, 1858), p. 45; *Journal of the Senate of the State of Georgia, 1858* (Columbus, 1858), p. 48; New York *Anti-Slavery Standard*, December 25, 1858.

[25] Atkinson, in New York *Anti-Slavery Standard*, December 25, 1858.

[26] Savannah *Morning News*, November 23, 1858; Milledgeville *Federal Union*, November 23, 1858; New Orleans *Picayune*, December 11, 1858; Washington *National Intelligencer*, November 27, 1858; *Georgia Senate Journal, 1858*, pp. 211–212. Subsequently the senate adopted a motion to reconsider the bill. This reconsideration, however, was based on the understanding that the bill should lie on the table and not be called up that year. See *Georgia Senate Journal, 1858*, pp. 214–215.

many Georgia legislators considered the African slave trade morally repulsive. Consequently, though they knew the Luffman and Atkinson bills could not actually reopen the African slave trade, they still found it impossible to vote for the repeal of the state prohibition of the traffic. Thus the Georgia advocates of the African slave trade narrowly failed to blot out what they called "a *stain* of the fair *escutcheon* of Georgia." [27] In their disappointment, they undoubtedly wondered how the people of Georgia could tolerate a constitution condemning the institution.

The African slave-trade agitation in Louisiana was far more radical than Senator Atkinson's reformist movement aimed at constitutional revision in Georgia. Louisiana fire-eaters like Henry St. Paul, Edward Delony, and James Brigham were engaged in a daring strategy to evade the federal laws and import African slaves disguised as "apprentices." Their African apprentice scheme was designed to meet Louisiana's great demand for slave labor, arrest the monopolization of slaves in Louisiana, and check the slave drain from the border states.[28]

The storm center of the agitation for African "apprentices" was the Louisiana state legislature. On January 28, 1858, State Senator Henry St. Paul announced his intention to introduce an African apprentice bill. "The Hotspur of the Senate, Henry St. Paul of New Orleans," the Baton Rouge correspondent of the New Orleans *Daily Delta* reported, "today went through the preliminary form of initiating the boldest stroke of State policy known in the annals of Southern legislation for half a century. When the notice was read by the Secretary, such of the Senators as were not prepared for anything so utterly astounding gazed around them as though they were under the impression that a mine had exploded. It was the theme of much conversation and varied comments in the House." [29] On March

[27] Senator Billups, in Savannah *Morning News*, November 23, 1858.
[28] Brigham, in *De Bow's Review*, XXVI (April, 1859), p. 482; Delony, "The South Demands More Negro Labor," *ibid.*, XXV (1858), pp. 491–506.
[29] New Orleans *Daily Delta*, January 31, 1858, in Stella Herron,

3 the House passed a bill authorizing James H. Brigham and his associates to import 2500 "free" Africans indentured as apprentices for 15 years.[30] Clearly these Africans would not be "free." The supporters of the bill, the editor of the Baton Rouge *Advocate* observed, were openly discussing their plan to sell the Africans into *"servitude for life ... at $500 per head."* [31] Commenting on the Brigham bill in his diary, Edmund Ruffin candidly admitted that it was "very obvious that these 'free negroes' could only be obtained in slaves purchased from Africa." Since the term of apprenticeship could be extended from 15 to 50 years, Ruffin concluded, the Louisiana African apprentice system "for all practical purposes" would mean the renewal of the African slave trade.[32]

But the African apprentice bill still required the approval of the Louisiana Senate. On March 12 St. Paul and his colleagues asked the senate to consider the bill. After a 12 to 12 tie vote, Lieutenant Governor Charles H. Mouton, the president of the senate, dramatically gave the bill his blessing. "In giving my casting vote upon this question," he declared, "I feel the responsibility of the act; but having come to the conclusion that the time has arrived for the South to think, to act, and to provide for herself, I vote *yea.*" [33] Three days later Colonel B. B. Simms, who had voted for the bill, decided he should consult his constituents before the legislature took further action on the bill. Consequently he moved to postpone the bill indefinitely, and the senate adopted his motion by a vote of 15 to

"The African Apprentice Bill," *Proceedings of the Mississippi Valley Historical Association,* VIII (1914–15), pp. 138–139.

[30] *Official Journal of the House of Representatives of the State of Louisiana, Session of 1858* (Baton Rouge: Printed at the Office of the *Daily Advocate,* 1858), pp. 64–65; Jackson *Semi-Weekly Mississippian* March 23, 1858.

[31] Baton Rouge *Daily Advocate,* in Richmond *Enquirer,* April 9, 1858.

[32] Ruffin, Diary, March 5, 1858, Ruffin Papers, Library of Congress. See also New Orleans *Daily Delta,* February 5, 1858; Richmond *Whig,* March 16, 1858; Savannah *Morning News,* March 16, 1858; New Orleans *Picayune,* March 16, 1858.

[33] *Official Journal of the Senate of the State of Louisiana, Session of 1858* (Baton Rouge: Printed at the Office of the *Daily Advocate,* 1858), p. 115.

13.[34] Thus the advocates of the African slave trade almost won the support of the Louisiana legislature.

Angry opposition to the African apprentice bill came from Louisiana Whigs. The editor of the New Orleans *Bulletin,* a voice of Whig opinion in Louisiana, blasted the state house of representatives for its hasty passage of the bill. "We doubt whether a piece of higher-handed despotic usurpation was ever enacted by any State Legislature in this country, or one that exhibited more utter recklessness or disregard alike of the public interest or public opinion."[35] As supporters of Southern industrial development, many Whigs feared the African slave trade would help to perpetuate the old agricultural order in the South. In a protest against the proposal to import Africans, the editor of the New Orleans *Picayune* argued that it was "worse than folly to arrest the present direction of capital and enterprise by plans whose effect . . . would restore the former tendency of all Southern enterprise to the channel of agriculture."[36] As sugar planters and merchants, many Whigs in Louisiana were dependent on the sugar tariff and were commercially connected to the Mississippi Valley.[37] Economically committed to the preservation of the Union, Louisiana Whigs were anxious to suppress St. Paul's sectionalist agitation to reopen the African slave trade.

The boiling controversy over the African apprentice bill spilled over into the power struggle between the Pierre Soule and John Slidell factions of the Louisiana Democratic Party. During the 1850 crisis, the Louisiana Democrats had been divided into two factions: the Soule or anti-Compromise Democrats, and the Slidell or pro-Compromise Democrats. Slidell, a

[34] *Ibid.,* p. 118; Henry Hughes, *State Liberties, or, The Right to African Contract Labor* (Port Gibson: Office of the *Southern Reveille,* 1858), p. 5.

[35] New Orleans *Bulletin,* in Washington *National Intelligencer,* March 24, 1858; New Orleans *Picayune,* March 21, 1858, April 13, 1858; New Orleans *Bee* (French edition), January 30, 1858.

[36] New Orleans *Picayune,* May 28, 1858.

[37] Shugg, *Class Struggle in Louisiana,* pp. 152, 157–158. Much opposition to the bill came from senators representing the sugar parishes. *Louisiana Senate Journal, 1858,* p. 118.

moderate, believed the South should try to rule within the Union. In 1852 he told Howell Cobb: "As to the Rhetts, Yanceys, etc., the sooner and the more effectively we get rid of them the better. . . ." [38] A year later Soule accepted an appointment as minister to Spain; and Slidell, undoubtedly happy to "get rid" of his rival, became the boss of the Louisiana Democracy. In 1855 Soule returned to Louisiana and launched a determined effort to capture the party but Slidell quickly reinforced his control over the Louisiana Democratic Party. In 1856 he helped to secure the Presidency for James Buchanan and strategically tied his hegemony in Louisiana to the national administration and federal patronage.[39]

The agitation for the African apprentice bill in 1858 threatened this political alliance between Slidell and Buchanan. Newspaper correspondents for the New Orleans *Delta* and the New Orleans *Crescent* reported that pressure from Washington had persuaded Colonel Simms to withdraw his support from the bill and that senators were warned its passage would "seriously embarrass" President Buchanan.[40] In his criticism of the bill, the editor of the Baton Rouge *Daily Advocate,* a Slidell newspaper, argued that the measure would precipitate a collision between state and federal authorities.[41] Such a collision would strain the relationship between Slidell and Buchanan and endanger a basis of Slidell's political power—President Buchanan's patronage. The day after the Louisiana Senate voted to postpone the bill, State Senator Thomas O. Moore, one of Slidell's lieutenants, privately remarked: "Last night defeated the African bill. Thank God nearly through." [42]

[38] Slidell to Cobb, quoted in Louis M. Sears, *John Slidell* (Durham: Duke University Press, 1925), p. 89.

[39] P. Soule to G. N. Sanders, April 10, 1856, Soule Papers, Louisiana State University Library; Shugg, pp. 154, 158–59; Leon C. Soule, *The Know Nothing Party in New Orleans: A Reappraisal* (Baton Rouge: Louisiana Historical Association, 1961), p. 107; John Slidell, letter, April 11, 1856, B. F. Flanders Papers, Louisiana State University Library.

[40] New Orleans *Daily Delta*, March 16, 1858; New Orleans *Daily Crescent*, March 16 and 17, 1858; Herron, *op. cit.*, p. 140.

[41] Baton Rouge *Daily Advocate,* in Richmond *Enquirer*, April 9, 1858.

[42] T. O. Moore, remark by T. O. Moore, written on the back of a

Significantly two leading pro-Soule newspapers—the New Orleans *Crescent* and the New Orleans *Delta*—applauded the African apprentice bill. They praised Senator Henry St. Paul for his "pluck" and called the apprentice scheme legal and practical.[43] But their support for the African slave trade forced these pro-Soule editors into a contradictory situation. In his opposition to Slidell and Buchanan, Soule swung his support to Senator Stephen A. Douglas for the 1860 Democratic Presidential nomination. If Douglas won the nomination and election in 1860, Soule would have control over the federal patronage in Louisiana. If Soule possessed the federal patronage, he would have the power to wreck Slidell's party machine. Thus while the editors of the *Crescent* and *Delta* were demanding the importation of African apprentices, they were also endorsing Senator Douglas, an uncompromising critic of the African slave trade! [44]

Like Louisiania, Mississippi had highly complex patterns of African slave-trade support and opposition. The agitation for the reopening of the trade in Mississippi was linked to partisan as well as intraparty politics, concerns about the proper Southern strategy for the defense of slavery, and class and geographical divisions within the state.

Mississippi Whigs dominated the opposition to the African slave-trade agitation. Whigs like Henry S. Foote and I. M. Patridge battled against African slave-trade advocates like De Bow and Spratt in the Southern Commercial Conventions. They also addressed large public meetings and organized a determined movement against the trade issue. In their newspapers, they rapped the agitation to reopen the African slave trade as an effort to destroy the Union.[45] Since most of these Mississippi

letter by A. Miltenberger to Moore, March 15, 1858, Moore Papers, Louisiana State University Library.

[43] New Orleans *Daily Crescent,* March 22, 1858, in Herron, *op. cit.,* p. 143; New Orleans *Delta,* February 9, 1858, in Savannah *Morning News,* February 22, 1858.

[44] New Orleans *Daily Crescent,* May 11, and June 20, 1859; New Orleans *Delta,* June 1, 1858, May 10, 1859.

[45] Jackson *Semi-Weekly Mississippian,* June 21, 1859, and July 5,

Whigs were large slaveholders and since their plantations were located in the counties close to the Mississippi River and vulnerable to Northern military attack, they had a special commitment to the protection of slavery within the Union and a special anxiety about the prospect of secession and war. Leading African slave-trade critics William L. Sharkey of Warren County, owner of 65 slaves, expressed the fears of many Whig planters in Mississippi when he declared: "If a State goes out of the Union she must prepare to wade through blood. Are we prepared to give up all our comforts, all our prosperity, everything and plunge into fierce and unrelenting civil war, simply because a man is elected under the forms of the Constitution?" [46] As Southerners directly interested in the institution of slavery, many Mississippi Whig planters looked upon the destruction of the Union as "the greatest of calamities" and viewed the African slave-trade issue as a disunionist proposition and a prelude to disaster.[47]

But the Whigs did not have a monopoly on the African slave-trade opposition in Mississippi. Both leaders of the Mississippi Democratic Party—Senator Jefferson Davis and Senator Albert Gallatin Brown—were against the reopening of the African slave trade. Their opposition, however, was motivated by different concerns.

Senator Davis, formerly a leader of the Southern resistance against the Compromise of 1850, was now campaigning for a North-South Democratic coalition to defend Southern interests. During his visit to New England in 1858, he made a strong and friendly bid for the support of the Northern wing of the National Democratic Party. Consequently, while Davis criticized the "offensive" and "infamous" federal laws against the trade, he also called the agitation to repeal the laws "utterly

1859; Foote, *War of the Rebellion,* p. 256; Rainwater, *Mississippi,* pp. 77–79; Vicksburg *Whig,* in Jackson *Semi-Weekly Mississippian,* August 26, 1859.

[46] Sharkey, in Natchez *Courier,* October 25, 1860, quoted in Rainwater, p. 150; United States Census Bureau, 1860 Census Population Schedules, Mississippi Slave Schedule, Warren County, pp. 141–142.

[47] Vicksburg *Whig,* October 24, 1860, quoted in Rainwater, p. 141.

impracticable" and declared his opposition to the importation of African slaves.[48] Undoubtedly Davis saw the agitation as a threat to his coalition strategy. In a letter to Davis, one of his friends frankly expressed this concern for National Democratic unity. "You may have noticed that in the Southern Convention [at Vicksburg]," wrote H. J. Harris of the Vicksburg *Sentinel* on June 7, 1859, "I voted against repealing the laws against reopening the slave trade. It was a bitter pill to vote with Foote; but I honestly thought that the Democratic party would be destroyed by the agitation of the question *at the time. . . .*"[49]

Davis's arch political rival—Senator Brown—was also against the African slave trade. Unlike Davis, Brown believed the difference between the North and the South was "radical and irreconcilable."[50] Consequently, he was prepared to destroy the Union. But Brown could not agitate for the reopening of the African slave trade as a means to hasten the breakup of the nation. His constituents were largely yeoman farmers living on the poor piney woodlands of Southeastern Mississippi; they would not benefit from the introduction of African slaves. Many of Brown's supporters were intensely racist: they feared the Negro as a dangerous physical threat and as a despised economic competitor. Clearly they did not want "an influx of untold millions of wild Africans."[51]

Most Mississippi States Rights Democrats critical of the African slave-trade agitation feared that the trade issue jeopardized party unity. By June 1859, even Democratic advocates of the African slave trade like Ethelbert Barksdale of the Jackson *Semi-Weekly Mississippian* had begun to limit their support. If the African slave trade became a party issue, they argued, it could divide and distract the Democratic States Rights party, and thereby destroy the efficiency of the organiza-

48 Davis, in Rowland, *Davis,* IV, p. 69; Rainwater, p. 62.

49 Harris to Davis, in Rowland, *Davis,* IV, pp. 55–56.

50 Brown, quoted in Rainwater, p. 62.

51 Brown, speech at Monticello, in Jackson *Mississippian,* June 14, 1859; Brown, in Jackson *Semi-Weekly Mississippian,* June 28, 1859; Ranck, *Brown,* p. 3.

tion essential for the Southern defense of slavery.[52] After the Mississippi State Democratic Convention of 1859 took no action on the trade question, editor Barksdale commented: "The Convention simply determined not to make the issue in any of its forms, a part of the Democratic creed; but to leave each member of the party to exercise his own private judgment, and to freedom of action, entirely untrammelled by party obligation." [53]

This compromise helped to keep the Mississippi Democratic Party together and allowed certain Democrats to continue their agitation for the African slave trade. Support for the trade revival in Mississippi was drawn largely from the ranks of the Democratic Party and leaders like Richard T. Archer, Ethelbert Barksdale, John McRae, and Henry Hughes.[54] Strong support for the trade came from Democratic newspapers, including the influential Jackson *Semi-Weekly Mississippian,* the Yazoo *Democrat,* the Natchez *Free Trader,* the Holly Springs *Democrat,* and the Vicksburg *True Southerner.*[55] "Twenty Democratic papers in this State," observed the Oxford *Mercury* in 1859, "are in favor of re-opening the African Slave Trade. About three are opposed to it." [56] Though the 1859 State Democratic Convention chose to ignore the trade issue, many Democratic county conventions approved resolutions for the reopening of the African slave trade.[57]

[52] Jackson *Semi-Weekly Mississippian,* June 7, 1859, July 12, 1859.
[53] Jackson *Semi-Weekly Mississippian,* September 9, 1859.
[54] Jackson *Semi-Weekly Mississippian,* September 27, 1858; April 22, June 14, July 12, 1859; Jackson *Daily Mississippian,* November 24, 1859; Sydnor, *Slavery in Mississippi,* p. 143; Charleston *Mercury,* October 23, 1858.
[55] Jackson *Semi-Weekly Mississippian,* February 6, February 21, 1858; June 14, 1859; Sea Coast *Democrat,* in *Semi-Weekly Mississippian,* August 9, 1859; Yazoo *Democrat,* in *Semi-Weekly Mississippian,* June 17, 1859; Natchez *Free Trader,* February 5, 1859, in Rainwater, *Mississippi,* pp. 76–77; Holly Springs *Democrat,* in *Semi-Weekly Mississippian,* June 17, 1859; DeKalb *Democrat,* in *Semi-Weekly Mississippian,* June 7, 1859; Vicksburg *True Southerner,* in Phillips, *Plantation and Frontier Documents,* Vol. II, pp. 54–55.
[56] Oxford *Mercury,* in Jackson *Semi-Weekly Mississippian,* September 9, 1859.
[57] Meeting of the Democratic Party of Copiah County at Gallatin on April 25, 1859, in Jackson *Semi-Weekly Mississippian,* May 3, 1859;

In their response to the great demand for slave labor in their state, Henry Hughes and his colleagues designed a scheme for the circumvention of the federal laws against the African slave trade. Like State Senator Henry St. Paul and his fellow African slave-trade radicals in Louisiana, they proposed to import Africans as "apprentices" or "voluntary laborers" into Mississippi. On November 19, 1857, State Representative D. S. Pattison introduced a bill for the Charter of the African Labor Immigration Company. Pattison's bill authorized the company to transport Africans to Mississippi. These Africans would be bound and obligated by negotiable labor obligations to work for their masters for 29 years. In a letter to Ethelbert Barksdale, Senator Hughes explained that the Pattison bill violated neither the letter nor the spirit of the federal laws and that its passage would realize a prompt supply of African labor. Although the laws prohibited the importation of slaves, Congress had not outlawed the immigration of Africans voluntarily obligating themselves to labor for a term of years. Thus, Hughes concluded, the scheme to import "voluntary laborers" was legal. Of course these African immigrants, Hughes added frankly, would be slaves in actuality. "Some have asked what shall be done with the African negroes after their term of service has expired. It is answered that the State has the right and power to fix their status. I propose that they shall be elevated into slavery. . . ." [58] Senator Hughes and his friends found that the legislature had little real interest in their program to meet Mississippi's labor needs.[59]

But the African slave-trade movement in Mississippi repre-

Democratic Party meeting at Scooba on April 30, 1859; in *Semi-Weekly Mississippian*, May 10, 1859; Democratic Party meeting of Lawrence County on May 16, 1859, in *Semi-Weekly Mississippian*, May 28, 1859; Democratic Party meeting at Hancock, in *Semi-Weekly Mississippian*, June 17, 1859; Primary meeting of the Democratic voters of Beat No. 5, Choctaw Agency of Oktibbeha County, in *Semi-Weekly Mississippian*, July 29, 1859; meeting of the Democratic Party of Claiborne County at Port Gibson, in *Semi-Weekly Mississippian*, August 18, 1859.

[58] Hughes, in Jackson *Semi-Weekly Mississippian*, January 12, 1858.

[59] *Mississippi State Journal, 1858,* p. 68; *Mississippi House Journal, 1858,* pp. 95, 182

sented more than an economic demand for slave labor: it also served a psychological need to purge the federal as well as Mississippi laws stigmatizing the institution of slavery. In 1858 Mississippi advocates tried to persuade the state senate to accept a resolution demanding the repeal of the federal law making the African slave trade piracy. Their resolution was referred to the Committee on State and Federal Relations, where it remained. The editor of the Paulding *Clarion* reported that the resolution was "sent to sleep without a particle of encouragement." [60] A year later the advocates of the African slave trade made a new move: they attempted to repeal the state law prohibiting the importation of African slaves into Mississippi. In the Mississippi House of Representatives, D. C. Graham of Franklin introduced a bill to repeal the state law making it illegal to hold foreign-born slaves.[61] Unlike the immigration bill, the purpose of the Graham bill was not to reopen the trade but to remove a Southern law virtually declaring the African slave trade a moral and social evil. Like Georgia State Senator Alexander Atkinson, Mississippi legislators like Graham and Hughes were trying to abolish a moral contradiction of Southern society. But the Mississippi House of Representatives postponed the subject indefinitely by a vote of 68 to 22. The postponement of Graham's bill had a distressing and crucial meaning for Mississippi advocates of the African slave trade: Mississippi,

[60] *Mississippi Senate Journal, 1858,* pp. 6, 7, 125; Paulding *Clarion,* in New Orleans *Picayune,* May 29, 1859.

[61] *Mississippi House Journal, 1859–1860,* pp. 46, 227. "Art. 29. It shall not be lawful for any person whatsoever to bring into this State, or knowingly to hold therein, any slave born or resident out of the United States, or any slave that shall have been convicted of any offence and therefore transported by the laws of this State, territory or district, or that shall have been secretly or clandestinely run to avoid a prosecution for a criminal offence; and any such person who shall bring into this State, any such slave, or shall sell or purchase therein any such slave, knowing such slave to have been brought into this State contrary to the provisions for this act, shall forfeit and pay to the State, for each slave so brought in, sold or purchased, a fine of one thousand dollars, on conviction before a court of competent jurisdiction." From *The Revised Code of the Statute Laws of the State of Mississippi* (Jackson: E. Barksdale, 1857), p. 235.

like Georgia, had refused to repeal a Southern prohibition of the African slave trade and to repudiate a Southern moral indictment of slavery.[62]

While Mississippians were debating the immigration scheme and the proposal to repeal the state prohibition, Texans were locked in an acrimonious feud over the issue of the African slave trade. The feud broke out into open political warfare during the contest between States Rights Democrat Hardin R. Runnels and Independent Democrat Sam Houston for the governorship in 1859.

Runnels and many of his supporters had spearheaded the Texas agitation to import African slaves during the 1850's. As railroad builders and planters, African slave-trade advocates like Runnels, Francis Lubbock, and Willard Richardson of the Galveston *News* wanted a supply of cheap slaves for the expansion of cotton cultivation in Texas. Thus they clamored for the reopening of the African slave trade and also enthusiastically supported the filibuster campaign in Nicaragua—an effort to annex territory for the extension of Southern slavery and to establish a base for the African slave trade.[63] As African slave-trade advocates, they were also concerned about the need for a defense of slavery on moral grounds. Like Senator Atkinson in Georgia and Representative Graham in Mississippi, they sought to reform Southern society. Thus they demanded the removal of the African slave-trade prohibition from the Texas Constitution and the Texas code of laws. The Texas restriction on the African slave trade, they argued, represented an embarrassing self-condemnation. "The admonition that the slave trade is immoral is fatal to slavery," warned Richardson; "every editor

[62] Natchez *Free Trader*, November 5, 1859; *Mississippi House Journal, 1859–1860*, pp. 324–325; *Mississippi House Journal, 1859–1860*, pp. 324–325.

[63] Austin *State Gazette*, March 1, 1856, in Anna Irene Sandbo, "Beginnings of the Secession Movement in Texas," *The Southwestern Historical Quarterly*, XVIII, No. 1 (July, 1914), p. 60; Galveston *Weekly News*, February 26, June 20, July 2, August 6, 8, 22, 29, September 5, 1857; Houston *Telegraph*, September 19, 1856, March 18, July 1, 1857; Fornell, *The Galveston Era*, pp. 108, 144, 204.

who holds this view condemns slavery and Texas whether he knows it or not." [64] Like William Yancey of Alabama, Texas advocates used their agitation to expose Southern "unsoundness" on slavery; they even slandered slaveholding Texans like State Senator M. M. Potter, an African slave-trade critic, "for want of good Southern principles." [65]

During his campaign for the governorship in 1859, however, Runnels tried to avoid the African slave-trade issue.[66] His chief aim was to win the election, not to give the Texas electorate a pro-slavery education. Runnels knew most Texans were against the African slave trade. A committee of the Texas House of Representatives had recommended that the legislature should take no action on the proposal to reopen the African slave trade because "the public mind of the country is not prepared for such a measure at this time." [67] Runnels also knew the Texas Democratic Party was divided over the African slave-trade question. At the 1859 State Democratic Convention, a wrangling debate on the African slave trade threatened to splinter the party and forced Runnels to skirt the African slave trade as an issue in the coming election.[68]

But in their campaign against Runnels, Sam Houston and his supporters effectively exploited the African slave-trade issue. They skillfully linked Runnels with the African slave trade. The Galveston *Civilian,* a pro-Houston newspaper, reprinted an editorial from the Tyler *Reporter* supporting both the African slave trade and Runnels. "The advocates of the African slave trade," remarked the editor of the *Civilian,* "openly and con-

[64] Galveston *News,* quoted in Houston *Telegraph,* February 28, 1859, in Fornell, p. 223.

[65] William Pitt Ballinger, Diary, May 30, 1859, quoted in Fornell, p. 271.

[66] Runnels to John Marshall, in Francis R. Lubbock, *Six Decades: or Memoirs of Francis Richard Lubbock, Governor of Texas in War Time, 1861–1863. A Personal Experience in Business, War and Politics* (Austin: B. C. Jones and Company, 1900), p. 247.

[67] Galveston *Weekly News,* December 1, 1857, January 9, 1858.

[68] *Ibid.,* May 7, 1859; Peter Gray, *Address on the African Slave Trade,* p. 2.

tinually proclaim that Messrs. Runnels and Lubbock [candidate for lieutenant governor] are in favor of the measure, and these gentlemen utterly refuse to deny the allegation." [69] The editor of the Victoria *Advocate* challenged Runnels to declare he would vote against the African slave trade. In a letter published in the Galveston *Civilian*, a Houston campaigner declared: "It can be no longer contended that the *Slave Trade* issue is not impending, notwithstanding the efforts of its friends in the canvass to ignore it publicly. They well knew to make that issue openly and frankly, on its merits, would crush them; and as far as Governor Runnels' and Lubbock's answer on this subject is concerned, it is regarded as no answer—a dodge!" [70]

The Houston campaign was designed to construct a powerful coalition of Know Nothings, Unionists, National Democrats, nonslaveholders, and German immigrants. Houston and his managers knew these groups could be united in a pro-Houston political movement against Runnels and the reopening of the African slave trade. In his denunciation of Runnels, Houston declared that the African slave-trade advocates were demagogues seeking to agitate for the destruction of the Union. [71] National Democrats like ex-Governor Elisha M. Pease, Hamilton Stuart of the Galveston *Civilian*, and George H. Sweet of the San Antonio *Herald* advised Texans to vote against advocates of the African slave trade and to support Houston, a Union man. [72] While the Houston forces appealed to the nationalistic emotions of Texas voters, they also made a strong bid for work-

[69] Tyler *Reporter*, in Galveston *Civilian*, July 12, 1859.

[70] Victoria *Advocate*, in Galveston *Civilian*, August 2, 1859; M. T. Johnson, letter dated July 2, 1859, in Galveston *Civilian*, August 2, 1859.

[71] Houston, letter to Galveston *Union*, in Boston *Liberator*, July 29, 1859.

[72] Galveston *Civilian*, July 12, August 2, 1859; Austin *State Gazette*, in Galveston *Weekly News*, May 28, 1859; San Antonio *Herald*, in Galveston *Civilian*, July 19, 1859; Nacogdoches *Chronicle*, in Williams and Barker (eds.), *Writings of Houston*, VII, p. 387; McKinney *Messenger*, in Galveston *Civilian*, August 2, 1859; Victoria *Advocate*, in Galveston *Civilian*, August 2, 1859; Austin *Southern Intelligencer*, in *De Bow's Review*, XXVI (February, 1859), p. 235.

ing class and German support. Houston called the African slave trade detrimental to the interests of the poor workingman.[73] Since many Germans in Texas had anti-slavery sentiments and since many German workers were competing with slaves, Houton's campaigners like Ferdinand Flake of the influential German newspaper *Die Union* were able to rally German support for Houston. They argued that slave labor had "a tendency to take bread from the poorer or laboring class of the German population of the State." They warned that the Runnels party was trying to reopen the African slave trade and to bring "hordes of Negroes" into Texas to compete with white workers and depreciate wages.[74] In their appeals to white workers and Germans, the Houston men had fused economic self-interest with racism.

The Houston campaign was a success: Houston crushed Runnels by a vote of 36,257 to 27,500. The editor of the Austin *State Gazette*, an African slave-trade paper, quickly pointed out that the Democratic convention and Runnels had refused to make the African slave trade an issue, and that the trade question therefore was not an influence in the election.[75] In a letter to the Richmond *Enquirer*, a writer from Marshall, Texas, asserted that Texas voters were influenced by images, not issues. He explained that the Houston managers represented Runnels "to be a man of less than ordinary intelligence and talent . . . until the *people*, really and honestly mistaken, considered him unfit for the Gubernatorial chair." They portrayed Houston, on the other hand, as a wise statesman and a war hero. "Such balderdash as this has fooled the ear of many a true Democrat,

[73] Houston, speech at Nacogdoches, in Galveston *Weekly News*, July 21, 1859, and Galveston *Civilian*, July 26, 1859.

[74] Galveston *Union*, in Galveston *Civilian*, July 12, 1859; Galveston *Union*, in Galveston *Weekly News*, July 9, 1859; *The Campaign Union*, in Galveston *Civilian*, July 9, 1859; Olmsted, *Texas*, pp. 432, 435, 437–439; Galveston *Weekly News*, July 23, 1859; Waco *Southerner*, in Galveston *Weekly News*, June 25, 1859.

[75] Austin *State Gazette*, in Jackson *Semi-Weekly Mississippian*, September 6, 1859; see also Jackson *Semi-Weekly Mississippian*, August 30, 1859.

and led him to support Houston. No issue of federal politics influenced the people in this election." [76]

The claims of the Austin editor and the writer from Marshall, however, were misleading. Although Runnels had refused to make the African slave trade an issue, Houston had successfully forced the trade question into the contest. Although the Houston managers had used images to influence voters, they were effective because they had identified Runnels with the African slave trade. Their anti-African slave-trade campaign was the basis of a coalition of several voting blocs, including the Know Nothings as well as the German immigrants. Even Lubbock, the candidate for lieutenant governor buried with Runnels under the Houston landslide, admitted that the African slave trade was the foremost factor in the election. "The Independents charged on the Democracy the design of reopening the African slave trade. The approximate unanimity with which the convention tabled a resolution barely squinting in that direction should have convinced all honest minds to the contrary. Affecting, however, to believe the charge to be true, the opposition newspapers kept up the accusation, as it was a winning card, the popular disapproval of such an abomination being well known." [77]

Shortly after the Texas gubernatorial election, the editor of the secessionist Charleston *Mercury* offered a sobering analysis of the Houston victory.

> The States Rights party of Texas have brought defeat upon themselves by making an impracticable and mischievous issue [the African slave trade]. Let it be a lesson to be remembered. The people of the South should be informed on the subject; but to make it a matter for voting, and a living issue, dividing our people, is a foolish and fatal move. Let the subject be considered calmly and thoroughly sifted by discussion merely. When the South is in a position to act on it, it will be time enough

[76] Letter signed "Pym," in Richmond *Enquirer*, September 2, 1859.
[77] Lubbock, *Memoirs*, p. 246. See also Clarksville (Texas) *Standard*, in Charleston *Mercury*, October 5, 1859; Charleston *Mercury*, August 13, 1859; and Milledgeville *Federal Union*, August 23, 1859.

to make it an issue. But until then, such a use of it is only fraught with evil. In this instance, it has paralyzed the States Rights party of Texas, and raised to power one of the greatest enemies to the South . . .—a southern Freesoiler.[78]

Actually the editor's concern about political developments in the Lone Star State had an internal motivation: the editor of the Charleston *Mercury* was anxious about the power struggle between Southern Rights Democrats and National Democrats within his own state. Like the controversy over the African slave trade in Louisiana, Mississippi, and Texas, the trade issue in South Carolina was mired in intrastate political and social conflicts.

Politics within South Carolina during the decade before the Civil War was in great turbulence. After the death of their leader John C. Calhoun in 1850, after their failure to persuade the South Carolina convention of 1852 to support state secession, and after Robert B. Rhett's resignation from the Senate, the Southern Rights Democrats of South Carolina found the old Calhounite unity disintegrating and faced an insurgency of National Democrats led by Representative James L. Orr.[79] A new political alignment was in the making. In an 1854 editorial entitled, "Should we be sectional or not?" the editor of the Edgefield *Advertiser* defined the division this way: "Those who maintain the negative of this proposition would perhaps style themselves *National* Democrats; while those who uphold the affirmative prefer the appellation of *Southern Rights* Democrats. The former believe that the conservative element of Southern safety is the friendly disposition of the bulk of our Northern brethren. The latter feel confident that our surest, and in fact our only real protection is to rally the Southern people, in defence of Southern interests and Southern institutions, under

[78] Charleston *Mercury*, August 13, 1859.
[79] Lillian A. Kibler, "Unionist Sentiment in South Carolina in 1860," *Journal of Southern History*, IV, No. 3 (August, 1938), p. 346; Laura A. White, "The National Democrats in South Carolina, 1852 to 1860," *South Atlantic Quarterly*, XXVIII (October, 1929), p. 370; Schultz, *Nationalism and Sectionalism*, pp. 11–12, 14.

a Southern banner. . . ." [80] Thus the National and Southern Rights Democrats of South Carolina had different views on what should be the relationship between South Carolina and the Union.

Among the leaders of the National Democrats of South Carolina were James Orr, Benjamin F. Perry, James Farrow, Francis W. Pickens, A. G. Magrath, and J. J. Pettigrew. They found support in the upcountry and Charleston rather than the lowcountry, in the districts rather than the parishes, and in the areas against rather than the areas for unconditional secession in 1851.[81] During the crisis over the Compromise of 1850, Perry had excoriated the South Carolina secessionists in his editorial columns of the Greenville *Southern Patriot*. "Freemen of the Back Country! Your rulers are about to plunge you into the vortex of revolution. Will you fold your arms in silence until the catastrophe is completed? Speak out!" The state senate, he charged, was a "House of Lords" controlled by the disunionist parishes of the coast.[82]

The program of the South Carolina National Democrats was twofold: electoral reform and the return of South Carolina to the National Democracy. They demanded the democratization of the state political system. They sought to abolish property qualifications for legislators, to transfer the election of presidential electors and of the governor from the legislature to the people, and to increase the representation of the up-

[80] Edgefield *Advertiser*, September 28, 1854.

[81] J. L. Orr to J. J. Pettigrew, April 20, 1857, Pettigrew Papers, North Carolina Archives; Schultz, *Nationalism and Sectionalism*, p. 23; F. Lieber to G. S. Hillard, January 21, 1855, in Perry (ed.) *Lieber,* p. 277; C. S. Boucher, "South Carolina and the South on the Eve of Secession, 1852–1860." *Washington University Studies*, VI, No. 2 (April, 1919), p. 113; F. W. Pickens to J. L. Manning, May 16, 1856, Chesnut-Manning Papers, University of South Carolina Library; Kibler, *Perry,* pp. 284–285; R. B. Rhett, Jr., to M. C. M. Hammond, January 6, 1858, J. Hammond Papers, Library of Congress; S. M. McGowan to J. J. Pettigrew, June 23, 1856, Pettigrew Papers, North Carolina Archives; A. G. Magrath to J. Buchanan, June 9, 1857, Pettigrew Papers, North Carolina Archives.

[82] Perry, in C. S. Boucher, "Sectionalism, Representation, and the Electoral Question in Ante-Bellum South Carolina," *Washington University Studies*, IV, Part II, No. 1 (October, 1916), p. 43.

country.[83] "We do believe," Perry declared in 1856, "in the right of the people to govern themselves . . . there are, at this time, two antagonistic principles in South Carolina, contending against each other—the one an *aristocratic principle* . . . the other, a *Democratic principle*, which has contended for the power of the people. . . . In every other State in the Union, except South Carolina, the aristocratic principle has yielded and given way to the Democratic principle." [84] The National Democrats, furthermore, proposed that South Carolina send delegates to the National Democratic Convention at Cincinnati. Since the nullification crisis, South Carolina had refused to participate in the National Democracy; but in 1856 under Orr's influence some 40 of the 169 state legislators issued a call for a state convention to select delegates.[85] The convention was held, and Orr himself personally and triumphantly led the South Carolina delegation to Cincinnati.[86] Orr's motive behind the abandonment of South Carolina's isolationism involved more than party patronage: he wanted power to influence national politics. "No man now living in this Union," Orr explained, "has power to accomplish any great measure or policy without the aid of party, and if you desire influence in a party, it is only to be attained by affiliating heartily in its organization." [87] Like Senator James Hammond and the Gradys and Wattersons of a later day, Orr sought to rule the Union in the Union; unlike the doctrinaire and uncompromising style of extremists like Spratt, Orr's was the style of political pragmatism.

The Southern Rights Democrats of South Carolina fought back fiercely. The Charleston *Standard* rejected the proposals for electoral reform, and the Charleston *Mercury* warned that such reforms would lead to mob rule and the tyranny of the

[83] Charleston *Mercury*, January 9, 1856; White, "National Democrats," *South Atlantic Quarterly*, pp. 374–375.

[84] Perry, in Kibler, *Perry*, pp. 284–285. Italics added.

[85] White, "National Democrats," *South Atlantic Quarterly*, pp. 372–373.

[86] Edgefield *Advertiser*, June 4, 1856, S. M. McGowan to J. J. Pettigrew, June 23, 1856, Pettigrew Papers, North Carolina Archives.

[87] Orr, in Schultz, *Nationalism and Sectionalism*, p. 22.

majority.[88] In the South Carolina House of Representatives, Edward B. Bryan and the Southern Rights Democrats resisted the efforts of the National Democrats to change the electoral system and to send delegates to the national convention.[89] Bryan and his associates were apprehensive over the emergence of the Orr movement. In a letter to African slave-trade advocate M. C. M. Hammond, Robert Barnwell Rhett, Jr., expressed this concern in 1858:

> During the last few years, in the stagnation that has followed the failure of the secession movement, a Spoils Party has sprung up here. Power and Place, is the object; and the means of seeking these, is the performance of a service that is acceptable to National Democracy. . . . It is now attempted to hold up National Democracy as the hope and defence of the South, and to attach the state blindly in dependence upon Party. Success in thus emasculating her of the moral power of her independent position and past history, would be the destruction of a bulwark against Northern aggression. . . . This move is now backed by all the influence of the National Party and administration, and we already see in what quarter and how liberally its patronage is bestowed here . . . it would be folly to suppose this party weak throughout the State. It is strong, especially in Charleston and the upcountry. It is organized, and has skillful, energetic and successful leaders. It is sustained, too, by wealth; and, unless met and vanquished, must ultimately triumph.[90]

Ironically, almost on the very eve of secession, Rhett, editor of the Charleston *Mercury*, was worrying not only about the Republican Party in the North but also about the National Democracy in the heartland of nullification.

The National Democrats of South Carolina saw that the agitation to reopen the African slave trade would undermine their relationship with the national party. Benjamin F. Perry,

[88] White, "National Democrats," *South Atlantic Quarterly*, p. 375.
[89] Charleston *Mercury*, January 9, 1856; Schultz, *Nationalism and Sectionalism*, p. 104.
[90] Robert B. Rhett, Jr., to M. C. M. Hammond, January 6, 1858, J. Hammond Papers, Library of Congress.

editor of the Greenville *Southern Patriot,* issued one of the earliest denunciations of the African slave-trade proposal.[91] The National Democrats also considered purchasing the Charleston *Standard* in order to silence Spratt's shrill demand for Africans. In a private letter to J. J. Pettigrew in December 1856, James Conner wrote: "There is a plan I learn to buy out Spratt and make the paper a party organ—if it succeeds, Spratt and his Slave Trade will both be defunct. This is confidential." [92] The agitation for African slaves, the South Carolina National Democrats observed, was still largely the cacophony of one Southern radical—Spratt. If they could put him out of business, they could defuse the agitation to reopen the African slave trade.

But by that time Governor James H. Adams, a Southern Rights Democrat, had delivered his message favoring the reopening of the African slave trade. Now the National Democrats had to extinguish the flaming issue in the legislature, and James Orr assigned J. J. Pettigrew the job of presenting a report against Adams's proposal. "As to the report on the Slave Trade," Orr wrote to Pettigrew on April 20, 1857, "I think you had better prepare an elaborate report on the subject—there will be some who will press it and whether they do or not it is our policy to *force* them to defend the monstrous recommendation of their leader Governor Adams—If they recoil now it is only because they see that public opinion is adverse to it—when they get the strength depend upon it they will press it." [93] In a minority report to the South Carolina legislature, Pettigrew presented a detailed criticism of Governor Adams's message on the African slave trade.[94]

[91] Greenville *Southern Patriot,* October 12, 1854, in Kibler, *Perry,* p. 282.

[92] Conner to Pettigrew, December 5, 1856, Pettigrew Papers, North Carolina Archives.

[93] Orr to Pettigrew, April 20, 1857, Pettigrew Papers, North Carolina Archives; see also Orr to Pettigrew, October 30, 1857, Pettigrew Papers, North Carolina Archives; John Preston to Orr, December 4, 1857, Orr Papers, University of North Carolina Library.

[94] James Conner to J. J. Pettigrew, December 5, 1856, J. J. Pettigrew Papers, North Carolina Archives; J. J. Pettigrew, "Protest Against a Renewal of the Slave-Trade," *De Bow's Review,* XXV (August and Sep-

A year later, Pettigrew was defeated in his bid for reelection to the state legislature. In his Knoxville *Southern Citizen,* African slave-trade agitator John Mitchel commented that in the South Carolina elections Spratt, a trade advocate, won by a large majority, and Pettigrew, a trade opponent, lost. But Mitchel admitted that the African slave trade had not been expressly made an issue in the elections.[95] Nevertheless Adams and his colleagues claimed a victory for the African slave-trade party. "They are," Franklin Gaillard reported to Pettigrew, "particularly delighted at your defeat." [96] Pettigrew's friends were surprised at the defeat, and Pettigrew privately complained that the "City was actually bought, the lower sort with money. . . ." [97]

But the National Democrats of South Carolina had little time to mourn Pettigrew's political misfortune. The state legislature would elect a United States Senator within a few weeks, and one of the chief contenders in this election was James Adams, who was running with strong support from the African slave-trade advocates.[98] Thus the National Democrats were busily planning a stop-Adams effort. On October 18, 1858, Franklin Gaillard wrote to J. J. Pettigrew: "I want to see Governor Adams defeated and I am looking not for the man I prefer but for him who can beat Adams. I am disposed to think that

tember, 1858), pp. 166–185, 289–308. Pettigrew received much praise for his report. See J. J. Pettigrew to Carey, Christmas, 1857, J. J. Pettigrew Papers, University of North Carolina Library; Victor Barringer to Pettigrew, February 19, 1858, *ibid.;* James L. Orr to Pettigrew, October 30, 1857, and January 18, 1858, *ibid.;* W. W. Boyce to Pettigrew, December 17, 1857, *ibid.*

[95] Knoxville *Southern Citizen,* in Boston *Liberator,* November 26, 1858; see also James Farrow, in *De Bow's Review,* XXVII (September, 1859), pp. 364–365.

[96] Gaillard to Pettigrew, October 18, 1858, Pettigrew Papers, University of North Carolina Library.

[97] Pettigrew to William Pettigrew, October 24, 1858, Pettigrew Papers, University of North Carolina Library; J. Farrow to Pettigrew, October 21, 1858, Pettigrew Papers, North Carolina Archives; F. Gaillard to Pettigrew, October 18, 1858, Pettigrew Papers, University of North Carolina Library.

[98] Wade Hampton to Pettigrew, May 28, 1858, Pettigrew Papers, North Carolina Archives.

if our party could concentrate on Chestnut [*sic*] the object would be accomplished. He has always been conservative and is opposed to the Slave Trade." [99]

Meanwhile Senator James Hammond had joined the South Carolina opposition to the African slave trade. Hammond had been an aggressive pro-slavery writer and a leading South Carolina fire-eater. During the 1850's, however, he had turned to a different strategy for the defense of slavery: Southern support for the National Democratic Party and Southern rule within the Union. Nevertheless, the advocates of the African slave trade, aware of Hammond's impressive and sound pro-slavery credentials, thought he was sympathetic to their cause. [100] State Senator Edward B. Bryan even sought Hammond's permission to use his name on bank paper to finance an African slave-trade newspaper. [101] But Hammond could hardly have had a genuine and serious interest in the African slave trade; a few years earlier he had called the proposal a joke. To Marcus Hammond, he had remarked privately: "Your proposition for the restoration of the slave trade is doubtless badinage:—for the next propostion in due course would be for all the states to return to the colonial condition under Great Britain!" [102] In his Barnwell Court House speech of October 1858, Senator Hammond announced his conviction that the South could defend slavery within the Union, and attacked the agitation to reopen the importation of Africans. A month later he told Marcus Hammond that "Adams, Gregg & Co. have read me out of *their* State Rights Party, and the fire-eaters are organized against me. The Senatorial election is the issue. . . . If Adams is elected I shall resign." [103]

Thus in the senatorial election of 1858 the African slave

[99] Gaillard to Pettigrew, October 18, 1858, Pettigrew Papers, University of North Carolina Library.

[100] E. B. Bryan to Hammond, February 20, 1858, Hammond Papers, Library of Congress; J. H. Adams to Hammond, September 22, 1858, *ibid.*

[101] Bryan to Hammond, March 26, 1858, Hammond Papers, Library of Congress.

[102] J. Hammond to M. Hammond, July 24, 1854, J. Hammond Papers, Library of Congress.

[103] Hammond, "Barnwell Speech," in New York *Anti-Slavery Stan-*

trade was the central issue.[104] The National Democrats of South Carolina and Senator Hammond were determined to defeat Adams; the advocates of the African slave trade were equally determined to elect Adams. During the balloting, the National Democrats divided their votes between C. G. Memminger and John L. Manning, and on the seventh ballot they united behind Manning. The Southern Rights Democrats meanwhile divided their votes among Adams, Robert B. Rhett, John McQueen, and Lawrence Keitt. After the fifth ballot, it became clear that Adams would not be elected; yet the Adams men refused to shift their votes to another extremist candidate like Rhett or McQueen. The Keitt and McQueen supporters on the ninth ballot switched to James Chesnut, a compromise candidate representing a middle position between the National Democrats and the African slave-trade Democrats. Then on the tenth ballot the National Democrats threw their support to Chesnut and gave him the election.[105] After the election, *De Bow's Review* commented that Chesnut's victory was "an evident letting down" of South Carolina from her previous pro-slavery position.[106] The Charleston *News* declared: "The purport of this Senatorial election cannot be mistaken. . . . It absolutely condemned the agitation of the slave-trade question." [107]

Despite Adams's defeat, Spratt, Bryan, Mazyck, and other African slave-trade advocates continued to agitate the issue in the legislature, which had been a battleground for the con-

dard, November 20, 1858; J. Hammond to M. Hammond, November 28, 1858, J. Hammond Papers, Library of Congress.

[104] Richmond *Enquirer*, December 3, 1858; James Rogers to James Chesnut, February 15, 1859, Chesnut-Manning Papers, University of South Carolina Library; N. D. Porter to Hammond, December 7, 1858, Hammond Papers, Library of Congress; J. Adams to Hammond, September 22, 1858, *ibid.*

[105] Schultz, *Nationalism and Sectionalism*, pp. 175–177; White, "National Democrats," *South Atlantic Quarterly*, pp. 380–381; Charleston *Evening News*, in Charleston *Mercury*, December 8, 1858; Charleston *Mercury*, December 6, 1858.

[106] *De Bow's Review*, XXVI (February, 1859), p. 326.

[107] Charleston *News*, in Washington *National Intelligencer*, December 9, 1858; see also James Rogers to James Chesnut, February 15, 1859, Chesnut-Manning Papers, University of South Carolina.

troversy over the African slave trade since 1846. They had tried time and again to pass resolutions on the African slave trade in the legislature, but had been turned back by powerful resistance. In their protests against the federal prohibition of the trade, they were asking fellow South Carolinians to declare null and void the laws stigmatizing the African slave trade as piracy, and to affirm the integrity of their slaveholding society. Their resolutions, however, had more than moral significance. An analysis of the votes on several of their African slave-trade resolutions will throw further light on our discussion.

In 1860 South Carolina had 30 districts. They may be divided into three groups of ten according to the proportion of the slave population to the total population.[108] Group I includes the ten districts with the highest proportion of slaves to population, and their percentages of slave population range above 62 per cent. Group III includes the ten districts with the lowest proportion of slaves to population, and their percentages of slave population range below 48 per cent. Group II includes the ten districts between Groups I and III, and their percentages of slave population range between 48 per cent and 62 per cent. Using these three groups, the votes in the South Carolina Senate and House on four motions concerning the African slave trade can be analyzed.

In 1857 the senate voted on a motion to postpone indefinitely the report and resolutions on the African slave trade. The senate a year later voted on a motion to table a resolution which declared unconstitutional the federal law making the foreign slave trade the equivalent of piracy. Also that year the house voted on a motion to postpone indefinitely Spratt's resolutions on the trade. In 1859 the senate voted on a motion to table reports and all other matter connected with the subject of the African slave trade. The following table shows the proportion of votes for and against tabling or postponing to the total votes cast by senators or representatives from the districts comprised in each group.[109]

108 Schultz, *Nationalism and Sectionalism*, p. 91.
109 *Ibid.*, pp. 143, 161, 163, 184.

	Group I High Slave Population		Group II Middle Slave Population		Group III Low Slave Population	
	For Tabling or Postponing	**Against**	**For**	**Against**	**For**	**Against**
1857	45%	55%	62½%	37½%	100%	—
1858	48	52	57	43	78	22%
1858	44	56	66	34	65	35
1859	61	39	75	25	91	9

The high slave population group was divided on the question. Nevertheless, of the three groups, Group I gave the African slave trade the highest percentage of support. The middle slave population group tended to be against the trade. The low slave population group was overwhelmingly and consistently against it. The evidence indicates that the African slave trade received support from planters, though not all planters, and that it did not attract nonslaveholders, though it was a project avowedly for the benefit of that group.

The votes on two of these motions in the South Carolina legislature have been recorded on maps of South Carolina. Map I shows the 1857 senate votes, and Map II shows the 1858 house votes.[110] From the two maps it is evident that planter support and nonslaveowner opposition were arranged along an intrastate sectional division—the planter lowcountry parishes tended to favor the African slave trade, and the upcountry districts and Charleston city tended to oppose it. The lowcountry parishes, it will be remembered, had been able to maintain their slave population between 1840 and 1850 and had voted for secession in 1851. It is significant that the districts opposed to the African slave trade included the soil-exhausted upcountry and Charleston city which had a large white labor population, that "Brutus" had earlier directed his appeal to the

[110] Based on the votes recorded in the *South Carolina Senate Journal, 1857* (Columbia, 1857), p. 89; Schultz, *Nationalism and Sectionalism,* p. 159.

Map I
1857 Senate vote

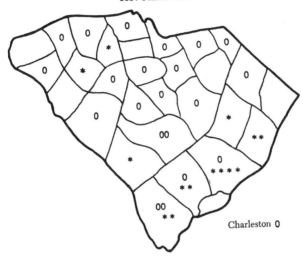

Map II
1858 Senate vote

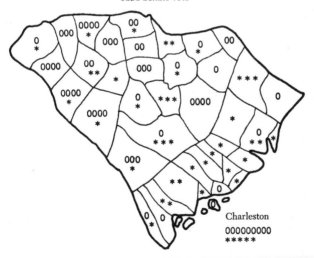

0 Voted for postponement or tabling of African slave trade resolution

* Voted against postponement or tabling of African slave trade resolution

Map III

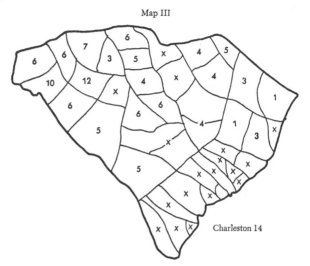

The figures indicate the number of delegates sent by the districts to the state convention in May, 1856 to elect delegates to the Democratic National Convention at Cincinnati. x Not represented.

Map IV

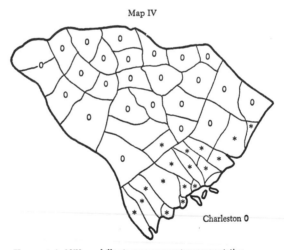

House vote in 1852 on a bill to increase upcountry representation

0 For
* Against

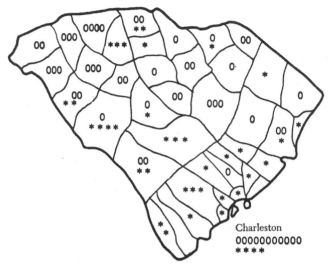

0 Voted to table resolution on Southern independence

* Voted against tabling resolution on Southern independence

people of these districts, and that they had rejected secession in 1851.

At this point let us juxtapose Maps I and II with Maps III, IV and V. Map III indicates the areas of support for and opposition to South Carolina's participation in the National Democratic Convention of 1856.[111] Map IV shows the house votes in 1852 on a bill to increase upcountry representation. And Map V shows the 1856 house votes on a motion to table a resolution proposing the southern states resume the powers they had delegated to the federal government.[112]

In general, support for the African slave trade can be correlated with opposition to the National Democratic party and to increased upcountry representation, and with support for

[111] Boucher, "South Carolina . . . Secession," *Washington University Studies*, p. 112.

[112] Boucher, "Sectionalism, Representation, and the Electoral Question in Ante-Bellum South Carolina," *Washington University Studies*, p. 51; Schultz, *Nationalism and Sectionalism*, p. 126.

Southern independence. Conversely opposition to the African slave trade can be correlated with support for the National Democratic party and for increased upcountry representation, and with opposition to Southern independence. Furthermore the relationships between African slave-trade support and secession and between African slave-trade opposition and anti-secession may be shown by a comparison between votes on African slave-trade and secession resolutions. For example, the 1858 senate vote on the motion to table a resolution on the foreign slave trade can be compared with the 1859 senate vote on the resolution to invite the slaveholding states to inaugurate a movement for Southern separation. Thirty senators voted on both motions. Of the 13 who voted against tabling the African slave-trade resolution, 10 voted for the resolution for separation. On the other hand, of the 17 who voted for tabling the African slave-trade resolution, 13 voted against the resolution for separation.[113] The divisions suggested in this analysis were not rigid. Many South Carolina secessionists like editor Rhett of the *Mercury* did not favor the agitation to reopen the trade. Nevertheless, as the analysis of voting patterns in South Carolina shows, the agitation for the African slave trade in the Palmetto State was associated with the radical pro-slavery movement for Southern independence.

Our study of South Carolina best illustrates the complexity of the African slave-trade agitations in the Southern states. Clearly the controversy over the reopening of the African slave trade was essentially a Southern turmoil. In their effort to assert the rightness of slavery, South Carolina advocates of the African slave trade were actually directing much of their pro-slavery aggressiveness at Southern society and its moral contradictions. Like State Senator Alexander Atkinson of Georgia and State Representative D. C. Graham of Mississippi, they were trying to erase the moral stigma certain laws had placed upon the peculiar institution. Furthermore, for South Carolinians, the African slave-trade agitation had internal political and social significance. While they were aware of the relationship

[113] *South Carolina Senate Journal, 1858* (Columbia, 1858), p. 120; *South Carolina Senate Journal, 1859*, p. 135.

between the trade proposal and the North-South conflict, they also viewed the issue in the context of certain regional, class, and political interests within the South and within their state. Like Albert Gallatin Brown and Henry Hughes in Mississippi or Sam Houston and Hardin Runnels in Texas, South Carolinians were conditioned by a vast array of factors in their behavior and thoughts on the African slave-trade question. Their responses to the trade issue were woven into the fabric of intrastate conflicts. Thus the African slave-trade controversy in the state was not only related to the tension between sectionalism and nationalism, but was also inextricably knotted into the rivalry between political forces as well as the sectional and class tensions between the upcountry and the lowcountry, and farmers and planters *within* South Carolina.

NINE

SOUTHERN
HIGHER LAWISM:
THE ILLEGAL
AFRICAN SLAVE TRADE

■

In 1859 Stephen A. Douglas claimed that over 15,000 African slaves had been imported into the South during the past year, and that he had seen "three hundred of those recently-imported, miserable beings, in a Slave-pen in Vicksburg, Miss., and also large numbers at Memphis, Tenn." [1] Actually such an extensive importation of African slaves had not occurred. No doubt the African slave trade was active during the late 1850's. Eighty-five slavers reportedly were fitted out in New York harbor in 1859–60, and twelve vessels filled with 3,119 Africans were

[1] Douglas, quoted in *27th Report of the American Anti-Slavery Society*, p. 20; also in Du Bois, pp. 181–182.

captured in 1860. This African slave-trade activity, however, was generally engaged in the transportation of slaves to Brazil and Cuba, not the United States.[2] Moreover, reports of African slaves in the South, including Senator Douglas's, almost invariably represented rumors and unconfirmable claims.[3] Nevertheless, Douglas's anxieties about the revival of the African slave trade were not completely unwarranted. Certain Southern fire-eaters were involved in the African slave trade; African slaves were being imported into the South; and African slave traders were being tried for the crime of piracy.

One evening in December 1858, Charles A. L. Lamar was on a steamer transporting about 170 newly imported African slaves up the Savannah River. The slaves were part of the "black cargo" carried across the Atlantic by the *Wanderer*, a 114 foot schooner that could fly along at twenty knots and leave pursuing United States cruisers trailing far behind its wake. Only a few days before, these unfortunate Africans, suffering from diarrhea, skin diseases, and the terrible trauma of the middle passage, had been landed on remote and lonely Jekyl Island, 65 miles south of Savannah. Now in the darkness Lamar was ferrying them past the port of Savannah to be distributed to plantations in the South.[4]

Lamar's daring act became a focus of the Southern controversy over the right of Southerners to disobey the federal law. The editor of the Savannah *Republican* condemned the schemers of the *Wanderer* for following in the footsteps of

[2] Du Bois, pp. 179, 180, 186, 187; *Hunt's Magazine*, Vol. 36 (January, 1857), p. 137; New Orleans *Picayune*, July 15, 1860; Washington *National Intelligencer*, May 21, 1860.

[3] In his evaluation of Douglas's claim, Charles Sydnor comments: "Such a statement is difficult to credit, for foreign-born negroes, particularly native Africans were rarely to be found." Sydnor, *Slavery in Mississippi*, p. 142.

[4] Savannah *Republican*, in Washington *National Intelligencer*, January 3, 1859; Charleston *Mercury*, January 1, 1859; Richmond *Whig*, January 4, 1859; Brunswick (Georgia) *Herald*, January 27, 1858, and March 9, 1859; Tom Henderson Wells, *The Slave Ship Wanderer* (Athens: University of Georgia Press, 1967), pp. 8, 24–29.

"northern higher-law men." [5] The editor of the Orangeburg [South Carolina] *Southern* also regretted the Southern violation of the law of the land. Though the law prohibiting the importation of Africans was "unjust," he argued, "as long as it remains a law let it be upheld: far better is it to obey even an unjust law than to subject the country to a reign of fanaticism and anarchy by trampling it under foot." [6] But the editor of the Augusta *Dispatch* defended the *Wanderer* and applauded Lamar's defiance of a "foolish law." [7] In his endorsement of the illegal African slave trade, the editor of the Griffin (Georgia) *Empire State* exclaimed: "We want, in the South, teachers of the Lamar stamp." [8] Thus Lamar had provoked a soul-searching debate over a deeply anxious question: should Southerners avow their allegiance to a "higher law" and violate the federal law stigmatizing the African slave trade and Southern society?

Charles Augustus Lafayette Lamar, according to a correspondent of the New York *Tribune,* was "a fair sample of a fast young Southern, belonging to one of the first families, very popular, and, no doubt, looked upon as a pattern man by the rising youth." [9] Indeed, the thirty-four-year-old Lamar undoubtedly wore his red mustache and carried his goldheaded cane with self-confidence and pride. He was not only the godson of Marquis de Lafayette but was also a member of a family distinguished for their political prestige and economic affluence. His kinsfolk included several Congressmen and a president of the Republic of Texas; his father was Gazaway Bugg Lamar, one of the wealthiest men in the South. [10]

The young and energetic Lamar had a flair for business

[5] Savannah *Republican,* quoted in Savannah *Daily News,* January 5, 1859.

[6] Orangeburg Southern, in Washington *National Intelligencer,* January 4, 1859; Columbia *South Carolinian,* in Washington *National Intelligencer,* January 4, 1859; Augusta *Chronicle,* in Charleston *Mercury,* December 17, 1858.

[7] Augusta *Dispatch,* in *American Anti-Slavery Society Report for 1859* (New York: 1859), p. 46; Macon *State Press,* in Savannah *Daily News,* December 18, 1858.

[8] Griffin *Empire State,* in Savannah *Daily News,* April 22, 1859.

[9] New York *Tribune,* April 1, 1859.

[10] Wells, *Slave Ship,* p. 4; Wells, "Charles Augustus Lafayette Lamar;

that made him seem less like a genteel Southern Cavalier and more like an acquisitive Northern Yankee.[11] Unlike Henry Hughes who scorned the world of moneymaking, Lamar was involved in a gigantic multiplicity of business enterprises. He was director of the Bank of Commerce, and of the Savannah, Albany and Gulf Railroad, the president of the Plank Road Company, and an agent for steamship lines, a cotton gin distributor, and the Lamar Insurance Company. He had interests in Savannah shipping wharves, a guano importing project, a gold mine in Georgia, a cotton press, and a six-story flour mill. His letters to his father reveal that he was a shrewd cotton speculator who attempted to corner part of the cotton market in order to sell when cotton prices were high. Often the enterprising young Lamar offered business advice to his wealthy father. "If you can make arrangements to hold it [cotton crop]," he wrote to his father in 1859, "go in & buy *double* the quantity you bought in the fall, & you will pay out, & make something." [12] Lamar also had an acute appetite for government contracts. In a letter to Navy agent George N. Sanders, he wrote: "I want a contract for making money. You have the power of disposing of the contract for the supplying of timber and lumber at the Navy Yard, and I have the means and ability of supplying. Will you give me the point to enable me to get it? I have 11,500 acres of pine land which is just the 'ticket'." [13]

Given young Lamar's keen business spirit, it should not

Gentleman Slave Trader," *Georgia Historical Quarterly*, Vol. 42 (June, 1963), pp. 158–159; Daniel P. Mannix, *Black Cargoes: A History of the Atlantic Slave Trade, 1518–1865* (New York: The Viking Press, 1965), p. 276.

[11] For discussions on the Southern Cavalier, see William R. Taylor's *Cavalier & Yankee: The Old South and American National Character* (Garden City, New York: Doubleday & Company, 1963); and Osterweis, *Romanticism and Nationalism in the Old South.*

[12] Deed between C. A. L. Lamar and Gazaway B. Lamar, October 16, 1857, C. A. L. Lamar Papers, Emory University Library; C. A. L. Lamar to G. B. Lamar, November 1, 1860, Lamar Papers, Emory University Library; Wells, *Slave Ship*, p. 4; Wells, "Lamar," p. 160; C. A. L. Lamar to G. B. Lamar, January 17 and 20, 1859, Lamar Papers, Emory University Library.

[13] Lamar to Sanders, April 1, 1857, reprinted in "A Slave-Trader's Letter-Book," *North American Review*, CXLIII (1866), p. 448.

be surprising to find him viewing his African slave-trade enterprises in terms of their profitability. In a letter to a William Roundtree of Nashville, Lamar showed that the profits of a proposed African slaving expedition would be enormous.[14]

Cost of the expedition	$300,000
Say we bring but 1,200 Negroes at $650	$780,000
Deduct 1st cost	$300,000
Leaves nett [sic] profit and steamer on hand	$480,000

But, for Lamar, the African slave trade was much more than a moneymaking scheme: it involved Southern honor. In their defense of slavery, Southerners had been extremely sensitive about questions of honor. During the debate over the Wilmot Proviso during the 1840's, John C. Calhoun had denounced the proposed prohibition of slavery in the territories acquired from Mexico. In Calhoun's judgment, such a prohibition would deny Southerners equality in the Union. "We ought rather than to yield an inch," he argued, "take any alternative, even if it should be disunion." [15] Southern honor was more important than the Union. Like Calhoun's struggle against the Wilmot Proviso, Lamar's effort to reopen the African slave trade involved a romantic obligation to assert "the rights" of the South. As Lamar's fellow African slave-trade advocate Leonidas W. Spratt declared to the Vicksburg Southern Commercial Convention in 1859: "There is *honor* [in the African slave trade], also, and my friend Lamar already hoists the slave-trade flag and floats it from his masthead." [16] In this respect, Lamar was indeed a Southern Cavalier. Like Hughes and many proud young men of the South, Lamar saw himself

[14] Lamar to Roundtree, and Lamar to C. C. Cook, June 20, 1859, in "Letter-Book," p. 459.

[15] Clement Eaton, *Freedom-of-Thought Struggle in the Old South* (New York: Harper, 1964), pp. 152–153.

[16] Spratt, in *De Bow's Review*, XXVII (August, 1859), p. 212. Italics added.

as a Southern gentleman fighting for principles—for the principles of slavery and the African slave trade.

Young Lamar knew that many of his best friends, including his father, differed with him on the question of the African slave trade. "An expedition to the moon," wrote Gazaway Bugg Lamar to his son, "would have been equally sensible, and no more contrary to the laws of Providence. May God forgive you for all your attempts to violate his will and his laws." [17] Unlike his father and many Southerners of an older generation, the young Lamar was aggressively demanding Southern moral consistency on the question of slavery. In a candid letter to his father, Lamar expressed the moral anxiety of many youthful fire-eaters like Spratt and Hughes. "Did not the negroes," Lamar sharply asked his father, "all come originally from the Coast of Africa? What is the difference between going to Africa and Virginia for negroes?" [18] The opposition of his father and friends did not seem to bother young Lamar. But perhaps it did. "I know," he told a friend, "that I am *right*." [19] Determined to show everyone, especially his father, he was "right," Lamar agitated for the reopening of the African slave trade even to the point of actually importing Africans in defiance of the federal government. And when Northern editors and critics made what he considered unkind remarks about his African slave-trade activities, the proud Lamar quickly challenged them to settle the matter on the "field of honor"—the dueling ground. Offended by William Raymond, editor of the New York *Times,* Lamar sought to confront his adversary personally. "I shall simply put an indignity upon him in a public manner—such for instance as slapping his face," the hurt and petulant Southern gentleman declared, "and then, if he don't resent it, why I shall take no further notice of him." [20] Lamar's was the style of

[17] G. B. Lamar, in C. A. L. Lamar to G. B. Lamar, in "Letter-Book," p. 449.

[18] C. A. L. Lamar to G. B. Lamar, October 31, 1857, in *ibid.,* p. 449.

[19] Lamar to B. R. Alden, July 30, 1859, Lamar to C. C. Cook, June 20, 1859, Lamar to Theodore Johnston, December 23, 1857, in "Letter-Book," pp. 460, 459, 451. Italics added.

[20] New York *Times,* April 5, 1859; Lamar to William Raymond,

chivalry seeking satisfaction for wounded honor with pistols at ten paces. In his disobedience of the federal laws against the African slave trade and in his devotion to the duel as a means to resolve conflict, Lamar viewed himself as a Cavalier, refined and civilized, above the law.

A few months before the *Wanderer* landed Africans on Jekyl Island, Lamar had been engaged in a heated public debate with Secretary of the Treasury Howell Cobb. Lamar had directed Lafitte and Company, a merchant firm, to make an application for the clearance of his ship the *Richard Cobden* for the coast of Africa to take on board African "emigrants" in accordance with the United States passenger laws, and to transport them to a port in the United States. William F. Colcock, the Collector of the Customs at Charleston, informed Lafitte and Company that their application was "of a novel character, and intimately connected with the grave issues now agitating the country." Hence he had decided to refer the matter to authorities in Washington, and to refuse clearance until he received instruction from the Secretary of the Treasury.[21]

About a month later, on May 22, 1858, Secretary Cobb firmly denied the application for clearance. Cobb, a Union Democrat in 1850, was now planning to be Georgia's favorite son candidate for the 1860 Democratic nomination for President; and he probably saw that Lamar's agitation could help to splinter the Democratic Party and threaten his presidential ambitions. In a letter to Collector Colcock that was widely reprinted in newspapers throughout the country, Cobb ex-

April 4, 1859; Lamar to B. R. Alden, and Lamar to L. Q. C. Lamar, June 12, 1860, in "Letter-Book," pp. 457–458, 460. For analyses of the significance of dueling in the Old South, see Daniel Boorstin, *The Americans: The National Experience* (New York: Vintage Books, 1967), pp. 206–212; Clement Eaton, *The Freedom-of-Thought Struggle in the Old South*, pp. 52–53; John Hope Franklin, *The Militant South* (Cambridge: Beacon Press, 1964), pp. 44–62; Charles S. Sydnor, "The Southerner and the Laws," *Journal of Southern History*, V (February, 1940), pp. 15–19.

[21] Letter of Messrs. Lafitte and Company, in Richmond *Enquirer*, June 11, 1858.

plained that the purpose of the applicants must be either to import Africans to be slaves or bound laborers, or to bring them into the country like other emigrants to be entitled to the rights and privileges of freemen. He then referred to the 1807 federal law forbidding the importation of Negroes, "whether introduced as slaves or *to be held to service or labor.*" He noted that the form of Lafitte's application would seem "to contemplate" the introduction of Negroes as emigrants having all the rights and privileges of freemen. But this proposition, Cobb argued, was absurd. The slaveholding states prohibited such introduction of free Negroes, and the nonslaveholding states would not welcome them. Thus, the Africans to be transported in the *Richard Cobden* to the United States must either be slaves or apprentices bound to service or labor. If so, Cobb concluded, the application for clearance was an attempt to evade the laws of the country, and must be refused.[22]

Cobb's denial outraged Lamar. In his response, Lamar impatiently explained that he was simply exercising a legal right, and that the question was whether or not he had the right to land Africans, bond or free, at any port in the United States. He charged that Cobb's assumption that the ship would return to a Southern port was not warranted by anything in the application, that Cobb had arrived at this conclusion only by an interpretation of the applicant's motives, and that Cobb had no right to make the interpretation. Upon the return of the ship to the United States, Lamar added, the status of the Africans on board and the legality of the voyage could have been tested in the Federal Courts. "You have undertaken to condemn the proposed voyage as illegal, and have closed the courts of the country against me, by depriving me of the only possible means of obtaining a hearing upon the merits of the question." [23] Lamar was trying to import Africans in order to test the constitutionality of the federal laws.

[22] Cobb to Colcock, May 22, 1858, in Brunswick *Herald*, June 16, 1858; in Jackson *Semi-Weekly Mississippian*, August 17, 1858.
[23] Lamar, reply to Cobb, in Jackson *Semi-Weekly Mississippian*, June 22, 1858.

But actually for Lamar, the controversy over the application of Lafitte and Company involved more than a constitutional issue: he was seeking to confront certain problems related to the internal crisis of Southern society. In his public exchange with Cobb, Lamar unveiled his reasons why the South had to import African slaves. The South, he argued, needed a tide of foreign labor to boost its prosperity. "This tide can only come from Africa, and it would be better perhaps that it would come in the form of slaves; but such persons whether slaves or free, will be *disfranchised;* they will thus be *more susceptible of government than is the hireling labor of Democratic States.*" [24] Like Governor James Adams and Leonidas Spratt, Lamar was concerned about a Southern dilemma—the need to have more laborers, but only controllable and politically powerless laborers. Hence they had to be black workers from Africa. Moreover, Lamar felt morally compelled to violate the federal law prohibiting the African slave trade. In his judgment, he had a choice between obedience to the federal law, to a "badge of servitude," to "a brand of reprobation," and to Northern sentiment, and obedience to "the truth" of the rightness of the African slave trade and the peculiar institution. Lamar's answer was clear and contemptuous: "Not only would I not sustain it [the federal law], but . . . I intend to violate it, if that shall be the only way by which *the South can come to right* upon this question, and I will reopen the trade in slaves to foreign countries; let your cruisers catch me if they can." [25] As a Southern Cavalier, Lamar felt his allegiance must be to Southern rights and the "Code of Honor" rather than to the written law.[26] As a defender of slavery, he chose to import African slaves in order to affirm the morality of slavery.

A few months later the audacious Lamar successfully took a boatload of the *Wanderer's* African slaves up the Savannah River, and people on the South Carolina side of the river were

[24] Lamar, letter to William Colcock, in Jackson *Semi-Weekly Mississippian,* August 17, 1858. Italics added.

[25] *Ibid.,* italics added.

[26] See Charles Sydnor, "The Southerner and the Laws," *Journal of Southern History,* V (February, 1940), p. 14.

excitedly asking: *"Have you seen the Africans?"* [27] But Lamar
soon found himself in serious trouble. On December 11, 1858,
three crew members of the *Wanderer* were arrested in Savannah,
and Lamar's personal attorney rushed to the jail to arrange
for their bail.[28] Lamar was worried. "I tell you things are in
a hell of a fix," he wrote to Nelson Trowbridge, an associate
involved in the *Wanderer* scheme. "The Government has employed H. R. Jackson to assist in the prosecution, and are
determined to press matters to the utmost extremity. The yacht
[*Wanderer*] has been seized. The examination commenced today. . . . They have all the pilots and men who took the yacht
to Brunswick, here to testify. *She will be lost certain and sure,*
if not the negroes. Dr. Hazlehurst [*sic*] testified that he attended
the negroes and swore they were Africans, and of recent importation. . . . All these men must be *bribed."* [29]

But Lamar's efforts to offer two witnesses $5000 not to
testify failed.[30] In February 1859, an admiralty court declared
that the *Wanderer* was an American-owned slaver, and that it
would be forfeited to the United States and condemned to
be auctioned. At the auction, Lamar announced to the crowd
that the *Wanderer* had been unjustly taken from him, and that
no one should bid against him. But Charles Van Horn, the
Savannah jailer, dared to offer a bid of $4000. The auctioneer
quickly accepted Lamar's counterbid of $4001. Amid cheers
from the crowd, Lamar then knocked Van Horn down. "The
authorities present," reported a witness, "looked quietly on, not
offering the slightest interference." [31] The Cavalier Lamar must
have thought Van Horn unworthy of a challenge to a duel.

The three *Wanderer* prisoners were indicted and tried for
piracy under the 1820 federal law prohibiting the African slave
trade. In his charge to the jury, Judge James M. Wayne ex-

[27] Edgefield *Advertiser,* in New York *Times,* December 31, 1858.
[28] Savannah *News,* in Charleston *Mercury,* December 21, 1858.
[29] Lamar to Nelson Trowbridge, December 18, 1858, in "Letter-
Book," p. 456. Lamar was referring to Dr. Robert Hazelhurst, a Brunswick physician, who gave medical care to the Africans on Jekyl Island.
[30] Lamar to N. D. Brown, January 28, 1859, in "Letter-Book," p. 457.
[31] Correspondent, in New York *Times,* April 1, 1858.

pressed the opinion that the accused men were "pretty plainly and conclusively shown to be connected with the *Wanderer*," and that the harshness of the penalty for piracy was not a concern of the jury. "That is a matter that rests with the makers of the law, and not with us. What right have you or I either to say we will not carry out the law, because of its severity?" [32] The next day the jury returned a verdict of not guilty. The conviction and execution of the *Wanderer* crewmen for importing African slaves would have been a bitter pill for a society already deeply implicated in the enslavement of blacks. As members of the jury, Southerners had refused to convict three African slave-traders for the crime of piracy and sentence them to death. They had in effect nullified the law of the land. "We cannot say," the editor of the Savannah *Republican* reported, "that the public expectation has been disappointed in this result." [33]

Meanwhile Charles A. L. Lamar himself had been indicted for violating the 1818 federal act that outlawed the holding of illegally imported African slaves. During the trial, the district attorney offered evidence showing that Lamar had hired a steamer and had taken Negroes from Jekyl Island to a place above Savannah. But after Judge Wayne explained that the evidence introduced by the prosecution was insufficient to connect Lamar with the *Wanderer*, the district attorney decided it would be useless to proceed further in the case.[34]

"I am afraid they will convict me," wrote Lamar to a friend before his trial, "but my case is only seven years and a fine. If I find they are likely to do so, I shall go to Cuba. . . ." But, though he worried about the possibility of a conviction, he also

[32] Charleston *Mercury*, February 14, 1859; Savannah *Morning News*, May 21, 1859; New York *Times*, November 23, 1859; Wayne, in Savannah *Republican*, November 23, 1859, in Alexander A. Lawrence, *James Moore Wayne; Southern Unionist* (Chapel Hill: University of North Carolina Press, 1943), p. 167.

[33] Savannah *Republican*, in Washington *National Intelligencer*, December 1, 1859.

[34] Brunswick *Herald*, April 20, 1859; Savannah *Republican*, May 22, 1860, in Washington *National Intelligencer*, June 1, 1860.

believed that it would be difficult to get a conviction. Four years earlier, he had doubted that he could be punished for his filibustering activities, for in a small place "a man of influence can do as he pleases." To a potential investor in an African slave-trade expedition, Lamar had explained in 1857: "One thing is certain. Nothing can be done in the way of conviction." And even after his arrest, Lamar told his father that the district attorney was "making a great ass of himself. I have no fears myself. I think all will go well—so far as trials? are concerned. . . ." [35] Lamar, moreover, believed that a Southern jury could not convict him without condemning slavery and the domestic slave trade. Significantly, after the grand jury had indicted Lamar for his complicity in the African slave trade, the members of that jury issued a signed protest against their own bill of indictment. The jurymen stated that they had been compelled against their will, by instructions from the court, to find a bill in accordance with the law prohibiting the African slave trade. Heretofore the people of the South, the grand jury concluded, "have failed to place the stamp of condemnation upon such laws as reflect upon the institution of slavery, but have permitted, unrebuked, the influence of foreign opinion to prevail in their support. Longer to yield to a sickly sentiment of pretended philanthropy . . . is weak and unwise. Regarding all such laws as tending to encourage such results . . . , we unhesitantly advocate their repeal because they directly or indirectly, *condemn this institution, and those who have inherited or maintain it. . . .*" [36] The disturbing implication of their protest was clear: in their indictment of Lamar for an act defined as a crime by federal law, the grand jury in effect had also indicted themselves and their Southern society.

Unlike the grand jury, however, Lamar had little interest

[35] Lamar to N. D. Brown, January 28, 1859, in "Letter-Book," p. 457; Lamar to J. S. Thrasher, February 25, 1855, in "Letter-Book," p. 448; Lamar to L. Viana, December 26, 1857, in "Letter-Book," p. 452; C. A. L. Lamar to G. B. Lamar, June 17, 1859, Lamar Papers, Emory University Library.

[36] In Savannah *Republican*, in Jackson *Semi-Weekly Mississippian*, June 10, 1859. Italics added.

in the repeal of the federal laws. What concerned him more was Southern independence from those laws. Like Edmund Ruffin and many advocates of the African slave trade, Lamar was confident that a Republican victory in the 1860 presidential election would force the Southern states into secession. "We shall have disunion certain if Lincoln is elected," he wrote to his father on the eve of the election. "I hope Lincoln may be elected. I want dissolution, & have I think contributed more than any man South for it." [37] Indeed, Lamar could proudly claim that his disobedience of the federal laws—his flagrant importation of African slaves—helped to ensure the success of the Republican Party and to fragment the nation.

Convinced the sectional conflict must be resolved through violence rather than politics, Lamar had already begun to organize a company of soldiers and had already ordered a hundred sabres and pistols. Like Henry Hughes, the advocate of military education for Southern children, Lamar had an obsession for the Southern cult of militarism. The Southern Cavalier was making military preparations in 1860 for a national duel to defend Southern honor and Southern principles. Shortly after Lincoln's election, Lamar told his father that Georgia must secede immediately. "If Georgia don't act promptly we, the military of Savh [*sic*], will throw her into Revolution, & we will be backed by the Minute Men all through the State. *We do not care for what the world may approve of—we know we are right* & will act regardless of consequences." [38] For Lamar, violence would be a means to express his repudiation of western civilization's anti-slavery values and to satisfy his compelling need to avow the rightness of slavery.

About three months before the *Wanderer* was anchored off Jekyl Island, a Charlestonian wrote to a friend: "You will see by this morning's Mercury that we have a slaver in our

---

[37] C. A. L. Lamar to G. B. Lamar, November 5, 1860, Lamar Papers, Emory University Library.

[38] *Ibid.*; C. A. L. Lamar to G. B. Lamar, November 26, 1860, Lamar Papers, Emory University Library. Italics added.

harbor. She has on board about 300 naked, native negroes, sixty of them women. Every one of whom is in the family way. Every body is talking about them. The yellow fever, the cables and Every other subject have faded before this. There is really and truly an Excitement among these cold, stolid Charlestonians." [39] The excited readers of the Charleston *Mercury* learned that the slaver was the brig the *Echo*, captured off the coast of Cuba by the *U.S.S. Dolphin* on August 21; that 141 of the original 455 slaves who had boarded the *Echo* on the west coast of Africa had died during the middle passage; that the captain of the slaver was a Yankee from Rhode Island; and that the U. S. officer of the prize crew sailing the captured *Echo* into Charleston was a Southerner from Alabama! But what must have concerned Charlestonians most of all was the fact that the crew would be tried in South Carolina as pirates.[40]

The editor of the Charleston *News* hoped that South Carolinians would have the moral courage and law-abiding sense to do their duty under the law and try the *Echo* crew for piracy, and a prominent Charlestonian privately assured President James Buchanan that the "thinking" part of the community would be faithful in performing their duty to enforce the law.[41] But the editor of the Philadelphia *American* predicted that it would "go hard with a Charleston jury to pronounce the slave trade in the same category of crimes as piracy, indeed, as piracy itself. Time, however, will soon disclose whether the law denouncing the slave trade as piracy, is in harmony with the feelings of the people in the Southern portion of our Union." [42] Indeed, the question raised by this Northern editor

[39] George A. Gordon to Krilla (a girlfriend), August 30, 1858, Gordon Papers, Duke University Library.

[40] Charleston *Mercury*, August 28, September 3, 1858; April 8, April 14, 1859; Charleston *Mercury*, in Richmond *Enquirer*, September 3, 1858.

[41] Charleston *News*, in Richmond *Enquirer*, September 7, 1858; Alfred Huger to J. Buchanan, August 30, 1858, Huger Papers, Duke University Library. See also Charleston *Courier*, in Washington *National Intelligencer*, September 3, 1858.

[42] Philadelphia *American*, in Charleston *Mercury*, September 7, 1858; also A. G. Magrath to James Hammond, January 21, 1859, Hammond Papers, Library of Congress.

forced to the surface the uncomfortable dilemma confronting Charlestonians who could see the *Echo* in their port and the illegally imported Africans on their wharves. Like the Savannah grand jury of the *Wanderer* case, Charlestonians and the South would have to answer a number of profound questions: should and could the South convict the *Echo* crew for piracy, a crime punishable by death? If the crew were convicted, what would be the meaning of such a conviction? Would it not mean in effect a conviction of slavery and the South? Could the South condemn itself?

But before Charlestonians could deal with these questions, they had to answer another but nonetheless related question: what should be done with the captured African slaves? For some Charlestonians, the answer was immediately clear. "All sorts of plans, schemes and projects, legal and illegal," reported a Charlestonian a few days after the arrival of the *Echo*, "are broached and discussed, as to the best means of getting them on shore, for once on shore they are free from the United States laws and must come under the jurisdiction of the state. They would find their way to the plantations rapidly there." [43] For President Buchanan the answer was also quite clear. According to the federal law of 1819, the captured African slaves would have to be returned to Africa. Thus the surviving *Echo* Africans again underwent the horrors of the middle passage, and 71 out of the 271 who left Charleston did not live to see their native land again. [44]

But meanwhile, many Charlestonians threw themselves into tantrums of protest against the federal law requiring the return of the Africans. "But why," asked "Curtius," an angry writer to the Charleston *Courier,* "should we send them back?" "Curtius" declared that the Africans were "here on the very threshold of civilization; shall we send them back to barbarism? They are

[43] Gordon to Krilla, *op. cit.*
[44] Charleston *Evening News,* August 30, 1858, in Washington *National Intelligencer,* September 2, 1858; New Orleans *Bee,* September 15, 1858, in Charleston *Mercury,* September 21, 1858; New York *Times,* December 13, 1858; W. H. Trescot to W. P. Miles, February 8, 1859, Miles Papers, University of North Carolina Library.

at the dawn of Christianity; shall we send them back to heathen darkness? . . . They are here almost within the pale of a society where they will be safe, and where every physical want will be surely supplied; will we send them back to the precarious subsistence snatched from wretches as starving as themselves?" Thus humanitarianism and paternalism demanded that the *Echo* Africans be kept in slavery and in the South and out of barbarism and Africa. But the real concern of "Curtius" was not the welfare of the Africans but the moral innocence of white Southerners. Like Charles A. L. Lamar, "Curtius" was extremely sensitive to the implications of actions related to the African slave trade, and he indignantly recognized that Buchanan's decision to return the African slaves implicitly condemned the South. "When these negroes shall be taken from the port of Charleston . . .," he explained, "it will be a brand upon our institutions that should fire the heart of every man that loves his country. It will be the declaration to the world that this condition in which our own negroes are, is so offensive to even our own government, that it is incumbent upon it to use its sovereign power in rescuing from the like condition all who come within its reach." [45] Indeed, the very integrity of Southern society was at stake.

The anguished cries of Southerners like "Curtius" went unheeded by the federal government. But if Southerners did not have the power to decide what should be done with the *Echo* Africans, they could decide the other important question: What should be done with the *Echo* crew?

On November 29, 1858, about five weeks after the captured Africans had left Charleston, bills for the indictment of the *Echo* crew on charges of piracy were presented to the Grand Jury of the United States Circuit Court at Colombia, South Carolina. The prisoners' leading counsel for defense was Leonidas W. Spratt. Spratt, of course, was an almost ubiquitous

[45] "Curtius," in Charleston *Courier*, in Richmond *Enquirer*, September 7, 1858; for further evidence, see "F. A. P." letter, in Charleston *Mercury*, September 17, 1858, Galveston *Weekly News*, December 4, 1858; Richmond *Enquirer*, September 3, 1858; J. L. Seward, in Savannah *Daily News*, February 2, 1859.

agitator for the reopening of the African slave trade, and his direct involvement in the defense of the *Echo* crew gave the court drama obvious political and ideological significance. After the grand jury received the bills, Justice James M. Wayne explained to the jury the provisions of the federal law declaring the African slave trade piracy. The next day the grand jury refused to indict the prisoners. Flushed with victory, lawyer Spratt then moved for their discharge on the grounds that the federal law against the African slave trade was unconstitutional. But United States District Attorney James Conner immediately asked that they be kept in jail to await future action of the grand jury, and argued that the law involved in the case was constitutional. Judges James M. Wayne and Alexander G. Magrath then rendered opinions in favor of the constitutionality of the law, and denied Spratt's motion. The *Echo* prisoners were returned to jail to await proceedings on a charge of piracy at the next circuit term of the Federal Court for South Carolina.[46] A few days later, the old and distinguished James L. Petigru privately complained to a friend: "There is a proverb that says, that crimes should be punished, deeds of shame buried. Yet History must have its rights, and sorry I am that one of its pages will be defiled by recording the depravity of the present day, when the laws against kidnapping of Africans . . . cannot be enforced."[47] The hoary South Carolina gentleman knew a Southern jury would not convict the *Echo* prisoners.

On April 2, 1859, the United States Circuit Court convened at Charleston. After the grand jury was sworn in, District Attorney Conner again presented bills to indict the *Echo* crew for piracy. Meanwhile, the Charleston *Mercury* announced that the majority of Southerners favoring the repeal of the federal

[46] New York *Times*, December 4 and 6, 1858; Charleston *Mercury*, September 9, 1858; Charleston *Mercury*, December 10, 1858, February 16, 17, 18, 24, 1859, April 8, 1859; Augusta *Constitutionalist*, in Washington *National Intelligencer*, December 28, 1858; and New Orleans *Picayune*, December 16, 1858; E. Ruffin, Diary, February 23, 1859, Library of Congress.

[47] J. L. Petigru to J. B. O'Neal, January 1, 1859, Petigru Papers, University of South Carolina Library.

laws against the African slave trade wanted indictments issued in order to test the constitutionality of the federal prohibition. This time the Charleston grand jury indicted the prisoners. The *Echo* crewmen were then tried and acquitted.[48]

The case of the *Echo* had become a topic of national interest, and many Americans, North and South, pondered the meaning of the verdict of the Charleston jury. On April 21, 1859, the New York *Tribune* offered a clue. The *Tribune* reported that the counsel had advanced two arguments in defense of the *Echo* prisoners. The counsel argued that the jury had the right to judge the constitutionality of the law, and that the act under which the *Echo* prisoners were indicted was unconstitutional. The counsel explained that the Constitution had given Congress the right to punish piracy, a term defined as robbery on the high seas, but that it did not give Congress any right to apply that term to slave-trading or to the transportation of persons with a view to sell them. The counsel also advanced the usual plea that the Government had not sufficiently made out a case. They argued that the bill of sale by which the vessel was conveyed to Captain Edward N. Townsend of the *Echo* was not sufficient to prove that the *Echo* belonged to Townsend, that there was no proof that the Townsend of Rhode Island was the same Townsend mentioned in the bill of sale, and that there was no evidence to show where the Negroes were taken on board and the intent to make them slaves.[49]

Possibly the jury made their decision only on the basis of the counsel's argument that the evidence was insufficient. A month after the jury had rendered their verdict, a South Carolinian told the Southern Commercial Convention at Vicksburg: "The jury never considered the constitutionality or the unconstitutionality of the *law*. In their judgment, the evidence was not sufficient to show that the defendants were truly charged. I have been credibly informed that this declaration

[48] New York *Tribune*, April 12, 1859; Charleston *Mercury*, in Washington *National Intelligencer*, April 7, 1859; New York *Times*, April 12, 1859; Charleston *Mercury*, April 15, 18, 21, 1859.
[49] New York *Tribune*, April 21, 1859.

had been made by every juror who was charged with the case." [50]

But whether or not the claim of this South Carolinian was true had only limited relevance to the meaning of the verdicts. More relevant was the fact that the *Echo* case had become a test of the constitutionality of the federal laws prohibiting the African slave trade. A few days after the *Echo* arrived in Charleston, a writer to the Charleston *Mercury* called the law of piracy unconstitutional and offered $50 to help defend the *Echo* crew.[51] The South Carolina Senate agreed to send to the Committee on Federal Relations Alexander Mazyck's extremist resolutions declaring that the federal laws against the African slave trade were unconstitutional, null, and void.[52] Three months before the *Echo* trial in Charleston, *De Bow's Review* published two articles on the issue of the constitutionality of the federal laws against the African slave trade. In "Is the Slave Trade Piracy?" D. S. Troy of Alabama asserted the term "piracy" as used in the Constitution did not include the African slave trade. Then where did Congress, he asked, obtain the power to punish American citizens as pirates for engaging in that trade?[53] In "Further Views of the Advocates of the Slave Trade," Thomas Walton of Mississippi went one step further than Troy. He called for the nullification of the "unconstitutional" federal prohibition of the African slave trade.[54] And "Van Tromp," a writer to the Charleston *Mercury*, suggested how this could be done. Laws must be based on the Constitution and citizens had the right to judge the constitutionality of the laws. "There is no sanction, legal or moral, by which a juryman can be com-

[50] James Farrow, in *De Bow's Review*, Vol. XXVII (September, 1859), p. 365; James Farrow to J. J. Pettigrew, May 23, 1859, Pettigrew Papers, North Carolina State Archives, Raleigh, North Carolina.

[51] Letter signed "A. W. D." in Charleston *Mercury*, September 15, 1858.

[52] Richmond *Enquirer*, December 3, 1858. See also Charleston *Mercury*, January 5, 1859; New York *Times*, December 1, 1858; Jackson *Semi-Weekly Mississippian*, May 10, 1859.

[53] Troy, in *De Bow's Review*, Vol. XXVI (January, 1859), p. 24.

[54] Walton, in *De Bow's Review*, Vol. XXVI (January, 1859), pp. 54–61; I. N. Davis, in Jackson *Semi-Weekly Mississippian*, April 26, 1859.

pelled to adopt the interpretation given to the Constitution by the Court, and intelligent and independent men will exercise their own judgment in spite of any refined theory to the contrary. . . ." [55]

The Charleston jury rendered their decision within the context of public and courtroom discussions on the constitutionality of the federal laws prohibiting the African slave trade. No wonder J. D. McRae of Mississippi declared to the Vicksburg Southern Commercial Convention that the *Echo* jury had based their verdict on their belief that the laws of Congress against the African slave trade were unconstitutional. A few weeks before the trial, Edmund Ruffin had predicted the exoneration of the *Echo* crewmen. The argument against the constitutionality of the federal prohibition, Ruffin wrote in his diary, was "so plausible" and concurred so well with the feelings, passions, and interests of Southerners. Consequently he was certain the jury would acquit every African slave-trader. "Never will a jury," Ruffin concluded, "be found to give a unanimous verdict against them." [56] Thus for many Southerners, one meaning of the *Echo* case was clear: the Charleston jury had tested the law's constitutionality, had defied the opinions of the federal judges, and had nullified the law of the land.

The *Echo* trial showed that African slave traders would not be punished in the South. The editor of the Jackson *Semi-Weekly Mississippian* openly invited Southerners to disobey the federal laws. "We venture to say," he shamelessly announced, "that the result of the judicial proceedings in Charleston are precisely what it would have been in almost any other community in the South. The enterprising trader who runs the gauntlet of the ocean police, need have no fears of serious molestation after he succeeds in landing his cargo upon the *terra firma* of a southern state." In a signed advertisement pub-

[55] "Van Tromp," in Charleston *Mercury*, March 23, 1859. For the Southern defense of the constitutionality of the laws, see Vicksburg *Whig*, in Jackson *Semi-Weekly Mississippian*, August 13, 1858; Savannah *Republican*, December 31, 1858.

[56] McRae, in *De Bow's Review*, XXVII (September, 1859), p. 362; Ruffin, Diary, February 23, 1859, Ruffin Papers, Library of Congress.

lished in a Mississippi newspaper, 18 Mississippi citizens declared they could not respect the "unconstitutional" laws against the African slave trade, and offered to pay $300 per slave for one thousand African slaves delivered in the South. The acquittal of the *Echo* prisoners and "the immunity of the crew of the Wanderer," Ruffin commented, demonstrated Southern refusal to enforce the federal laws and would probably promote an extensive importation of slaves from Africa.[57]

In their very expressions of scorn for the "unconstitutional" federal laws, many Southerners revealed an uneasiness, perhaps a guilt, about their gross defiance of the laws. Often they justified Southern defiance of the laws against the African slave trade as retaliation against Northern defiance of the Fugitive Slave Law of 1850. A Southern editor bluntly called it "Tit for Tat." [58] "What is the difference," asked the editor of the Brandon *Republican,* "between a Yankee violating the fugitive slave law in the North, and a Southern man violating . . . the law against the African slave trade in the South?" [59] In his address to South Carolina planters, a Dr. Bradford explained that there was an underground railroad to transport stolen slaves from the South to Canada, and that consequently there should be opened a "submarine railroad" from Africa to the South.[60] In their defense of the African slave trade, Southerners were not content simply to declare the federal laws "unconstitutional": they also had to blame Northerners for Southern violations of the laws.

Significantly many defenders of the *Echo* went farther: they justified the *Echo* on the basis of Southern "higher law."

[57] Jackson *Semi-Weekly Mississippian,* April 19, 1859; Enterprise *Weekly News,* in Charleston *Mercury,* May 25, 1859; Ruffin, Diary, April 22, 1859; Ruffin Papers, Library of Congress.

[58] *Cross City,* in Jackson *Semi-Weekly Mississippian,* May 24, 1859; Charleston *Mercury,* October 22, 1859; Galveston *Weekly News,* January 18, 1859.

[59] Brandon *Republican,* in Jackson *Semi-Weekly Mississippian,* June 7, 1859; Richmond *Whig,* in Jackson *Semi-Weekly Mississippian,* September 20, 1859; John Cunningham to J. Hammond, January 15, 1859, Hammond Papers, Library of Congress.

[60] Brunswick *Herald,* September 21, 1859.

The Southern defense of slavery included an appeal to a higher law—a law transcending the Constitution. Pro-slavery polemicist John Taylor of Caroline believed in the "right, anterior to every political power whatsoever, and alone sufficient to put the subject of slavery at rest; the natural right of self-defence." William Yancey declared that the "laws of nature in their majesty stand out from the issue more imperative than the obligations due to . . . Constitutions." Alexander Stephens also expressed a commitment to higher lawism. "I, too," he explained, "believe in the higher law—the law of the Creator. . . . Upon this, our cause eminently rests. . . . I would not swear to support any constitution inconsistent with this higher law." [61] Southerners, too, had a higher law.

In their defense of the *Echo* violation of the federal laws, many Southerners turned to this higher law doctrine. Like Charles A. L. Lamar, they declared their commitment to the rightness of the African slave trade and slavery rather than to the federal law. After congratulating the Charleston jury for the acquittal of the *Echo* prisoners, the editor of the Jackson *Semi-Weekly Mississippian* solemnly announced: "While [William] Seward sacrilegiously invokes the 'higher law' in behalf of his efforts to destroy the South, we have sanctioned the 'higher law' of self-protection against the assault of fanatical and unscrupulous enemies who are bent upon her destruction. We have said that if they violate the Constitution and steal her slaves to destroy her labor system, we are justified, if the necessity exists, in disregarding the laws which would prevent her from repairing the injury thus created; and that we would be the more justified in this course because the slave traffic finds its sanction in the examples of all Christian nations and 'in the Code of Laws that have emanated from a higher authority than man'." [62] Here the Mississippi editor was distinguishing between two forms of higher lawism. While Northern higher

[61] Taylor, quoted in Phillips, *The Course of the South to Secession,* p. 99; Yancey, Stephens, quoted in Carpenter, *South as a Conscious Minority,* pp. 199–200.
[62] Jackson *Semi-Weekly Mississippian,* April 22, 1859.

lawism involved sacrilege, fanaticism, and destruction, Southern higher lawism, on the other hand, signified self-protection and divine sanction and authority. To be sure, the editor had presented a highly distorted view of abolitionist higher law, and had also failed to make clear the relationship between the law of self-protection and the law of God.[63] Nevertheless, in the editor's judgment, Southern higher law had given Southerners a moral justification to violate unjust federal laws: they could reopen the African slave trade with God on their side.

Southerners who identified themselves with the *Echo* prisoners and who projected their own anxieties onto the men on trial for piracy had to ask themselves the awesome question: what should be their relationship with the federal laws against the African slave trade? Addressing himself to this issue, a writer to the Charleston *Mercury* queried: "Now, what is the meaning of this word guilty? . . . It means that a wrong has been done and that the wrong doer must suffer. It is not sufficient, therefore, to take the facts alone into consideration, but the moral characters of the acts. If the man who carries negroes from Virginia to Louisiana for sale is an innocent man, he cannot be a guilty man who buys them in Africa and sells them in Cuba. It is impossible that one can be right and the other wrong. But the law has made it wrong. The law is absurd which attempts to create such distinctions. Both parties are alike negro traders; both are alike innocent or alike guilty. No sensible body of men can be expected to give efficacy to an absurd law."[64] Like Charles A. L. Lamar, this writer to the *Mercury* insisted there should be no distinction between the domestic and African slave trades. Thus if the slave trades, African and Southern, were right, if the federal law were "absurd," then Southerners should have no loyalty to an "absurd" law. They had to do what they thought was right.

[63] For a discussion of abolitionist higher law, see Russel B. Nye, *Fettered Freedom: Civil Liberties and the Slavery Controversy, 1830–1860* (East Lansing: Michigan State University Press, 1949), pp. 192–195; Timothy L. Smith, *Revivalism and Social Reform* (New York: Harper & Row, 1965), pp. 205–206.
[64] "F. A. P." in Charleston *Mercury*, September 29, 1858.

But if Southerners obeyed the federal law, if they convicted the *Echo* prisoners, many Southerners realized, then they
would not only be supporting the law which they condemned
but also condemning themselves. "Ought Negro-traders to be
hung?" asked a Louisiana defender of the *Echo* crew. His
answer was pointed: "Is any slaveholder in favor of thus branding himself as a pirate?" [65] Immediately after the *Echo* jury
rendered the not guilty verdict, the Charleston *Mercury* explained that the jurymen probably thought it would be "inconsistent" and "hypocritical" for them, "as members of a community where slaves are bought and sold every day, and are
as much and as frequently articles of commerce as the sugar
and molasses which they produce, to pass condemnation and
a verdict of guilty of death upon men whose only crime was
that they were going to a far country, to bring in more supplies
of the articles of trade, these *commodities. . . .*" [66] In a letter
to William Porcher Miles, written about two months before the
Echo trials in Charleston, defense counsel Leonidas W. Spratt
revealed what he considered was one of the significant meanings
of the *Echo* trial. "It will not be whether we shall nullify an
act of Congress but whether we shall let individuals be punished for an act which *we cannot condemn without concurring
in the censure upon our institution.*" [67] In the Charleston court
house, Southerners and their slaveholding civilization were on
trial.

Southern defenders of the *Echo* prisoners obeyed a Southern
higher law rather than an "absurd" federal law, and sought to
acquit themselves from their own crimes and guilts of slave
trading and slaveholding. And from their self-constructed moral
fortress, they could scorn Republican David Kilgore of Indiana,
whose anguish over the *Echo* case led him to introduce in
Congress the resolution that "no legislation can be too thorough

[65] "The South," in Richmond *Enquirer*, October 19, 1858.
[66] Charleston *Mercury*, April 29, 1859. Italics added.
[67] Spratt to Miles, February 12, 1859, Miles Papers, University of
North Carolina Library. Italics added. See also Philadelphia *North American*, in Charleston *Mercury*, May 7, 1859.

in its measures, nor can any penalty known to the catalogue of modern punishment for crime be too severe against a traffic so inhuman and unchristian." They could also scorn Senator William Seward and his demand for ten war steamers to patrol the African and American coasts in order to suppress the outrageous illegal importation of African slaves. They could also scorn the New York State Senate and its resolution condemning the illegal African slave trade as an "invasion of our laws, of our feelings, and of the dictates of Christianity. . . ."[68] Yet, in their rebellious protest against the federal law and the moral sentiments of the North, these defiant fire-eaters were also trying to discipline white Southerners. If Southerners believed in slavery, they declared, then Southerners must condemn the federal law as a "lie." On the other hand, if Southerners respected the federal law, then they must be condemned as "abolitionists."[69] Thus these Southern radicals were also aiming their barbed defense of the African slave trade at Southerners themselves.

But many Southerners found that they could not share nor support what they considered the frantic and raving defiance of the *Echo* apologists. The editor of the New Orleans *Picayune* accused the Charleston jury of practicing the dangerous belief of "higher laws." This, he added, was the "worst sort of policy —as it is morally wrong—for us of the South to weaken ourselves by countenancing, in any way, a denial of the obligations to support the laws, or by encouraging the higher law theories of the supremacy of popular sentiment over statutes and constitutions. These constitute the law of order, protection and safety for minorities. . . ."[70] In a speech at Monticello, Mississippi, Senator Albert Gallatin Brown declared that he "utterly

[68] Jackson *Semi-Weekly Mississippian*, February 4, 1859; in Du Bois, *Suppression of the African Slave Trade*, p. 175; New York *Times*, April 15, 1859.

[69] Letter signed "A Pirate," in Jackson *Semi-Weekly Mississippian*, June 17, 1859.

[70] New Orleans *Picayune*, April 30, 1859; S. B. Newman, in Jackson *Daily Mississippian*, November 10, 1859; Baltimore *American*, in Washington *National Intelligencer*, April 26, 1859.

repudiated the doctrine that juries might acquit on the ground that *they* thought the law unconstitutional. This was the higher law. It was too high for him to stand upon. If he stood upon its summit his head would grow dizzy in contemplating the mischief it would inflict on the country." [71] But the editor of the *Picayune* and Brown had not answered the essential question raised by *Echo* defenders: would not the conviction and hanging of the *Echo* prisoners signify the condemnation of the South and its peculiar institution?

For years, the advocates of the reopening of the African slave trade had been insisting that if slavery were right, then the African slave trade must be right. Thus they proposed to transform the African slave trade into a new symbol aggressively affirming the morality of the peculiar institution in order to convince Southerners of the rightness of slavery, and possibly also to help mitigate their own psychological and moral uneasiness caused by the contradiction of slavery, an institution that ambivalently recognized the slave as property and yet as person. Like the *Wanderer*, the *Echo* gave to this new symbol an unmistakable concreteness. And the advocates sought to use the *Echo* to press their point. They contemptuously invoked a Southern higher law to justify Southern disobedience of federal laws "dictated by a false and foreign sentiment." [72]

But, for some Southerners, the *Echo* only caused greater distress because they found it impossible to reconcile the newly defined and fantastic moral meaning of the African slave trade with the brutal and hideous realities of the traffic in human bodies. One such Southerner was D. H. Hamilton. Like Charles A. L. Lamar, Hamilton was an advocate of the African slave trade. As the United States Marshal in Charleston, he had been placed in charge of the *Echo* Africans while they were in port. His horrible encounter with the surviving Africans who

[71] Brown, in Jackson *Semi-Weekly Mississippian*, June 14, 1859; Nashville *Banner*, in Nashville *Union*, May 25, 1859; Milledgeville *Federal Union*, July 5, 1859.

[72] Resolution passed at meeting held at Edgefield Court House, South Carolina, in Jackson *Semi-Weekly Mississippian*, April 22, 1859.

had been reduced to mere fragments of humanity shattered his belief in the African slave trade and left him badly shaken. He knew the *Echo* slaves were property, but above all, he knew they were human beings. And unlike Lamar, he realized he could no longer ride the hobbyhorse of the African slave-trade fantasy. In a private letter to a friend, the anguished Hamilton confessed: "Thirty-five [*Echo* slaves] died while in my custody, and at one time I supposed that one hundred would have fallen a sacrifice to the cruelties, to which the poor creatures had been subjected on board the Slaver. I wish that everyone in So. Ca. who is in favour of the re-opening of the Slave-trade, could have seen what I have been compelled to witness for the three weeks of their stay at Fort Sumter. It seems to me that I can never forget it." [73] For Southerners like Hamilton, the pro-slavery crusade of fire-eaters like Lamar and Hughes did not help them overcome their moral dilemma concerning slavery. The agitation to reopen the African slave trade offered them anxiety rather than therapy.

[73] Hamilton to Hammond, September 24, 1858, Hammond Papers, Library of Congress; D. H. Hamilton to W. P. Miles, February 27, 1860, Miles Papers, University of North Carolina Library.

THE
SOUTHERN
DILEMMA

b ut a far greater irony was still to occur.

The men of the pro-slavery crusade did not know this as they pursued their course towards secession, and as Alabama advocates of the African slave trade planned to divide the National Democratic Party in the presidential election of 1860. The aim of their conspiracy was obvious: they wanted to "open the door of the Executive Mansion to the Black Republicans" in order to drive the Southern states into secession.[1] Clearly the issue of the African slave trade could be used to block the nomination of Senator Stephen A. Douglas and to disrupt the

[1] Montgomery *Confederation*, in Galveston *Civilian*, July 19, 1859.

National Democracy at the Charleston Convention. Senator Douglas, the only leader who could possibly hold together the Southern and Northern wings of the Democratic Party, was firmly committed to the prohibition of the African slave trade. He had declared that he was "irreconcilably opposed to the revival of the African slave trade in any form and under any circumstances." Moreover, Senator Douglas had warned his party he definitely could not accept the presidential nomination if the Charleston Democratic Convention included the demand for the reopening of the African slave trade in the party's platform.[2] Thus Douglas and the party were in an extremely vulnerable situation. If the Alabama African slave-trade advocates could force their demand for the trade into the party's platform at Charleston, they could politically destroy Douglas and guarantee a Republican victory in 1860. If they lost the fight over the platform, they could walk out of the convention in protest and possibly initiate a general Southern bolt and the disruption of the National Democracy.

While Alabama African slave-trade advocates were plotting to take their issue to Charleston, Southern fire-eaters like Robert Barnwell Rhett, Jr., fearful of the African slave trade as a divisive issue in Southern politics, were trying to suppress the trade agitation. Rhett, the editor of the Charleston *Mercury*, closed all discussion on the African trade in his newspaper in late 1859. The African slave-trade agitation, he argued, could splinter and paralyze the movement for Southern secession in the crisis of 1860.[3] In a letter signed "Philo St. James Santee," a writer to the Charleston *Mercury* outlined the strategy of fire-eaters like Rhett. "Philo" urged Southerners to leave the trade issue alone and concentrate on the election of 1860. "We cannot dissolve the Union on the issue of the African slave

---

[2] Douglas to Dorn, June 22, 1859, in Jackson *Semi-Weekly Mississippian*, July 1, 1859; New York *Tribune*, June 24, 1859; Douglas to Peyton, August 2, 1859, in Washington *National Intelligencer*, August 13, 1859.

[3] Charleston *Mercury*, October 13 and 15, 1859; R. B. Rhett, Jr., to James Chesnut, October 17, 1859, Chesnut-Manning Papers, University of South Carolina Library.

trade; but we may do so by the Presidential election." "Philo" suggested that Southerners nominate a Southern rights, slave-holding candidate for President. If they won, then the South could rule within the Union; if they failed to capture the Presidency, they would have a united sectional movement to carry the South out of the Union.[4] Concerned about their plan of Southern action for the Presidential election, these Southern radicals sought to muffle the African slave-trade agitation, for they viewed it as a threat to Southern unity.

Thus both Senator Douglas and many Southern fire-eaters were against the agitation for the reopening of the African slave trade; both wanted to keep the trade issue out of the Charleston Democratic Convention. But they were not entirely successful. Four days after the opening of the convention, Leroy Pope Walker of Alabama presented a resolution declaring that the Federal Government must offer "protection and equal advantage to all descriptions of property recognized as such by the laws of any of the States as well within the Territories as *upon the high seas. . . .*"[5] This was in effect an African slave-trade resolution, for the statement "all descriptions of property . . . upon the high seas" could be applied to African slaves.[6] Thus Walker was asking the Democratic Party to support a proposal for the federal protection of slavery in the territories and of the African slave trade. Undoubtedly he did not expect the convention, controlled by Douglas, to approve his explosive resolution. After the Douglas forces defeated the Alabama effort

[4] Charleston *Mercury,* in Savannah *Morning News,* October 14, 1859. William Yancey, on the other hand, was reluctant to use the presidential election to justify secession. "I say it, with all deference to my colleagues," Yancey argued, "that no more inferior issue could be tendered in the South, upon which we should dissolve the Union, than the loss of an election." Galveston *Civilian,* November 13, 1860.

[5] In Murat Halstead, *A History of the National Political Conventions of the Current Presidential Campaign . . .* (Columbus: Follett, Foster & Co., 1860), pp. 39–43. Italics added.

[6] Benjamin F. Butler of Massachusetts pointed out that the phrase the "rights of persons and property on the high seas" was "capable of a construction . . . to assert the duty of Government to protect the African slave-trade," and that such a construction would "do the Northern Democracy incalculable mischief." In *ibid.,* p. 46.

to force the African slave trade into the party's platform, and after the convention adopted the Douglas platform, Walker led the Alabama delegation out of the convention. As they stormed out of the hall, crowds of excited Charlestonians in the galleries burst into applause. Amidst more cheering, the delegates from Mississippi, Louisiana, South Carolina, Florida, and Texas arose and followed Walker's fateful footsteps.

After the Southern walkout, William B. Goulden of Georgia addressed the convention to criticize the actions of Walker and the Southern bolters, and to express his commitment to the Union and the African slave trade. Goulden was both a Unionist and an African slave-trade advocate. Like James Hammond and Howell Cobb, Goulden supported the Southern efforts to cooperate with the National Democratic Party and to defend slavery within the Union. But like Leonidas W. Spratt and Henry Hughes, Goulden was an agitator for the reopening of the African slave trade. Goulden's strategy was to set up a coalition between Southern and Northern Democrats to repeal the federal laws against the African slave trade, import African slaves for Southern expansion into the territories, and restore Southern political power in the Federal Government. For Goulden, the African slave trade would be the means to preserve the peculiar institution and the Union.[7]

But Walker and his associates had used the African slave-trade issue to help bring about the disruption of the National Democracy at Charleston, and had helped to place a "Black Republican" in the executive mansion. Shortly after the election, Robert Barnwell Rhett visited the British Consul at Charleston to discuss the coming secession and the future relationship between the Southern Confederacy and Great Britain. In their conversation, both men candidly discussed the question of the African slave trade. Consul Robert Bunch explained that the Southern efforts to revive the African slave trade horrified the British government. Thus to make certain the new Southern government would neither encourage nor tolerate the traffic,

[7] Goulden, in Washington *National Intelligencer*, May 5, 1860.

Great Britain would require from the Confederacy a distinct assurance the trade would remain closed. Otherwise, Bunch warned, his government would not enter cordially into communication with the Confederacy. "No Southern State, or Confederacy," Rhett snapped back, "would ever be brought to negotiate upon such a subject," for "to prohibit the Slave Trade was, virtually, to admit that the Institution of Slavery was an evil and a wrong, instead of, as the South believed it, a blessing to the African Race and a system of labour appointed of God." [8] Like Lamar and Fitzhugh, the South Carolina secessionist recognized a moral equation between the African slave trade and slavery. For Rhett, the seceding Southern states could not condemn the very reason for secession—the rightness of slavery.

Two months later, however, the Montgomery Convention, assembled to write a constitution and establish the Confederacy, prohibited the African slave trade. In the Constitution for the Confederate States of America, the Convention not only forbade the importation of slaves from Africa but also required the Confederate Congress to enact legislation to outlaw the trade.[9]

This was, for Rhett, the "most unkindest cut of all." His fellow secessionists had branded the African slave trade and slavery. But many Southern supporters of the Confederate Constitutional prohibition of the African slave trade had not intended to stigmatize the trade. In their movement to write the prohibition into the Confederate Constitution, Southern leaders like William R. Smith of Alabama insistently affirmed their belief in the rightness of the African slave trade. "The question of morality," secessionist Smith explained, "does not of necessity arise here. As a matter of opinion, I do not believe that the African Slave Trade would in itself be immoral. . . . I hold that the African taken from his native wilds and placed in ranks that march onward from savage to civilized life is greatly

[8] Rhett, in "Dispatch from the British Consul at Charleston to Lord John Russell, 1860," *The American Historical Review,* XVIII (July, 1913), p. 786.

[9] Constitution for the Provisional Government of the Confederate States of America, in Edgefield *Advertiser,* February 20, 1861.

benefitted—He is humanized and christianized." [10] Like Rhett, Smith juxtaposed the African and Africa against himself and the South. Thus, for both Rhett and Smith, the African slave trade served to confirm their identity as civilized and Christian men.

The editor of *The Southern Episcopalian*, however, failed to see this consensus between Southerners like Rhett and Smith. In his applause for the Confederate prohibition of the African slave trade, he interpreted the prohibition as a moral protest against the trade. Like Thomas Jefferson and Emerson Etheridge, the editor of the *Episcopalian* had a moral abhorrence for the African slave trade. Commenting on the Montgomery Convention, he declared: "Our fathers, slaveholders like ourselves, decided upon moral grounds, that this traffic was inadmissible, and put a stop to it half a century ago." [11] Actually the actions of the Montgomery Convention against the African slave trade were based largely upon tactical rather than "moral grounds." The Confederate prohibition was designed to appease European sentiments against the traffic. Many founders of the Confederacy were anxious to show the new government's orthodoxy on the African slave trade. In the Georgia secession convention, T. R. R. Cobb argued that an ordinance against the African slave trade should be promptly passed to assure the world that the people of Georgia had not dissolved their political connection with the Federal Union in order to reopen the African slave trade. In the Alabama secession convention, William R. Smith asked: Would it be wise for a newly formed nation "to bid defiance to the whole civilized world? Have we grown so great in the brief period of a single week, that we shall court the frowns of all Christendom, and bring down upon our earliest deliberations the anathemas of all Europe?" [12]

Concerned about world opinion, these Southern leaders

10 Smith, *Convention of Alabama*, p. 201.
11 *The Southern Episcopalian*, VII, No. 12 (March, 1861), p. 655.
12 Cobb, in Milledgeville *Federal Union*, January 29, 1861; Smith, *Convention of Alabama*, pp. 204–205. See also R. Simms to Alexander Stephens, January 25, 1861, Stephens Papers, Library of Congress.

suppressed the African slave trade in order to facilitate English and French diplomatic recognition of the Confederacy. But they were also worried that the African slave trade, if it were reopened, would lead the Confederacy into armed conflict with Britain. The editor of the Augusta *Constitutionalist* warned that such a confrontation would be disastrous for the South. If the Southern Congress declared the trade legal, he argued, then the Confederate government would have the responsibility to protect its citizens engaged in the trade. "As, then, we have no navy . . . are not able to whip the world, and have plenty to do in regulating our domestic matters," he asked, "is it not wise in Congress—at least till after we get Sumter and Pickens —to keep people out of difficulties, piracy, hanging, etc., by telling them *for the present to be content with what slaves they have?*" [13] William Smith of Alabama put it this way: If the Confederacy refused to prohibit the African slave trade, then the interception of a Southern slave ship by a foreign power would be an act hostile to Confederate commerce and equivalent to a declaration of war.[14] Faced with the prospect of war with the North, the Confederacy could not afford to risk the possibility of war with England.

More important than the need to win European diplomatic recognition and to avoid an armed clash with the English navy was the fear that the border states would not join the new and insecure Confederacy. The Southern leaders who engineered the Confederate prohibition of the African slave trade were worried about the antagonism between the border states and the cotton states. Aware of the border states' vested interest in the domestic slave trade, they knew that these states would not tolerate the reopening of the African slave trade. They knew that the African slave trade, if it were reopened, could force the border states into the Yankee camp. They could remember the Richmond *Enquirer's* sober warning in 1858. "We can see no good whatever to be accomplished by the continued

13 Augusta *Constitutionalist*, in Washington *National Intelligencer*, February 25, 1861.
14 Smith, *Convention of Alabama*, p. 205.

discussion of this question [African slave trade]," the editor threatened. "If the cotton States are determined to revive the slave trade, and thus to destroy the value of slavery in every non-cotton-growing State, it will demonstrate a selfishness of which we have believed Southern States incapable. If a dissolution of the Union is to be followed by the revival of the slave trade, Virginia had better consider whether the South of a Northern Confederacy would not be far more preferable for her than the North of a Southern Confederacy. In the Northern Confederacy, Virginia would derive a large amount from the sale of her slaves to the South, and a gain in the increased value of her lands from Northern emigration—while in the Southern Confederacy, with the African slave trade revived, she would lose two-thirds of the value of her slave property, and derive no additional increase to the value of her lands." [15]

During the final crisis of 1860–61, Southern secessionists nervously noticed that Virginia seemed to show great concern for the protection of the domestic slave trade and little enthusiasm for joining the Confederacy. Their fears were not imaginary. In December 1860 the editor of the Charlottesville *Review* proposed that the border states seek from the Northern states guarantees for the preservation of slavery in order to remain in the Union. In January Congressmen from border and free states met, elected John F. Crittenden their chairman, and appointed a committee to study several compromise propositions. In their report, the committee recommended a Constitutional amendment to forbid the abolition of slavery, and a prohibition of the African slave trade.[16]

[15] Richmond *Enquirer*, in Boston *Liberator*, June 18, 1858. See also Richmond *Enquirer*, in Charleston *Mercury*, June 2, 1858; Richmond *Enquirer*, June 1 and 4, 1858; Thomas J. Kirkpatrick to A. H. Stephens, March 2, 1861, Stephens Papers, Library of Congress; Henry E. Colton to J. De Bow, January 15, 1860, De Bow Papers, Duke University Library; W. G. Simms to W. P. Miles, February 22, 1861, Miles Papers, University of North Carolina Library.

[16] Charlottesville *Review*, December 14, 1860, in Washington *National Intelligencer*, December 15, 1860; Charlottesville *Review*, November 30, 1860; John Bach McMaster, *A History of the People of the United States*,

The wavering of Virginia panicked the deep South. "I look with intense anxiety to the actions of the border States," wrote Hershel Johnson to Alexander Stephens, who was attending the Montgomery Convention. "If they join us, we will constitute a respectable power among nations. . . . If they adhere to the old Union, I shall regard it as a precursor of their emancipating, at an early day. This will be a calamity on us." [17] Sharing a similar anxiety, William Yancey told the Alabama secession convention that he would propose a prohibition of the African slave trade at the Montgomery Convention "because we should offer inducements to the slaves States, which have not yet seceded, to do so." [18] Underlying the need to draw Virginia into the Confederacy was the great fear of war with the North. For William Smith, a leading supporter of the Confederate prohibition of the African slave trade, war was a certainty. "If this war is expected," he declared, "and who does not expect it?" [19] Clearly the Confederacy needed Virginia as a source of industrial support for Dixie's war machine and as a buffer against Northern invasion. Thus many secessionists were willing to offer the prohibition of the African slave trade as a bribe to buy Virginia's support for the Confederacy. In January 1861 the editor of the *Southern Literary Messenger* announced that leading men in the Gulf states were willing to incorporate a provision against the African slave trade into the Confederate Constitution in order to assure Virginians the trade would remain closed. "Can Virginia ask more?" [20]

[17] Johnson to Stephens, February 13, 1861, Hershel Johnson Papers, Duke University Library. See also R. Simms to A. Stephens, January 25, 1861, Stephens Papers, Library of Congress; T. Kirkpatrick to A. Stephens, March 2, 1861, *ibid.,* A. Miltenberger to T. O. Moore, February 25, 1861, Moore Papers, Louisiana State University Papers, E. Ruffin to J. Perkins, Jr., March 2, 1861, Perkins Papers, University of North Carolina Library.

[18] Yancey, in Smith, *Convention of Alabama,* p. 251.

[19] Smith, in *ibid.,* p. 260.

[20] *Southern Literary Messenger* (January, 1861), p. 76. See also the Augusta *Chronicle & Sentinel,* February 20, 1861, in Washington *National*

But the Montgomery Convention attached a threat to this bribe. The second part of the Constitutional prohibition gave Congress the power to prohibit the introduction of slaves from non-Confederate states. This provision was intended to coerce the border states into joining the Confederacy. The prohibition of the domestic slave trade from Virginia would force the Old Dominion into a distressing predicament. "If . . . we shall simply prohibit the trade in slaves from any quarter outside the limits of the Southern Confederacy," explained Yancey of Alabama, "then will those border States have presented to them this grave issue: shall they join the South and keep their slaves, or sell them, as they choose—or shall they join the North, and lose their slaves by abolition?" [21] A Southerner present at the Montgomery Convention observed that the Convention had forbidden the foreign slave trade and had provided for the prohibition of slave importations from "other slave states not members of the Confederacy, which will not suit Virginia, if she does not come in." [22] In February 1861, Henry L. Benning, the commissioner from Georgia, informed hesitant Virginians that the Montgomery Convention had placed a Constitutional ban upon the African slave trade in order to expel "the illusion" deterring "some timid persons from uniting with us." But, he bluntly added, if Virginia would not join the Confederacy, the Confederate Congress would close the Virginia slave trade.[23]

Clearly Southerners of the new Confederacy faced a profound dilemma. Afraid to provoke the moral and military wrath of England and afraid to alienate the border states, the Confederacy had prohibited the African slave trade. The reopening

Intelligencer, February 25, 1861; J. T. Morgan and H. C. Jones, in Smith, *Convention of Alabama,* pp. 199, 206.

[21] Confederate Constitution, in Edgefield *Advertiser,* February 20, 1861; Yancey, in Smith, *Convention of Alabama,* p. 252. See also Governor of Mississippi, in Richmond *Enquirer,* January 8, 1861; Governor of South Carolina, in Richmond *Enquirer,* November 30, 1860.

[22] James Deas to James Chesnut, February 12, 1861, Chesnut Papers, Duke University Library. See also William Smith, in Easby-Smith, *William Russell Smith,* p. 114; J. T. Morgan, in Smith, *Convention of Alabama,* p. 198.

[23] Benning, in Richmond *Enquirer,* February 22, 1861.

of the trade would have meant national suicide for the South. If the Confederacy were forced into a war against both the North and England, and if it did not have the enlistment of Virginia, the new slaveholding nation would have quickly ended with a whimper. But, as the basis of a slaveholding nation, the Confederate Constitution was a moral disaster: the Constitutional prohibition of the trade represented the Confederacy's failure to offer moral leadership in the defense of slavery. Thus the action of the Montgomery Convention outlawing the trade appalled many Southerners. "For God's sake," exclaimed the editor of the Jacksonville *Southern Confederacy*, "and for the sake of consistency, do not let us form a Union for the express purpose of maintaining and propagating African slavery, and then, as the Southern Congress have done, confess our error by enacting a constitutional provision abolishing the African slave trade." [24] The editor of the Bellefonte (Alabama) *Era* lamented: "We must regard the Constitutional prohibition . . . as a more fatal stab at slavery than was ever inflicted upon it by its outside enemies. Such a prohibition would soon put an end to the Government or to slavery or to both." [25] The editor of the Charleston *Mercury* angrily declared: *"We deem it also unfortunate and mal apropos that the stigma of illegitimacy should be placed upon the institution of slavery by a fundamental law against the slave trade."* [26] In the judgment of these unhappy Southerners, the Confederacy's action on the African slave trade was a moral blunder: the pro-slavery government had condemned slavery.

South Carolina was the storm center of the protest against the Confederate Constitutional prohibition of the African slave trade. The Southern cult of chivalry was more extreme in South

[24] Jacksonville *Southern Confederacy*, in J. E. Cairnes, *The Slave Power*, p. 290.

[25] Bellefonte *Era*, February 21, 1861, in Washington *National Intelligencer*, February 26, 1861.

[26] Charleston *Mercury*, February 12, 1861, in Washington *National Intelligencer*, February 15, 1861. See also Charleston *Mercury*, February 16, 1861, and February 25, 1861.

238

Carolina than in any other Southern state.[27] Obsessively committed to honor and integrity, many proud and haughty Palmetto Cavaliers despised the Montgomery Convention's concern for expediency rather than principle. For them, the Confederate Constitution was worse than an embarrassment: it was an abomination. In the South Carolina secession convention, they furiously attacked the Confederate Constitutional provision against the importation of Africans. In their defiant resolutions, ardent secessionists and African slave-trade advocates like Gabriel Manigault and John I. Middleton declared that South Carolina could not ratify the Confederate Constitution unless it allowed the African slave trade.[28]

But the prospect of a certain event was making this debate irrelevant. Ten days before the bombardment of Fort Sumter, a delegate to the South Carolina secession convention told his wife: "The debates are going on upon the ratification of Confederate constitution. . . . The ratification will be nearly unanimous, and without amendments." [29] The following day the South Carolina convention ratified the Constitution by a vote of 138 to 21. Among the delegates voting against ratification were African slave-trade advocates like James H. Adams, Maxcy Gregg, Gabriel Manigault, Alexander Mazyck, John I. Middleton, and Leonidas W. Spratt. Later that day James Hammond observed: "I see the Constitution has been adopted by an overwhelming majority against Rhett & Co., Slave traders . . . fire eaters, and extremists, and I suppose this is an end of them. It is certain that these men brought on this great movement." [30]

But the South Carolina African slave-trade extremists refused to surrender. They had brought on the "great movement"

[27] For a study of the Southern cult of chivalry in South Carolina, see Osterweis, *Romanticism and Nationalism in the Old South*, pp. 111–154.

[28] *Journal of the Convention of the People of South Carolina, Held in 1860–1861* (Charleston: Evans & Cogswell, 1861), pp. 219–227.

[29] John L. Manning to wife, April 2, 1861, Chesnut-Manning Papers, University of South Carolina Library.

[30] *Journal of the Convention of South Carolina*, pp. 240–250; Hammond to J. D. Ashmore, April 23, 1861, Hammond Papers, Library of Congress.

for Southern secession in order to proclaim the rightness of the African slave trade and slavery. Thus they agitated for amendments to strike out the African slave-trade prohibition even after the South Carolina convention had ratified the Confederate Constitution. Finally, on April 5, they won a limited victory. The convention resolved that as soon as the Confederacy was securely established and in peaceful operation, South Carolina should call for the meeting of a national convention to consider the repeal of the Confederate Constitutional prohibition of the African slave trade.[31]

The Confederate Constitutional prohibition of the African slave trade was a bitter and painful disappointment for Palmetto son Leonidas W. Spratt, "the philosopher of the new African slave trade." Spratt had been an uncompromising prophet of the new proslavery crusade. Like many Southern fire-eaters of the 1850's, he was a graduate of the College of South Carolina, a sectionalist-oriented school for "children of . . . Nullifiers." Like many young men of the South in the decade before the Civil War, Spratt became involved in a pro-slavery crusade to confront the perplexing moral contradictions of his slaveholding society and to educate Southerners about "The Destiny of the Slave States." [32]

It was indeed fitting that pro-slavery philosopher Spratt was the author of the most eloquent protest against the Confederate Constitutional prohibition of the African slave trade. In a letter to one of the delegates to the Montgomery Convention, he expressed the deep anxieties of many Southerners, anxieties secession alone could not relieve. Like Henry Hughes, James Adams, and many Southern fire-eaters of his day, Spratt was distressed about the *internal crisis* of Southern society—a crisis based essentially on the fear of white class struggle and potential anarchy within the South, and on the need to establish the rightness of slavery as well as the identity of Southerners as both slaveholding and moral.

[31] *Journal of the Convention of South Carolina*, p. 261 ff.

[32] New York *Tribune*, in Boston *Liberator*, August 19, 1859; Osterweis, p. 141; Charleston *Southern Standard*, June 25, 1853.

The real contest, Spratt observed, was not between two geographical sections but between "the two forms of society which have become established, the one at the North, and the other at the South." [33] In the North, society was composed of one race; in the South, society was composed of two races. These racial realities had crucial social and political significance. While Northern society was bound together by "the two great social relations of husband and wife and parent and child," Southern society was united by "the three relations of husband and wife, parent and child, and master and slave." Furthermore the North had hireling labor and the South had slave labor. In the North, the white laborers had "the power to rise and appropriate by law the goods protected by the State"; in the South, the black laborers were controlled and powerless. Thus the Southern "ship of State has the ballast of a disfranchised class: there is no possibility of political upheaval." The two forms of society were thus antithetical, and the "natural expansion of the one must become encroachment on the other, and so the contest was inevitable."

But, Spratt declared, "the contest is not ended with a dissolution of the Union," and "the agents of the contest still exist *within* the limits of the Southern States." He warned that the monopolization of slaveholding and the increasing intenseness of Southern social conflicts could destroy Southern society. The 500,000 nonslaveholders in Virginia, he pointed out, were in competition with slaves and did not constitute a part of slave society. Even in South Carolina the "process of disintegration" had commenced. Foreign laborers within the last ten years had settled in Charleston to take the places of 10,000 slaves drawn away from the city by the attractive slave prices of the West. These white workers represented a worrisome threat to the slaveholding society of South Carolina. They sought to exclude slaves from the trades, public works, drays, and hotels. And when more white workers come South, Spratt fearfully predicted, "they will question the right of masters to employ

[33] Spratt to John Perkins, in Charleston *Mercury*, February 13, 1861. Italics added.

their slaves in any works that they may wish for; they will invoke the aid of legislation; they will use the elective franchise to that end, they may acquire the power to determine municipal elections; they will inexorably use it; and thus this town of Charleston, at the very heart of slavery, may become a fortress of democratic power against it." Indeed, Spratt declared, "having achieved one revolution to escape democracy at the North, it [the South] must still achieve another to escape it at the South."

Spratt then posed the "impending question": will slavery be established as a *"normal"* institution of society? *"I regard the slave trade,"* he anxiously exclaimed, *"as the test of its integrity. If that be right, then slavery is right, but not without."* Thus he condemned the Confederate Constitutional prohibition of the African slave trade as "a great calamity," as a "brand" upon slavery. The Confederacy, Spratt argued, should avow slavery "as a living principle of social order, and assert its right, not to toleration only, but to extension and political recognition among the nations of the earth." Above all, the new slaveholding nation of the South should not be ashamed of "its nature and destiny."

The message of Spratt's somber protest was clear. The Confederate Constitution provided little security against the threatening anarchy of social conflicts within Southern white society. If the African slave trade remained closed, if Southern class turmoil intensified, and if the relation between master and slave were abolished, then the biracial society of the South would have only "the two great social relations of husband and wife and parent and child." Like the Alabama farmer who did not want to "hev a niggar steppin' up" to his "darter," and like Henry Hughes who wanted to protect the "purity of the females of one race," Spratt believed that the master–slave relation was crucial for the preservation of the Southern white identity and destiny.[34]

But Spratt's disgust for the Confederate Constitution in-

[34] Alabama farmer, in Olmsted, *Seaboard*, Vol. II, p. 219; Hughes, *Treatise on Sociology*, p. 288.

volved more than a concern for the preservation of slaveholding class hegemony and Southern white supremacy. The new constitution, in his judgment, offered Southerners little peace of mind on the vexatious question of the institution's rightness. In their new Constitution, Southerners had trapped themselves in an intolerable moral contradiction. They had reaffirmed the rightness of slavery but had reprobated the means to the formation of the institution. They had implicitly repudiated slavery as a *"normal"* institution of society. They had condemned themselves. This, to Spratt, was a grievous mistake. As slaveholders and as Southern gentlemen concerned about principle and integrity, Southerners of the new Confederacy should realize and accept who they were or should be. They must not stand at the pinnacle of secession only to remain mired in moral confusion over slavery. While they could not repeal history, they should break radically from that Southern past condemning the African slave trade. The problem for slaveholders was not the defense of the world they had made, but the need to create a new and logical world for slaveholders—where they could be both slaveholding and moral men. Like the Southern Methodists demanding the expunction of the church rules on slavery, like the Yanceyites seeking to expose "unsoundness in our midst on the question of slavery," and like the members of the grand jury protesting against their own indictment of Lamar for his involvement in the *Wanderer* slave importations, Spratt believed that Southerners should aggressively and confidently claim their moral innocence.[35] For Spratt, the Confederacy should be the national model of the Southern Commercial Conventions: it should be an asylum for pro-slavery men.

In the depths of his anguish, Spratt recognized the terribly ironic significance of the Confederate Constitution: on the eve of the violent Civil War, white Southerners had, in the supreme moment of defiance, denied the rightness of the peculiar institution. The Confederacy itself was unsound on slavery. Unless the Confederacy endorsed the norms and values essential to

[35] Yancey, in Charleston *Mercury,* July 9, 1859.

Southern society, unless the Confederacy enabled Southerners to live *with themselves* as well as by themselves, unless the Confederacy reopened the African slave trade, Southerners would never realize their "destiny" as a slaveholding nation. At the end of his letter, in bitter protest against the irony of Southern secession, Spratt again called for "another revolution. It *may be painful,* but we must make it."

BIBLIOGRAPHY

PRIMARY SOURCES

Manuscripts

Bell, John. Library of Congress.

Branch, L. O'B. Duke University Library.

Breaux, Gustave A. Tulane University Library.

Brown, Albert G. Mississippi Department of Archives and History.

Burt, Armistead. Duke University Library.

Chesnut, James. Duke University Library.

————. Letterbook, South Caroliniana Library, University of South Carolina.

Chesnut-Manning-Williams. South Caroliniana Library, University of South Carolina.

Claiborne, John F. H. Library of Congress.
——. Mississippi Department of Archives and History.
——. University of North Carolina Library.
Clay, Clement Claiborne. Duke University Library.
Cobb, Howell. Duke University Library.
Crittenden, John J. Library of Congress.
De Bow, James Dunwoody Brownson. Duke University Library.
Flanders, Benjamin F. Louisiana State University Library.
Gordon, George A. Duke University Library.
Graham, William A. North Carolina Historical Association Archives.
Green, Thomas Jefferson. University of North Carolina Library.
Gregg, Maxcy. South Caroliniana Library, University of South Carolina.
Hammond, James. Library of Congress.
Hampton, Wade III. South Caroliniana Library, University of South Carolina.
Huger, Alfred. Duke University Library.
Hughes, Henry. Mississippi Department of Archives and History.
Johnson, Andrew. Library of Congress.
Johnson, Hershel V. Duke University Library.
Johnson, Reverdy. Library of Congress.
Jones, Charles Colcock. Tulane University, New Orleans.
Keitt, Lawrence Massillon. Duke University Library.
King, Thomas Butler. University of North Carolina Library.
Lamar, Charles A. L. Emory University Library. Microfilm; originals in possession of Mrs. Albert Howell, Jr., 601 Peachtree Battle Avenue, N.W., Atlanta 5, Georgia.
Lieber, Francis. South Caroliniana Library, University of South Carolina.
McCalla, John M. Duke University Library.
Mangum, Willie P. Library of Congress.
Mazyck family. South Caroliniana Library, University of South Carolina.
Meade, Rt. Rev. William. Library of Congress.
——. Typescript copy may be found in the Virginia Diocesan Library, 110 West Franklin Street, Richmond, Virginia. Originals are in the General Theological Seminary, New York.
Memminger, Christopher. University of North Carolina Library.
Miles, W. Porcher. University of North Carolina Library.
Moore, Thomas O. Louisiana State University Library.
Orr, James L. University of North Carolina Library.
——. South Caroliniana Library, University of South Carolina.
Perkins, John. University of North Carolina Library.

Perry, Benjamin F. South Caroliniana Library, University of South Carolina.
———. University of North Carolina Library.
Petigru, James Louis. South Caroliniana Library, University of South Carolina.
Pettigrew family. University of North Carolina.
Pettigrew, James Johnston. North Carolina Historical Association Archives.
Pickens, Francis Wilkinson. Duke University Library.
Polk, Leonidas. University of North Carolina Library.
Preston, William C. South Caroliniana Library, University of South Carolina.
Quitman, John. Mississippi Department of Archives and History.
———. University of North Carolina Library.
Ramsey, J. G. M. University of North Carolina Library.
Rhett, Robert Barnwell. Duke University Library.
———. University of North Carolina Library.
Ruffin, Edmund. Library of Congress.
———. University of North Carolina Library.
Seymour, William. Louisiana State University Library.
Slidell, John. Tulane University Library.
Soule, Pierre. Louisiana State University Library.
Stephens, Alexander H. Duke University Library.
———. Library of Congress.
———. Manhattanville College of the Sacred Heart, Manhattanville, New York; microfilm copy, Library of Congress.
Terry, William. Louisiana State University Library.
Thornwell, James H. University of North Carolina Library.
Wailes, B. L. C. Duke University Library.
Wigfall family. Library of Congress.
Wilson, J. Leighton. Letter to James Lennox, New York, December 29, 1859. Letter on his article "The Foreign Slave-Trade" attached to copy of the article in the New York Public Library.
Wise, Henry A. Library of Congress.

Newspapers
Boston *Liberator*. 1850–1861.
Brunswick (Georgia) *Herald*. 1857–1859.
Charleston *Courier*. 1856–1858.
Charleston *Mercury*. July, 1854–December, 1859.
Charleston *Southern Standard*. 1853–1857.
Charlotte *North Carolina Whig*. January–February, 1859.
Charlottesville (Virginia) *Review*. November, 1860.
Edgefield (South Carolina) *Advertiser*. 1850–1861.

Galveston *Civilian*. 1857–April, 1861.
Galveston *Weekly News*. 1856–March, 1861.
Houston *Telegraph*. 1856–1859.
Jackson *Semi-Weekly Mississippian*. July, 1854–December, 1860.
Milledgeville (Georgia) *Federal Union*. August, 1853–April, 1861.
Mobile *Daily Register*. September, 1855–June, 1860.
Nashville *Republican Banner and Nashville Whig*. 1856–1858.
Nashville *Union and American*. November, 1856–June, 1859.
Natchez *Daily Free Trader*. May, 1858–June, 1860.
New Orleans *Bee*. January–June, 1858.
New Orleans *Daily Crescent*. January–June, 1859.
New Orleans *Daily Delta*. January, 1858–June, 1859.
New Orleans *Picayune*. January, 1856–April, 1861.
New York *Herald*. 1858–1860.
New York *National Anti-Slavery Standard*. June, 1853–January, 1859.
New York *Times*. 1858–1859.
New York *Weekly Tribune*. 1858–1860.
Newbern (North Carolina) *Daily Progress*. January–February, 1859.
Raleigh *North Carolina Tri-Weekly Standard*. January–February, 1859.
Richmond *Enquirer*. 1853–1861.
Richmond *Whig and Public Advertiser*. 1857–1861.
Savannah *Daily Morning News*. November, 1856–March, 1861.
Vicksburg *Daily Whig*. September, 1859–March, 1861.
Washington *National Intelligencer*. November, 1856–May, 1861.

Magazines and Reports
The African Repository. Washington, 1853–1860.
The American Colonization Society. *Forty-third Annual Report*. Washington, 1860.
The American Cotton Planter. Montgomery, 1853–1860.
The American Farmer. Baltimore, 1853–1860.
Annals of Southern Methodism. Nashville, 1855–1857.
The Cotton Planter. Montgomery, 1857–1860.
De Bow's Review. New Orleans, 1845–1861.
Hunt's Merchants' Magazine and Commercial Review. New York, 1849–1859.
The Plantation. Eatanton, Georgia, 1860.
The Quarterly Review of the Methodist Episcopal Church, South. Richmond, 1854–1861.
Russell's Magazine. Charleston, 1859–1860.
Southern Cultivator and Dixie Farmer. Augustus, Athens, and Atlanta, Georgia, 1853–1861.
The Southern Episcopalian. Charleston, 1861.

The Southern Literary Messenger. Richmond, 1858–1861.
The Southern Planter. Richmond, 1853, 1854, 1858–1861.
The Southern Presbyterian Review. Columbia, 1857–1861.
The Southern Literary Quarterly. Charleston, 1853.

Statistical and Census Information

De Bow, James D. B. *Encyclopædia of the Trade and Commerce of the United States, more particularly of the southern and western states: giving a view of the commerce, agriculture, manufacturers, internal improvements, slave and free labour, slavery institutions, products, etc.* (London, 1854).
United States Bureau of the Census. *Historical Statistics of the United States, Colonial Times to 1957.* Washington, 1960.
———. *Negro Population, 1790–1915.* Washington, 1918.
United States Census Office. *Sixth Census, 1840.* Washington, 1841.
———. *Seventh Census, 1850.* Washington, 1853.
———. *Eighth Census, 1860.* Washington, 1864.
———. *1860 Census Population Schedules, Alabama Slave Schedules,* MSS. Microfilm copy in the University of North Carolina Library.
———. *1860 Census Population Schedules, Georgia Slave Schedules,* MSS. Microfilm copy in the University of North Carolina Library.
———. *1860 Census Population Schedules, Louisiana Slave Schedules,* MSS. Microfilm copy in the University of North Carolina Library.
———. *1860 Census Population Schedules, Maryland Slave Schedules,* MSS. Microfilm copy in the University of North Carolina Library.
———. *1860 Census Population Schedules, Mississippi Slave Schedules,* MSS. Microfilm copy in the University of North Carolina Library.
———. *1860 Census Population Schedules, South Carolina Slave Schedules,* MSS. Microfilm copy in the University of North Carolina Library.
———. *1860 Census Population Schedules, Tennessee Slave Schedules,* MSS. Microfilm copy in the University of North Carolina Library.
———. *1860 Census Population Schedules, Texas Slave Schedules,* MSS. Microfilm copy in the University of North Carolina Library.
———. *1860 Census Population Schedules, Virginia Slave Schedules,* MSS. Microfilm copy in the University of North Carolina Library.

Federal Official Records and Documents

The Congressional Globe, 1855–1861. Washington: John C. Rives, 1855–1861.

The Debates and Proceedings in the Congress of the United States, 1789–1807, 1818–1823. Washington: Gales and Seaton, 1834.

State Official Records and Documents

Journal of the Sixth Biennial Session of the House of Representatives of the State of Alabama, Session of 1857–58. Montgomery: N. B. Cloud, 1858.

Journal of the Sixth Biennial Session of the Senate of the State of Alabama, Session of 1857–58. Montgomery: N. B. Cloud, 1858.

Journal of the Seventh Biennial Session of the House of Representatives of the State of Alabama, Session of 1859–60. Montgomery: Shorter & Reid, 1860.

Journal of the Seventh Biennial Session of the Senate of the State of Alabama, Session of 1859–60. Montgomery: Shorter & Reid, 1860.

Journal of the House of Representatives, for the Twelfth Session of the General Assembly of the State of Arkansas. Little Rock, 1859.

Journal of the Senate, for the Twelfth Session of the General Assembly of the State of Arkansas. Little Rock, 1859.

Journal of the Proceedings of the House of Representatives of the General Assembly of the State of Florida at its Ninth Session. Tallahassee, 1858.

Journal of the House of Representatives of the State of Georgia, 1858. Columbus, 1858.

Journal of the Senate of the State of Georgia, 1858. Columbus, 1858.

Official Journal of the House of Representatives of the State of Louisiana, Session of 1858. Baton Rouge: Office of the *Daily Advocate,* 1858.

Official Journal of the Senate of the State of Louisiana, Session of 1858. Baton Rouge: Office of the *Daily Advocate,* 1858.

Official Journal of the House of Representatives of the State of Louisiana, Session of 1859. Baton Rouge: J. M. Taylor, 1859.

Official Journal of the Senate of the State of Louisiana, Session of 1859. Baton Rouge: J. M. Taylor, 1859.

Journal of the Senate of the State of Mississippi, 1856–1861. Jackson: E. Barksdale, 1856–1861.

Journal of the House of Representatives of the State of Mississippi, 1856–1861. Jackson: E. Barksdale, *1856–1861.*

The Revised Code of the Statute Laws of the State of Mississippi. Jackson: E. Barksdale, 1857.

Journal of the House of Commons of North Carolina, 1859. Raleigh: Holden & Wilson, 1859.

Journal of the Senate of North Carolina, 1858–1859. Raleigh: Holden & Wilson, 1859.

Journal of the House of Representatives of South Carolina, 1849–1860. Columbia, 1849–1860.

Journal of the Senate of South Carolina, 1849–1860. Columbia, 1849–1860.

Report of the Special Committee of the House of Representatives, of South Carolina, on so much of the Message of his Excellency Gov. James H. Adams, as Relates to Slavery and the Slave Trade. Columbia, 1857.

Report of the Minority of the Special Committee of Seven to whom was Referred so much of his late Excellency's Message No. 1, as Relates to Slavery and the Slave Trade. Columbia, 1857.

Journal of the Senate of Texas, Seventh Biennial Session. Austin, 1857.

Secession Conventions

Smith, William R. *History and Debates of the Convention of Alabama, 1861.* Montgomery: White, Pfister & Co., 1861.

Journal of the Public and Secret Proceedings of the Convention of the People of Georgia, Held in Milledgeville and Savannah in 1861. Milledgeville: Boughton, Nisbet and Barnes, 1861.

Proceedings of the Louisiana State Convention Together with the Ordinances Passed by Said Convention and the Constitution of the State as Amended. New Orleans: J. O. Nixon, 1861.

Journal of the Mississippi State Convention, and Ordinances and Resolutions adopted in January, 1861. Jackson: E. Barksdale, 1861.

Journal of the Mississippi State Convention, and Ordinances and Resolutions adopted in March, 1861. Jackson: E. Barksdale, 1861.

Journal of the Convention of the People of South Carolina, Held in 1860–61. Charleston: Evans and Cogswell, 1861.

Journal of the Conventions of the People of South Carolina, Held in 1860, 1861, and 1862, together with Ordinances, Reports, and Resolutions. Columbia, 1862.

Winkler, Ernest W. (ed.). *Journal of the Secession Convention of Texas.* Austin, 1912.

Journal of the Acts and Proceedings of the General Convention of the State of Virginia, Assembled at Richmond . . . 1861. Richmond, 1861.

Journal of the Convention Assembled at Wheeling, West Virginia, June 11, 1861. Wheeling: Daily Press, 1861.

252

Published Correspondence and Speeches, Articles, Travellers' Reports, Reminiscences, Books, etc.

Adger, John B. *My Life and Times.* Richmond: Presbyterian Committee of Publication, 1899.

———. *A Review of Reports to the Legislature of South Carolina on the Revival of the Slave Trade.* Columbia: A. W. Gibbes, 1858.

"B" *Notice of the Rev. John B. Adger's Article on the Slave Trade.* Charleston, 1858.

Baldwin, Joseph G. *The Flush Times of Alabama and Mississippi.* New York: D. Appleton, 1853.

Benjamin, J. P. *The African Slave Trade. The Secret Purpose of the Insurgents to Revive It. No Treaty Stipulations against the Slave Trade to Be Entered into with the European Powers, Etc.* Philadelphia: C. Sherman, Son & Co., 1863.

Botts, John Minor. *The Great Rebellion: Its Secret History, Rise, Progress, and Disastrous Failure.* New York: Harper & Bros., 1866.

Bremer, Fredrika. *The Homes of the New World; Impressions of America.* 3 Vols. London: Arthur Hall, Virtue and Co., 1853.

British and Foreign State Papers, 1854–1855. Vol. LXV. London, 1865.

Bryan, E. B. *Letters to the Southern People Concerning the Acts of Congress and Treaties with Great Britain, in Relation to the African Slave Trade.* Charleston: Walker, Evans & Co., 1858.

Bryan, Edward B. *The Rightful Remedy.* Addressed to the Slave-holders of the South. Charleston, 1850.

———. *Scrap Book,* n.p. n.d., contains 10 Vols. of pamphlets collected by Bryan. Vols. 3–8 may be found in the University of North Carolina Library.

Bunch, Robert. "Dispatch from the British Consul at Charleston to Lord John Russell, 1860." (December 15, 1860), reprinted in the *American Historical Review,* XVIII, No. 5 (July, 1913), pp. 783–787.

Cairnes, J. E. *The Slave Power.* London: Parker, Son, and Bourn, 1863.

Carey, Henry C. *The Slave Trade, Domestic and Foreign: Why It Exists and How It May Be Extinguished.* Philadelphia: A. Hart, 1853.

Chambers, William. *American Slavery and Colour.* London: W. & R. Chambers, 1857.

Claiborne, John F. H. *Life and Correspondence of John A. Quitman.* 2 Vols. New York: Harper & Brothers, 1860.

Clark, Rufus. *The African Slave Trade.* Boston: American Tract Society, 1860.

Cluskey, Michael W. *The Political Textbook, or Encyclopedia . . . for the Reference of Politicians and Statesmen.* Philadelphia: J. B. Smith, 1860.

Cox, R. W. *The Present State of the African Slave Trade: an Exposition of Some of the Causes of Its Continuance and Prosperity with Suggestions as to the Most Effectual Means of Repressing and Extinguishing it.* Washington: L. Towers, 1858.

Davis, Reuben. *Recollections of Mississippi and Mississippians.* New York: Houghton, Mifflin and Co., 1891.

Delony, Edward. "The South Demands More Negro Labor," *De Bow's Review,* XXV (1858), pp. 491–506.

Dew, Thomas R., *et al. The Pro-Slavery Argument.* Charleston: Walker, Richards, 1852.

Douglass, Frederick. *Life and Times of Frederick Douglass.* New York: Crowell-Collier, 1962.

Dumond, Dwight L. *Southern Editorials on Secession.* New York: The Century Co., 1931.

Elliott, E. N. (ed.). *Cotton Is King, and Pro-Slavery Arguments.* Augusta: Pritchard, Abbott & Loomis, 1860.

Estes, Matthew. *A Defense of Slavery As It Exists in the United States of America.* Montgomery: Press of the Alabama Journal, 1846.

Fitzhugh, George. "The Administration and the Slave Trade," *De Bow's Review,* XXVI (1859), pp. 144–148.

———. (Edited by C. Van Woodward.) *Cannibals All! or Slaves without Masters.* Cambridge, Mass.: The Belknap Press of Harvard University Press, 1960.

———. "The Conservative Principle; or, Social Evils and Their Remedies," Part II—"Slave Trade," *De Bow's Review,* XXII (May, 1857), pp. 449–462.

———. *Sociology for the South or the Failure of Free Society.* Richmond: A. Morris, Publisher, 1854.

Foote, Henry S. *The Bench and Bar of the South and Southwest.* St. Louis: Soule, Thomas & Wentworth, 1876.

———. *Casket of Reminiscences.* Washington: Chronicle Publishing Co., 1874.

———. *War of the Rebellion.* New York: Harper & Brothers, 1866.

Goodwin, Daniel R. *Southern Slavery in Its Present Prospects.* Philadelphia: J. B. Lippincott & Co., 1864.

Gray, Peter W. *An Address of Judge Peter W. Gray to the Citizens of Houston, on the African Slave Trade.* n.p., May 30, 1859.

Halstead, Murat. *A History of the National Political Conventions of the Current Presidential Campaign.* . . . Columbus: Follett, Foster & Co., 1860.

Hammond, James H. *Selections from the Letters and Speeches of the Hon. James H. Hammond, of South Carolina.* New York: J. F. Trow & Co., 1866.

————. *Speech of Hon. James H. Hammond, Delivered at Barnwell Court House,* October 29, 1858. Charleston, 1858.

Harper, Robert G. *An Argument against the Policy of Reopening the African Slave Trade.* Atlanta: C. R. Hanleiter, 1858.

Hayne, Isaac W. *Argument before the United States Circuit Court, by I. M. Hayne, on the Motion to Discharge the Crew of the Echo.* Albany: Weed, Parsons & Co., 1859.

Helper, Hinton R. *The Impending Crisis of the South: How to Meet It.* New York: Burdick Bros., 1857.

Hughes, Henry. *State Liberties; or, The Right to African Contract Labor.* Port Gibson: Office of the *Southern Reveille,* 1858.

————. *Treatise on Sociology.* Philadelphia: J. B. Lippincott, 1854.

Hundley, D. R. *Social Relations in Our Southern States.* New York: Henry B. Price, 1860.

Ingraham, J. H. *The Southwest by a Yankee.* 2 Vols. New York: 1835.

Lamar, C. A. L. "A Slave-Trader's Letter-Book," *North American Review,* CXLIII (1886), pp. 447–461.

Las Casas, pseud. of Alexander Mazyck. *The Courier and the Slave Trade.* n.p., 1858.

Lieber, Francis. *Plantations for Slave Labor the Death of the Yeomanry.* New York: Loyal Publication Society, No. 29, 1865.

Lubbock, Francis Richard. *Six Decades: or Memoirs of Francis Richard Lubbock, Governor of Texas in War Times, 1861–1863. A Personal Experience in Business, War and Politics.* Austin: B. C. Jones and Company, 1900.

Lyell, Charles. *A Second Visit to the United States of America.* London: J. Murray, 1855.

Mackay, Charles. *Life and Liberty in America: or, Sketches of a Tour in the United States and Canada in 1857–8.* New York: Harper & Brothers, 1859.

McKitrick, Eric L. (ed.). *Slavery Defended: the Views of the Old South.* Englewood Cliffs: Prentice-Hall, Inc., 1963.

Miller, C. W. *Address on Re-opening the Slave Trade . . . to the Citizens of Barnwell at Wylde-Moore.* Columbia, August 29, 1857.

Mitchel, John. *Jail Journal.* London: T. Fisher Unwin, 1913.

Moore, Frank. *The Rebellion Record: A Diary of American Events with Documents Narrative, Illustrative, Incidents, etc.* Vols. I and II. New York: G. P. Putnam's Sons, 1862–1864.

Oliphant, Mary C., Alfred Taylor Odell, and T. C. Duncan Eaves (eds.). *The Letters of William Gilmore Simms*. 4 Vols. Columbia: University of South Carolina, 1955.

Olmsted, Frederick Law. *The Cotton Kingdom*. New York: Alfred A. Knopf, 1853.

———. *A Journal in the Back Country*. New York: Mason Brothers, 1863.

———. *A Journey in the Seaboard Slave States in the Years 1853–1854 with Remarks on Their Economy*. 2 Vols. New York: G. P. Putnam's Sons, 1904.

———. *A Journey Through Texas*. New York: Dix, Edwards & Co., 1857.

———. *The Slave States before the Civil War*. New York: G. P. Putnam's Sons, 1859.

Perry, Benjamin F. *Biographical Sketches of Eminent American Statesmen, with Speeches, Addresses and Letters by Ex-Governor B. F. Perry of Greenville, South Carolina*. Philadelphia: Ferree Press, 1887.

———. *Reminiscences of Public Men*. Philadelphia: J. D. Avil & Co., 1883.

Perry, Thomas S. (ed.). *The Life and Letters of Francis Lieber*. Boston: J. R. Osgood & Co., 1882.

Pettigrew, J. J. "Protest Against the Slave-Trade Revival." *De Bow's Review*, XXV (August and September, 1858), pp. 166–185, 289–308.

Phillips, Ulrich Bonnell. *Correspondence of Robert Toombs, Alexander H. Stephens, and Howell Cobb*. Annual Report of the American Historical Association, 1911.

Phillips, Ulrich Bonnell (ed.). *Plantation and Frontier Documents: 1649–1863*. 2 Vols. Cleveland: Arthur H. Clark Co., 1909.

Pollard, Edward Albert. *Black Diamonds Gathered in the Darkey Homes of the South*. New York: Pudney & Russell, 1859.

———. *A New Southern Policy, or the Slave Trade as Meaning Union and Conservatism*. n.p., 185?

The Rebuke of Secession Doctrines by Southern Statesmen (William B. Goulden's speech at the Democratic National Convention, 1860), Philadelphia, 1863.

Richardson, James D. (ed.). *Messages and Papers of the Confederacy*. Nashville, 1906.

Rowland, Dunbar (ed.). *Jefferson Davis Constitutionalist: His Letters, Papers and Speeches*. 10 Vols. Jackson, Mississippi: Mississippi Department of Archives, 1923.

Russell, Robert. *North America: Its Agriculture and Climate, . . .* Edinburgh: A. & C. Black, 1857.

Sawyer, George S. *Southern Institutions; or an Inquiry into the Origins and Early Prevalence of Slavery and the Slave-Trade . . . with Notes and Comments in Defense of the Southern Institutions.* Philadelphia: J. B. Lippincott and Co., 1859.

Smith, William R. *Reminiscences of a Long Life.* Washington, D.C.: Rufus H. Darley Press, 1889.

Spratt, Leonidas W. *The Foreign Slave Trade, the Source of Political Power—of Material Progress, of Social Integrity, and of Social Emancipation of the South.* Charleston, 1858.

————. "The Philosophy of Secession, Being a Protest against the Decision of the Southern Congress," reprinted in J. E. Cairnes, *The Slave Power.* London, 1863, pp. 390–410.

————. "Report on the Slave Trade Made to the Southern Convention at Montgomery, Alabama," *De Bow's Review,* XXIV (June, 1858), pp. 473–491.

————. *A Series of Articles on the Value of the Union to the South, Lately Published in the Charleston Standard. By . . . One of the Editors.* Charleston: James, Williams & Gitsinger, 1855.

————. *Speech upon the Foreign Slave Trade before the Legislature of South Carolina.* Columbia: Southern Guardian, 1858.

Stanton, R. L. *The Church and the Rebellion.* New York: Derby & Miller, 1864.

Stirling, James. *Letters from the Slave States.* London: John W. Parker and Son, West Strand, 1857.

Townsend, John. *The South Alone Should Govern the South and African Slavery by Those Friendly to It.* Charleston: Evans & Cogswell, 1860.

————. *The Southern States, Their Present Peril.* Charleston: E. C. Councell, 1850.

Troy, D. S. "Is the Slave Trade Piracy?" *De Bow's Review,* XXVI (January, 1859), pp. 23–28.

Walton, Thomas. "Further Views of the Advocates of the Slave Trade," *De Bow's Review,* XXVI (January, 1859), pp. 51–66.

Wayne, James M. "Charge to the Grand Jury of the Sixth Court of the United States, for the Southern District of Georgia," Delivered November 14, 1859. Reprinted in *African Repository,* XXXVI, No. 4 (April, 1860), pp. 98–114.

Williams, Amelia W., and Eugene C. Barker. *The Writings of Sam Houston, 1813–1863.* 8 Vols. Austin: University of Texas Press, 1938–1943.

Wilson, Rev. J. Leighton. "The Foreign Slave Trade. Can It Be Revived without Violating the Most Sacred Principles of Honor, Humanity, and Religion?" Reprint from the *Southern Presbyterian Review,* Charleston, 1859.

Wish, Harvey (ed.). *Ante-Bellum, Writings of George Fitzhugh and Hinton Rowan Helper on Slavery.* New York: G. P. Putnam's Sons, 1960.

SECONDARY SOURCES

Ambler, Charles Henry. *Sectionalism in Virginia, 1776–1861.* Chicago: University of Chicago Press, 1910.

Aptheker, Herbert. *American Negro Slave Revolts.* New York: Columbia University Press, 1943.

Bancroft, Frederic. *Slave-Trading in the Old South.* Baltimore: J. H. Furst Company, 1931.

Barker, E. C. "The African Slave Trade in Texas," *Quarterly of the Texas State Historical Association,* VI (1902), pp. 145–158.

Beals, Carleton. *War within a War: The Confederacy against Itself.* New York: Chilton Books, 1965.

Benson, Lee, and Thomas J. Pressly. "Can Differences in Interpretations of the Causes of the American Civil War Be Resolved Objectively?" Paper discussed at a session of the American Historical Association, December 29, 1956.

Bernstein, Barton J. "Southern Politics and Attempts to Reopen the African Slave Trade," *The Journal of Negro History,* LI, No. 1 (January, 1966), pp. 16–35.

Blake, William O. *The History of Slavery and the Slave Trade, Ancient and Modern.* Columbus, Ohio: H. Miller, 1860.

Boucher, Chauncey S. "The Secession and Co-operation Movements in South Carolina, 1848 to 1852," *Washington University Studies,* V, No. 2 (April, 1918), pp. 65–138.

———. "Sectionalism, Representation, and the Electoral Question," *Washington University Studies,* IV. Part II, No. 1 (October, 1916), pp. 3–62.

———. "South Carolina and the South on the Eve of Secession, 1852–1860," *Washington University Studies,* VI, No. 2 (April, 1919), pp. 77–127.

Bruce, Kathleen. *Virginia Iron Manufacture in the Slave Era.* New York: The Century Co., 1931.

Campbell, Mary Emily Robertson. *The Attitude of Tennesseans Toward the Union, 1847–1861.* New York: Vantage Press, 1961.

Carnathan, W. J. "The Proposal to Reopen the African Slave Trade in the South, 1854–1860," *The South Atlantic Quarterly,* XXV, No. 4 (October, 1926), pp. 410–429.

Carpenter, Jesse T. *The South as a Conscious Minority, 1789–1861.* New York: New York University Press, 1930.

Carson, James P. *Life, Letters and Speeches of James Louis Petigru, the Union Man of South Carolina.* Washington, 1920.

258

Cash, Wilber, J. *The Mind of the South.* New York: Vintage Books —Alfred Knopf, 1941.

Caskey, Willie M. *Secession and Restoration of Louisiana.* Baton Rouge: Louisiana State University Press, 1938.

Cate, Wirt A. *Lucius Q. C. Lamar.* Chapel Hill: University of North Carolina Press, 1935.

Cauthen, Charles E. "South Carolina's Decision to Lead the Secession Movement," *North Carolina Historical Review,* XVIII (October, 1941), pp. 360–372.

Chenault, William W., and Reinders, Robert C. "The Northern-born Community of New Orleans in the 1850's," *The Journal of American History,* LI, No. 2 (September, 1964), pp. 232–238.

Clark, Robert T., Jr. "The German Liberals in New Orleans (1840–1860)," *Louisiana Historical Quarterly,* XX, No. 1 (January, 1937), pp. 137–151.

————. "The New Orleans German Colony in the Civil War," *Louisiana Historical Quarterly,* XX (1937), pp. 990–1015.

Cleveland, Henry. *Alexander H. Stephens in Public and Private.* Chicago: National Publishing Co., 1866.

Coleman, J. Winston, Jr. *Slavery Times in Kentucky.* Chapel Hill: University of North Carolina Press, 1940.

Collins, Winfield H. *The Domestic Slave Trade of the Southern States.* New York: Broadway Publishing Co., 1904.

Connor, Henry Groves. *John Archibald Campbell, Associate Justice of the United States Supreme Court, 1853–1861.* New York: Houghton Mifflin Co., 1920.

Conrad, Alfred H., and John R. Meyer. "The Economics of Slavery in the Ante-Bellum South," *Journal of Political Economy,* LXVI, No. 2 (April, 1958), pp. 95–130.

Couch, W. T. (ed.). *Culture in the South.* Chapel Hill: The University of North Carolina Press, 1934.

Coulter, E. Merton. *The Confederate States of America.* Baton Rouge: Louisiana State University Press, 1950.

Craven, Avery O. *Civil War in the Making, 1815–1860.* Baton Rouge: Louisiana State University Press, 1959.

————. *The Coming of the Civil War.* Chicago: University of Chicago Press, 1966.

————. *Edmund Ruffin: A Study in Secession.* New York: D. Appleton and Co., 1932.

————. *The Growth of Southern Nationalism, 1848–1861.* Baton Rouge: Louisiana State University Press, 1953.

————. *Soil Exhaustion as a Factor in the Agricultural History of Virginia and Maryland, 1606–1860.* Urbana: *University of Illinois Studies in Social Sciences,* XIII, 1926.

Crenshaw, Ollinger. *The Slave States in the Presidential Election of 1860.* Baltimore: Johns Hopkins Press, 1945.

Current, Richard. *John C. Calhoun.* New York: Washington Square Press, 1963.

Dabney, Thomas E. *One Hundred Great Years: The Story of the Times-Picayune from Its Founding to 1940.* Baton Rouge: Louisiana State University Press, 1944.

Davis, David Brion. *The Problem of Slavery in Western Culture.* Ithaca: Cornell University Press, 1966.

Davis, W. W. "Ante-Bellum Southern Commercial Conventions," *Alabama Historical Society Transactions,* Vol. V, 1904, pp. 153–202.

Denman, Clarence Phillips. *The Secession Movement in Alabama.* Norwood, Massachusetts: Norwood Press, 1933.

Dillon, William. *Life of John Mitchel.* 2 Vols. London: Kegan Paul, French & Co., 1888.

Dodd, William E. *The Cotton Kingdom.* New Haven: Yale University Press, 1919.

Doyle, B. W. *The Etiquette of Race Relations in the South.* Chicago: University of Chicago Press, 1937.

Du Bois, W. E. B. *The Suppression of the African Slave Trade to the United States of America.* New York: Russell & Russell, 1965.

Du Bose, John Witherspoon. *The Life and Times of William Lowndes Yancey.* 2 Vols. New York: Peter Smith, 1942.

Duignan, Peter, and Clarence Clendenen. *The United States and the African Slave Trade, 1619–1862.* Stanford, California: Stanford University Press, 1963.

Easby-Smith, Ann. *William Russell Smith of Alabama, His Life and Works.* Philadelphia, 1931.

Easterby, J. H. "The Charleston Commercial Convention of 1854," *The South Atlantic Quarterly,* XXV, No. 2 (April, 1926), pp. 181–197.

Eaton, Clement. *Freedom of Thought in the Old South.* Durham: Duke University Press, 1940.

Elkins, Stanley M. *Slavery: A Problem in American Institutional & Intellectual Life.* New York: Grosset & Dunlap, 1963.

Elliott, Charles. *South-Western Methodism—A History of the Methodist Episcopal Church in the South-West, from 1844–1864.* Cincinnati: Poe & Hitchcock, 1868.

Erikson, Erik H. *Young Man Luther: A Study in Psychoanalysis and History.* New York: Norton, 1958.

Erikson, Kai T. *Wayward Puritans: A Study in the Sociology of Deviance.* New York: Wiley, 1966.

Fitts, Albert N. "The Confederate Convention: The Constitutional Debate," *The Alabama Review*, II (July, 1949), pp. 189–210.

———. "The Confederate Convention: The Provisional Constitution," *The Alabama Review*, II (April, 1949), pp. 83–101.

Flanders, Ralph B. *Plantation Slavery in Georgia.* Chapel Hill: University of North Carolina Press, 1933.

Flippin, Percy Scott. *Hershel V. Johnson of Georgia: State Rights Unionist.* Richmond: Dietz Press, 1931.

Fornell, Earl W. *The Galveston Era, the Texas Crescent on the Eve of Secession.* Austin: University of Texas Press, 1961.

Franklin, John Hope. *The Militant South, 1800–1861.* Cambridge: Belknap, 1956.

Freehling, William. *Prelude to Civil War: The Nullification Controversy in South Carolina.* New York: Harper & Row, 1966.

Friedman, Lawrence. *The White Savage: Racial Fantasies in the Post-Bellum South.* (To be published by Prentice-Hall.)

Genovese, Eugene. *The Political Economy of Slavery: Studies in the Economy and Society of the Slave South.* New York: Random House, 1966.

———. *The World the Slaveholders Made.* New York: Random House, 1969.

Gray, Lewis Cecil. *History of Agriculture in the Southern United States to 1860.* 2 Vols. Washington: Waverly Press, 1933.

Green, Fletcher M. *Constitutional Development in the South Atlantic States, 1776–1860.* Chapel Hill: University of North Carolina Press, 1930.

Greer, James K. "Louisiana Politics, 1845–1861," *Louisiana Historical Quarterly*, XII and XIII, Nos. 3 and 4 and 1–4 (July, October, 1929; January, April, July, October, 1930).

Hacker, Louis M. *The Triumph of American Capitalism.* New York: Simon and Schuster, 1940.

Hamilton, William Baskerville. "Holly Springs, Mississippi, to the Year 1876." Unpublished M.A. Thesis. University of Mississippi, 1931. (Copy on file University of North Carolina.)

Hearon, Cleo. *Mississippi and the Compromise of 1850. Publications of the Mississippi Historical Society.* Vol. XIV. University: University of Mississippi, 1914.

Hendrix, James Paisley, Jr., "The Efforts to Reopen the African Slave Trade in Louisiana," *Louisiana History.* Vol. X, No. 2 (Spring, 1969), pp. 97–124.

Herron, Stella. "The African Apprentice Bill," *Proceedings of the Mississippi Valley Historical Association*, VIII (1914–1915), pp. 135–145.

Hodgson, Joseph. *The Cradle of the Confederacy or, The Times of Troup, Quitman and Yancey.* Mobile: Register Publishing Office, 1876.

Hofstadter, Richard. *The American Political Tradition.* New York: Vintage, 1960.

Hollis, Daniel Walker. *University of South Carolina.* 2 Vols. Columbia: University of South Carolina Press, 1951.

Hull, Augustus Longstreet (ed.). "The Making of the Confederate Constitution," *Publications of the Southern History Association,* IX, (1905), pp. 272–292.

Jackson, Henry R. *The Wanderer Case.* Atlanta: E. Holland, 1903.

Jenkins, William S. *Pro-Slavery Thought in the Old South.* Chapel Hill: University of North Carolina Press, 1935.

Jervey, Theodore D. *The Slave Trade.* Columbia: The State Company, 1925.

Jordan, Weymouth T. *Rebels in the Making: Planters' Conventions and Southern Propaganda.* Tuscaloosa, Alabama: Confederate Publishing Company, 1958.

Jordan, Winthrop D. *White Over Black: American Attitudes Toward the Negro.* Chapel Hill: University of North Carolina Press, 1968.

Kendall, John S. "George Wilkins Kendall and the Founding of the New Orleans *Picayune,*" *Louisiana Historical Quarterly,* II, No. 2 (April, 1928), pp. 261–285.

———. "New Orleans' 'Peculiar Institution,'" *Louisiana Historical Quarterly,* XXIII, No. 2 (July, 1940), pp. 864–886.

Kendall, Lane C. "Interregnum in Louisiana, 1860–1861," *Louisiana Historical Quarterly,* XVI, (April, July, October, 1933), pp. 175–208, 374–408, 639–669; XVII (January, April, July, 1934), pp. 124–138, 339–348, 524–536.

Kibler, Lillian. *Benjamin F. Perry: South Carolina Unionist.* Durham: Duke University Press, 1946.

———. "Unionist Sentiment in South Carolina in 1860," *Journal of Southern History,* IV, No. 3 (August, 1938), pp. 346–366.

Landry, Harral E. "Slavery and the Slave Trade in Atlantic Diplomacy, 1850–1861," *Journal of Southern History,* XXVII, No. 2 (May, 1961), pp. 184–207.

Landry, Thomas R. "The Political Career of Robert Charles Wickliffe, Governor of Louisiana, 1856–1860," *Louisiana Historical Quarterly,* XXV, No. 3 (July, 1942), pp. 670–727.

Lapp, Rudolph M. "The Ante-Bellum Poor Whites of the South Atlantic States." Unpublished Ph.D. Thesis, University of California, Berkeley, 1956.

Lee, Charles Robert, Jr., *The Confederate Constitutions.* Chapel Hill: University of North Carolina Press, 1963.

Locke, Mary Stoughton. *Anti-Slavery in America; from the Introduction of African Slaves to the Prohibition of the Slave Trade (1619–1808).* Gloucester, Mass.: Peter Smith, 1965.

Lonn, Ella. *Foreigners in the Confederacy.* Chapel Hill: University of North Carolina Press, 1940.

Lynch, James D. *Bench and Bar of Mississippi.* n.p. n.d.

McColley, Robert. *Slavery and Jeffersonian Virginia.* Urbana: University of Illinois Press, 1964.

McConnell, Rowland Calhoun. "The Reopening of the African Slave-Trade to the United States of America, 1850–1860," unpublished M.A. thesis, Howard University, 1933.

McLure, Mary L. "The Elections of 1860 in Louisiana," *Louisiana Historical Quarterly,* IX (October, 1926), pp. 602–702.

Mandel, Bernard. *Labor: Free and Slave; Workingmen and the Anti-Slavery Movement in the United States.* New York: Associated Authors, 1955.

Mannix, Daniel Pratt. *Black Cargoes, a History of the Atlantic Slave Trade 1518–1865.* New York: Viking Press, 1962.

Martin, Thomas P. "Conflicting Cotton Interests at Home and Abroad, 1848–1857," *Journal of Southern History,* VII, No. 2 (May, 1941), pp. 173–194.

Mathieson, William Law. *Great Britain and the Slave Trade, 1839–1865.* London: Longmans, Green & Co., 1929.

May, John Amasa, and Joan Reynolds Faunt. *South Carolina Secedes.* Columbia: University of South Carolina Press, 1960.

Mayes, Edward. *Lucius Q. C. Lamar: His Life, Times and Speeches, 1825–1893.* Nashville: Publishing House of the Methodist Episcopal Church, South, 1896.

Menn, Joseph Karl. *The Large Slaveholders of Louisiana—1860.* New Orleans: Pelican Publishing Company, 1964.

Merritt, Elizabeth. *James Henry Hammond, 1807–1864.* Baltimore: Johns Hopkins University Press, 1923.

Mitchell, Broadus. *William Gregg: Factory Master of the Old South.* Chapel Hill: University of North Carolina Press, 1928.

Montgomery, Horace. *Cracker Parties.* Baton Rouge: Louisiana State University Press, 1950.

Mooney, Chase C. *Slavery in Tennessee.* Bloomington: Indiana University Press, 1957.

Munford, Beverley B. *Virginia's Attitude Towards Slavery and Secession.* Richmond: J. H. Jenkins, 1915.

Nau, John Frederick. *The German People of New Orleans, 1850–1900.* Leiden, Netherlands: E. J. Brill, 1958.

Nevins, Allan. *The Emergence of Lincoln.* 2 Vols. New York: Charles Scribner's Sons, 1950.

————. *The Ordeal of the Union.* 2 Vols. New York: Charles Scribner's Sons, 1947.

Nichols, Roy Franklin. *The Disruption of American Democracy.* New York: Macmillan Co., 1948.

Niehaus, Earl F. *The Irish in New Orleans, 1800–1860.* Baton Rouge: Louisiana State University Press, 1965.

Norton, Clarence C. *The Democratic Party in Ante-Bellum North Carolina, 1835–1861.* Chapel Hill: The University of North Carolina Press, 1930.

O'Connor, Mary D. *The Life and Letters of M. P. O'Connor.* New York: Dempsey & Carroll, 1893.

Odom, Van D. "The Political Career of Thomas Overton Moore, Secession Governor of Louisiana," *Louisiana Historical Quarterly,* XXVI (October, 1943), pp. 975–1054.

Osterweis, Rollin G. *Romanticism and Nationalism in the Old South.* Baton Rouge: Louisiana State University Press, 1967.

Overdyke, W. Darrell. "History of the American Party in Louisiana," *Louisiana Historical Quarterly,* XV, No. 4 (October, 1932), pp. 581–588; XVI, No. 1 (January, 1933), pp. 84–91; XVI, No. 2 (April, 1933), pp. 256–279; XVI, No. 3 (July, 1933), pp. 409–426.

————. *The Know-Nothing Party in the South.* Baton Rouge: Louisiana State University Press, 1950.

Pearce, Roy Harvey. *Savagism and Civilization: A Study of the Indian and the American Mind.* Baltimore: Johns Hopkins, 1967.

Pendleton, Louis B. *Alexander H. Stephens.* Philadelphia: George W. Jacobs & Co., 1908.

Phillips, Ulrich Bonnell. *American Negro Slavery.* Gloucester, Mass.: Peter Smith, 1959.

————. *The Course of the South to Secession.* New York: D. Appleton-Century Co., 1939.

————. *A History of Transportation in the Eastern Cotton Belt to 1860.* New York: Columbia University Press, 1908.

————. *Life and Labor in the Old South.* Boston: Little, Brown, and Company, 1930.

Purifoy, Lewis M. Jr. "The Methodist Episcopal Church, South and Slavery, 1844–1865." Unpublished Ph.D. Dissertation, University of North Carolina, 1965.

Rainwater, Percy Lee. "An Analysis of the Secession Controversy in Mississippi, 1854–1861," *Mississippi Valley Historical Review,* XXIV, No. 1 (June, 1937), pp. 35–42.

————. "Economic Benefits of Secession: Opinions in Mississippi in the 1850's," *Journal of Southern History,* I (1935), p. 466.

————. *Mississippi, Storm Center of Secession, 1856–1861*. Baton Rouge: Otto Claitor, 1938.

Ramsdell, Charles W. "The Natural Limits of Slavery Expansion," *Mississippi Valley Historical Review*, XVI (September, 1929), pp. 151–171.

Ranck, James B. *Albert Gallatin Brown: Radical Southern Nationalist*. New York: D. Appleton-Century, 1937.

Rhett, Robert G. *Charleston: An Epic of Carolina*. Richmond: Garrett and Massie, 1940.

Robert, Joseph C. *The Road from Monticello: A Study of the Virginia Slavery Debate of 1832*. Durham: Duke University Press, 1941.

Rowland, Dunbar. *History of Mississippi: The Heart of the South*. 2 Vols. Chicago: J. S. J. Clark, 1925.

————. *Mississippi*. 3 Vols. Atlanta: Southern Historical Publishing Association, 1907.

Russel, Robert R. *Economic Aspects of Southern Sectionalism 1840–1861*. New York: Russell & Russell, 1960.

Sandbo, Anna Irene. "Beginnings of the Secession Movement in Texas," *The Southern Historical Quarterly*, XVIII, No. 1 (July, 1914), pp. 41–73.

————. "First Session of the Secession Convention in Texas," *The Southern Historical Quarterly*, XVIII, No. 2 (October, 1914), pp. 162–195.

Sargent, F. W. *England, the United States, and the Southern Confederacy*. London: Hamilton, Adams and Company, 1864.

Saxton, Alexander. "An Examination of the Secession Crises of 1850 and 1860–1861 in Louisiana in Terms of Parish Voting Records," unpublished seminar paper for Dr. Charles G. Sellers, Jr., University of California, Berkeley, May, 1963.

Schaper, W. A. *Sectionalism and Representation in South Carolina*. *American Historical Association Report*, 1900, Vol. I, Washington, 1901.

Schultz, Harold S. "Movement to Revive the Foreign Slave Trade, 1853–1861." Unpublished M.A. thesis, Duke University, 1940.

————. *Nationalism and Sectionalism in South Carolina, 1852–1860*. Durham: Duke University Press, 1950.

Sears, Louis Martin. *John Slidell*. Durham: Duke University Press, 1925.

Sellers, Charles G., Jr., "The Travail of Slavery," in Sellers, ed., *The Southerner as American*. Chapel Hill: University of North Carolina Press, 1961.

Sellers, James Benson. *Slavery in Alabama*. University of Alabama: University of Alabama Press, 1950.

Shanks, Henry T. *The Secession Movement in Virginia, 1847–1861.* Richmond: Garrett & Massie, 1934.

Shryock, Richard H. *Georgia and the Union in 1850.* Durham: Duke University Press, 1926.

Shugg, Roger W. *Origins of Class Struggle in Louisiana: A Social History of White Farmers and Laborers during Slavery and After, 1840–1875.* Baton Rouge: Louisiana State University Press, 1939.

Simms, Henry H. *A Decade of Sectional Controversy, 1851–1861.* Chapel Hill: University of North Carolina Press, 1942.

Sitterson, Joseph C. *The Secession Movement in North Carolina.* Chapel Hill: University of North Carolina Press, 1939.

Skipper, Ottis Clark. *J. D. B. De Bow, Magazinist of the Old South.* Athens: University of Georgia Press, 1958.

Soule, Leon C. *The Know-Nothing Party in New Orleans: A Reappraisal.* Baton Rouge: Louisiana Historical Association, 1961.

Soulsby, Hugh G. *The Right of Search and the Slave Trade in Anglo-American Relations, 1814–1862. The Johns Hopkins University Studies in Historical and Political Science,* Series LI, No. 2. Baltimore: Johns Hopkins University Press, 1933.

Spears, John Randolph. *The American Slave-Trade: an Account of its Origin, Growth and Suppression.* London: Beckers and Son, 1901.

Stampp, Kenneth M. "An Analysis of T. R. Dew's Review of the Debates in the Virginia Legislature," *The Journal of Negro History,* XXVII, No. 4 (October, 1942), pp. 380–387.

————. *The Peculiar Institution.* New York: Knopf Vintage edition, 1964.

Staudenraus, P. J. *The African Colonization Movement, 1861–1865.* New York: Columbia University Press, 1961.

Strode, Hudson. *Jefferson Davis.* 3 Vols. New York: Harcourt, Brace & World, 1955–1964.

Swaney, Charles Baumer. *Episcopal Methodism and Slavery.* Boston: Gorham Press, 1926.

Sydnor, Charles S. *Slavery in Mississippi.* New York: D. Appleton-Century Company, 1933.

Tatum, Georgia Lee. *Disloyalty in the Confederacy.* Chapel Hill: University of North Carolina Press, 1934.

Taylor, Joe Gray. *Negro Slavery in Louisiana.* Baton Rouge: Louisiana Historical Association, 1963.

Taylor, Orville W. *Negro Slavery in Arkansas.* Durham: Duke University Press, 1958.

Taylor, Rosser Howard. *Ante-Bellum South Carolina: A Social and*

Cultural History. Chapel Hill: University of North Carolina Press, 1942.

Taylor, William R. *Cavalier & Yankee: The Old South and American National Character.* New York: Doubleday, 1963.

Thompson, Ernest T. *Presbyterians in the South, 1607–1861.* Richmond: John Knox Press, 1963.

Trent, William P. *William Gilmore Simms.* New York, 1892.

Trescot, William Henry. *Memorial of the Life of J. Johnston Pettigrew.* Charleston: J. Russell, 1870.

Urban, C. Stanley. "The Ideology of Southern Imperialism: New Orleans and the Caribbean, 1845–1860," *The Louisiana Historical Quarterly,* XXXIX, No. 1 (January, 1956), pp. 48–73.

Van Deusen, John G. *The Ante-Bellum Southern Commercial Conventions.* Durham: Duke University Press, 1926.

————. *Economic Bases of Disunion in South Carolina.* New York: Columbia University Press, 1928.

Venable, Austin L. *The Role of William L. Yancey in the Secession Movement.* Nashville: The Joint University Libraries, 1945.

Wade, Richard C. *Slavery in the Cities: The South, 1820–1860.* New York: Oxford, 1964.

Weaver, Herbert. *Mississippi Farmers, 1850–1860.* Nashville: The Vanderbilt University Press, 1945.

Wells, Thomas Henderson. *The Slave Ship Wanderer.* Athens: University of Georgia Press, 1967.

Wender, Herbert. *The Southern Commercial Conventions. Johns Hopkins University Studies in Historical and Political Science,* Vol. XLVIII, No. 4, Baltimore: Johns Hopkins University Press, 1930.

White, Laura A. "The National Democrats in South Carolina, 1852–1860," *South Atlantic Quarterly,* XXVIII (October, 1929), pp. 370–389.

————. *Robert Barnwell Rhett: Father of Secession.* New York: The Century Company, 1931.

White, M. J. "Louisiana and the Secession Movement of the Early Fifties," *Mississippi Valley Historical Association Proceedings,* VIII (1914–1915), pp. 278–288.

Whittington, G. P. "Thomas Overton Moore, Governor of Louisiana, 1860–1864," *Louisiana Historical Quarterly,* XIII (January, 1930), pp. 5–31.

Williams, Eric. *Capitalism and Slavery.* New York: Russell & Russell, 1961.

Williams, Jack K. "The Southern Movement to Reopen the African Slave Trade, 1854–1860: A Factor in Secession," *South Carolina Historical Association Proceedings,* 1960.

Wish, Harvey. *George Fitzhugh*. Baton Rouge: Louisiana State University Press, 1943.

———. "The Revival of the African Slave Trade in the United States," *Mississippi Valley Historical Review* (March, 1941), pp. 569–588.

Yearns, Wilfred Buck, Jr. *The Confederate Congress*. Athens: The University of Georgia Press, 1960.

INDEX